Professional Development: What Works

Second Edition

Sally J. Zepeda
University of Georgia

EYE ON EDUCATION
6 DEPOT WAY WEST, SUITE 106
LARCHMONT, NY 10538
(914) 833–0551
(914) 833–0761 fax
www.eyeoneducation.com

A sincere effort has been made to supply the identity of those who have created specific strategies. Any omissions have been unintentional.

Sponsoring Editor: Robert Sickles
Production Editor: Lauren Davis
Copyeditor: Richard Adin, Freelance Editorial Services
Designer and Compositor: Richard Adin, Freelance Editorial Services
Cover Designer: Knoll Gilbert
Cover Images: Compass, Sashkin/Shutterstock; Map, Robert Adrian Hillman/ Shutterstock

Library of Congress Cataloging-in-Publication Data

Zepeda, Sally J., 1956–
  Professional development : what works / Sally J. Zepeda. — 2nd ed.
    p. cm.
  ISBN 978-1-59667-193-5
  1. Teachers—Training of—United States. 2. School principals—Training of—United States. 3. Career development—United States. 4. Educational leadership—United States. I. Title.
  LB1715.Z46 2011
  370.71'1—dc23

                                                          2011023524

10 9 8 7 6 5 4 3 2 1

Also Available from EYE ON EDUCATION

The Principal as Instructional Leader:
A Handbook for Supervisors, 2nd Edition
Sally J. Zepeda

Informal Classroom Observations On the Go:
Feedback, Discussion, and Reflection, 3rd Edition
Sally J. Zepeda

Supervision Across the Content Areas (with R. Stewart Mayers)
Sally J. Zepeda

Instructional Leadership for School Improvement
Sally J. Zepeda

The Call to Teacher Leadership
(with R. Stewart Mayers and Brad N. Benson)
Sally J. Zepeda

Instructional Supervision:
Applying Tools and Concepts, 2nd Edition
Sally J. Zepeda

What Great Principals Do Differently:
15 Things That Matter Most
Todd Whitaker

Leading School Change:
9 Strategies to Bring Everybody on Board
Todd Whitaker

Rigorous Schools and Classrooms: Leading the Way
Ronald Williamson and Barbara R. Blackburn

Classroom Walkthroughs to Improve Teaching and Learning
Donald Kachur, Judith Stout, and Claudia Edwards

Help Teachers Engage Students: Action Tools for Administrators
Annette Brinkman, Gary Forlini, and Ellen Williams

Motivating & Inspiring Teachers:
The Educational Leader's Guide for Building Staff Morale, 2nd Edition
Todd Whitaker, Beth Whitaker, and Dale Lumpa

What's New

The updated second edition of *Professional Development: What Works* offers the following changes and additions:

- Expanded coverage of job-embedded learning, which is a cost-effective way for administrators to enhance professional development of their staff;

- More information on the theoretical grounding of professional development;

- Updated references and figures throughout the book, to reflect newly published literature on the topics covered;

- Inclusion of the 2011 *Standards for Professional Learning* by Learning Forward;

- User-friendly tabs for easy reference; and

- Downloadable tools for your own use, available on www.eyeoneducation.com (see page xix).

Acknowledgments

There are many people who provided assistance as I was writing this book, and I hope I pay a befitting tribute to the contributions each person has made during this journey. I want to thank my research assistants, Oksana Parylo and Lauren Moret. Oksana sought new articles and references to update this edition of the book. Both Oksana and Lauren pitched in on so many of the tasks associated with writing a book—proofing drafts, updating the references, asking me the tough and probing questions about the content of the book, and formatting figures, were just a few of the many tasks that they gave so freely of their time to do. With admiration for their work ethic, I believe that Oksana and Lauren represent the next generation of professional developers.

No book is ever complete without the thoughtful and reflective insights provided by reviewers. The external reviewers poured over the first draft of this manuscript. This manuscript is much better as a result of their keen insights and critical but constructive feedback. The reviewers included

- ◆ Dr. Lea Arnau, former Director of Professional Learning for Gwinnett County Public Schools (GA), independent consultant

- ◆ Mary Hasl, Mentor Coordinator, Poudre School District, Fort Collins, CO

- ◆ Dr. Gale Hulme, Executive Director of Programs and Systemic Initiatives at Georgia's Leadership Institute for School Improvement, Atlanta, GA

- ◆ Joellen Killion, Deputy Executive Director, Learning Forward, Oxford, OH

- ◆ Dr. Mike Mattingly, Assistant Superintendent for Curriculum, Instruction, and Staff Development, Denton Independent School District, Denton, TX

- ◆ Kathy O'Neill, Director, SREB Learning-Centered Leadership Program and Executive Director of the Georgia Learning Forward (Formally Georgia Staff Development Council), GA

- ◆ Daniel I. Vorhis, Director of Professional Education, Bucks County Intermediate Unit, PA

- Richard Jones, Executive Director, Learning Forward New York, NY

I am also indebted to the teachers, professional development consultants, principals, and higher education faculty who allowed their practices to be included in this book. These practices are exemplary. Hopefully, their collective voices will be heard by those who want to continue to expand professional development in schools. Of special note are the contributions, lively and informative phone discussions, and e-mail exchanges with the following professionals who graciously agreed to share best practices about professional development.

- Dr. Dana L. Bickmore, Assistant Professor in Educational Leadership at Louisiana State University and former Executive Director, Curriculum and Staff Development, Jordan School District, Sandy, UT

- Kelly Nagle Causey, former Principal, Sonny Carter Elementary School, Bibb County School District, Macon, GA

- Linda Gerstle, Executive Director, ATLAS Learning Communities, Cambridge, MA

- Neal Guyer, Director of School Improvement, Regional School Unit No. 13, Rockland, ME

- Judith Harvey, former Superintendent, Maine School Administrative District No. 50, Thomaston, ME

- Dr. Bill Kruskamp, former Principal, Creekland Middle School, Gwinnett County Public Schools, Lawrenceville, GA

- Mr. Stan Lewis, Principal, Adairsville High School, Bartow County Schools, Adairsville, GA

- Dr. Scott McLeod, Associate Professor, Iowa State University, Coordinator, Educational Administration Program; Director CASTLE; UCEA Associate Director, Communications and Marketing

- Dr. Carter McNamara, cofounder and partner, Authenticity Consulting, LLC, Minneapolis, MN

- Kaite Mediatore, Readers' Services Librarian, main branch of Kansas City, Kansas Public Library, Kansas City, KS

- North Carolina Department of Public Instruction

- Kathy Ridd, Elementary Language Arts and Early Childhood Consultant, Jordan School District, Sandy, UT

- Dr. Brenda Schulz, Director of Teaching and Learning, Forsyth County Schools, Cumming, GA

- Steven Strull, Director, National School Reform Faculty, Bloomington, IN

- Dr. Thomas Van Soelen, Assistant Superintendent, Curriculum, Assessment, Instruction, and Professional Learning, City Schools of Decatur, Decatur, GA

- Dr. Judith Vinson, Director of Human Resources, Peach County Schools, Fort Valley, GA

- Dr. John R. Ward, Associate Professor and Department Chair, Educational Foundations, School of Education, Millersville University, Millersville, PA

- Barry Zweibel, Founder and ICF-Certified Master Coach, GottaGettaCoach!, Incorporated, Northbrook, IL

This book has been a positive experience because of the continual encouragement and goodwill from Bob Sickles, president and publisher of Eye On Education. Your commitment to education and to educators is inspiring, and that is why writing for "Eye" has always been a privilege. The words "fly off the pages" because of the editorial, layout, and production skills of Richard Adin and Lauren Davis.

My family, Daniel R. Zepeda and Robin A. Zepeda, have always been in the background supporting me in so many ways as I finish "one last paragraph."

Sally J. Zepeda, Ph.D.

Professor, Program in Educational Administration and Policy, Department of Lifelong Education, Administration, and Policy, the University of Georgia

About the Author

Dr. Sally J. Zepeda, a former K–12 administrator and teacher, is a professor at the University of Georgia in the Department of Lifelong Education, Administration, and Policy and in the Program in Educational Administration and Policy. She teaches courses related to instructional supervision, professional development, and learning communities.

Sally has written numerous articles in such journals as the *Journal of Curriculum and Supervision*, the *Journal of Staff Development*, the *Journal of School Leadership*, the *High School Journal, NASSP Bulletin, Kappa Delta Pi Forum*, the *International Journal of Management*, the *National Journal of Urban Education and Practice, Review of Educational Research, International Journal of Educational Management*, and *The Rural Educator*.

Sally Zepeda has also authored and coauthored 18 books including the highly acclaimed second edition of *The Principal as Instructional Leader: A Handbook for Supervisors*, the second edition of *Instructional Supervision: Applying Tools and Concepts*, the third edition of *Informal Classroom Observations On the Go: Feedback, Discussion, and Reflection*, and *Instructional Leadership for School Improvement* with Eye On Education.

She served for nine years as the book and audio review column editor for the *Journal of Staff Development*, and she served as chair of the American Education Research Association Supervision SIG.

Sally is a member of the Council of Professors of Instructional Supervision (COPIS) and a lifetime Fellow in the Foundation for Excellence in Teaching. She also serves on the editorial boards for several scholarly and practitioner journals, including *the International Journal of Mentoring and Coaching in Education* and the *International Journal of Teacher Leadership*.

In 2005, Sally received the inaugural Master Professor Award from the University Council of Educational Administration. Sally received the 2010 Russell H. Yeany, Jr., Research Award that honors outstanding contributions to research, and in 2011, she received the Distinguished Research Mentor Award from the University of Georgia.

As a professor-in-residence with the Clarke County School District (Athens, GA), Sally is assisting with the rollout of a teacher evaluation system and providing professional development for school leaders as they work with teachers to improve student learning.

Contents

Free Downloads

Some of the tools discussed and displayed in this book are also available on Eye On Education's Web site as Adobe Acrobat files. Permission has been granted to purchasers of this book to download these tools and print them.

You can access these downloads by visiting Eye On Education's Web site: www.eyeoneducation.com. Click FREE DOWNLOADS or search or browse our Web site to find this book, and then scroll down for downloading instructions.

You'll need your book buyer access code: PDW-7193-5

Index of Downloads

Foreword to the First Edition

Professional Development: What Works by Sally Zepeda reminds me of *Betty Crocker's Cookbook*, the first cookbook I owned. An aunt gave it to me as a wedding shower gift. While I was touched, I remember thinking, "I can cook. My mother taught me basically all I need to know." As a gracious gift recipient, I thanked my aunt and stored the book in the cookbook cupboard that today includes an array of companion books such as *Cooking Italian, Rachael Ray's 365, Silver Palate,* and *The Joy of Cooking.*

Today *Betty Crocker's Cookbook* is one of the most frequently referenced books in my personal library next to my dictionary. It is a staple for holiday baking, cooking, and roasting and for days when I am ready to take my culinary responsibilities seriously. My copy is tattered, stuffed with notes and untried recipes clipped from newspapers, and it continues to have the answer to the question: What if I don't have buttermilk?

Professional Development: What Works will become for many educators their own *Betty Crocker's Cookbook* for all things related to professional development. It is comprehensive enough to serve as the single resource on the shelf of a school principal who is unfamiliar with his or her responsibilities related to teacher professional development, or to refine and extend his or her professional development leadership. It is informative enough to provide school and district professional development committees a broad view of the complexity of the field of professional learning and the stream of decisions and resulting actions that influence its effectiveness. It is sophisticated enough to guide the director of professional development to create a program framework, to determine what to include in a district professional development plan, and to explore how to build the skill of other professional development leaders within the school district.

Professional Development: What Works provides a robust balance of research, theory, and practice. This is its strength. Author Sally Zepeda speaks from a platform of authority, experience, and passion. She holds a single driving assumption that is evident in each chapter: Student learning depends on teacher learning.

Joellen Killion, Deputy Executive Director
Learning Forward

Introduction to the Second Edition

Why Does Professional Development Matter?

The primary ideas promoted in this book resonate with what Tienken and Stonaker (2007) so aptly share, "every day is a professional development day" (p. 24). For principals and other leaders, the direction is clear: schools that succeed are schools in which every participant is a learner. Atrophy and stagnation begin where growth ceases. Although no principal can "do it all," the principal is the *point of convergence* for all that the school is and does. The principal sets the tenor in all facets of the school. Students, teachers, and staff reflect the direction and motivation demonstrated by the principal, and as Darling-Hammond (2003) says, "Great school leaders create nurturing school environments in which accomplished teaching can flourish and grow" (p. 13).

Who Is Responsible for Professional Development?

This book is for leaders who support and promote collaborative and ongoing professional learning and development for and with teachers. Recent studies emphasize the importance of collaborative inquiry to teacher professional development (Levine, 2010; Levine & Marcus, 2010; Musanti & Pence, 2010). One common form of teacher collaboration is participating as a member of a learning community (Skerrett, 2010) or a professional learning community (Jacobson, 2010). Having identified teacher learning and professional development as a complex process, it is time to recognize the need to acknowledge the importance of job-embedded, ongoing, and career-long professional development for teachers. This entire book amplifies that "good" professional development is job-embedded. Therefore, the notions surrounding job-embedded learning are trumpeted because of their great importance.

The responsibility of planning professional development for school personnel is no longer a job for one central office leader. In the past, the central office and the building level were disconnected in the planning of meaningful and relevant professional development; to ensure effectiveness, a bridge must be built to connect those two sides. It is important for many people across site and district levels to promote, create, and facilitate professional development for school personnel. Although not exhaustive at the site level, this list of professionals includes teachers, principals, assistant principals, grade-level leaders, team leaders, department chairs, mentors, and instructional and subject-specific coaches. Because of budget austerity, it is urgent that we all (superintendents, human resources directors, principals, the ninth grade physical education teacher, instructional coaches, the fifth grade art teacher, and so on) take on a part of the responsibility to create meaningful professional learning. The time is now. We cannot wait any longer.

Although we are all accountable for professional learning, the responsibilities may look quite different across jobs. There are personnel whose primary work at the central office is to support professional development and learning. Given the subject matter in this book, regardless of one's title, we are all responsible for planning and implementing quality professional development. Titles can be used interchangeably. The message is that professional development is an inclusive, highly collaborative adventure in which a variety of site-based and central office personnel provides the leadership, imagination, support, and mechanisms to help school personnel grow. As a learning tool, this book serves as a roadmap to a never-ending but fruitful journey.

In *Professional Development: What Works,* the reader is led through the necessary ingredients to promote teacher growth and development. This book assists principals and other school leaders in understanding several key concepts that support learning. Attending to professional learning is more than just arranging for professional development to occur on certain days. That type of professional development is counterproductive to what we know about how teachers learn. Moller and Pankake (2006) state:

> Professional learning models are tools to be used, but the real learning happens in the cycle of conversations, actions, evaluation, and new actions that is supported through intentional leadership that gently pressures and nurtures teachers. This inquiry process must be organizationally embedded rather than externally imposed to build teachers' knowledge and skills or increase human capital, within the school's social networks. (pp. 128–129)

It is this gentle pressure along with nurture, affirmation, and support that teachers will champion learning from each other, themselves, and the children they teach.

Effective professional development is learning at the site from the work teachers do. More importantly, however, effective professional development occurs in the company of others who support, encourage, and learn along in partnership. Professional development today is much different from yesterday. The stakes are higher, accountability has led to frenetic methods to find the magic bullet, and often teachers and administrators are looking for answers to bigger-than-life questions related to school improvement, issues of diversity, and student achievement and performance on standardized tests.

Principals need hope; they need to see that there is a way to deal with change; and they need to understand that their response to change sets the tempo for how others will respond to change. The issues and challenges that school leaders and teachers face can be vexing, trying even the most patient and optimistic. The way that schools can thrive and go beyond the status quo is to challenge the status quo by supporting each other, by finding creative solutions, and by creating a forum for teachers to learn from each other—everyday. The principal is called to the challenge to cast a safety net in which teachers can learn from their work and conversations. Principals who accept this challenge become the warriors championing professional development and learning as the primary arsenal.

Teachers and students will become the benefactors of these efforts. Leading and learning to promote growth and development will be a tremendous journey for you and your faculty and staff. I am glad you are here with a boarding pass for the nuggets of information in this book, *Professional Development: What Works.*

Organization of This Book

The journey now begins for the practitioners reading this book. The struggle was more in deciding on a title that would fit accurately the contents of this book. The title, *Professional Development: What Works,* suggests that professional development is a journey. The chapters in this book serve as a compass to guide principals, teachers, and other leaders in the work of designing professional development that supports learning. The first six chapters serve as a road map. They describe how to find time for professional development, how to plan it, how to support teachers, and how to evaluate and assess professional development efforts.

Chapters 7 through 13 explore very specific forms of professional development that can complement the overall learning needs of adults. These forms of professional development can stand alone or can be used in conjunction with other professional development initiatives. These forms of professional development are highly collaborative and rest on the premise that professional learning is job-embedded. Chapter 14 provides final perspectives about professional development and the work that needs to be sustained to ensure that learning opportunities support the high-stakes nature of learning in a standards-based environment.

With seat belts on, a full tank of gas, and a roadmap and compass, we begin the journey of learning together.

Getting Ready to Champion Professional Development

In This Chapter…

♦ Bringing Out the Best in Teachers

♦ Supporting Student and Teacher Learning

♦ Lessons Learned from the Research on Professional Development

♦ Linking Professionalism and Teacher Quality to Professional Development

♦ Learning Forward—The Standard-Bearer for Professional Development

Bringing Out the Best in Teachers

In a seminal work, Flexner (1915) suggested six major characteristics that should be present for an occupation to be called a profession:

> …professions involve essentially intellectual operations with large individual responsibility; they derive their raw material from science and learning; this material they work up to a practical and definite end; they possess and educationally communicable technique; they tend to self-organization; they are becoming increasingly altruistic in motivation. (p. 904)

Teachers are professionals. Teachers grow, evolve, and emerge as professionals through the long-term and day-to-day work they do, and that is why job-embedded learning opportunities need to be the focal point of all professional development efforts. Teachers need support from school leaders and from their peers throughout these opportunities.

Build a Culture to Support Professional Learning

Tienken and Stonaker (2007) report the research that helped their school system change the culture in which professional learning opportunities were offered. They share:

♦ Teachers learn best outside of the constraints of large-group workshops.

♦ Participants in professional learning activities should demonstrate mutual respect.

♦ Learning is an outcome of personal interactions.

♦ Teachers are motivated by participating in a community of learners where knowledge is created and shared among its members.

♦ Small groups facilitate communication and learning. (p. 25)

Additional cultural changes resulted from recent technological advances and the increased use of technology in our schools. Polly and Hannafin (2010) asserted, "To facilitate learner-centered, technology-rich instruction to K–12 students, teachers must be afforded opportunities to develop key understandings and skills, rarely evident in most professional development programs" (p. 557). To meet the needs of distance learners, new online degrees and programs are offered yearly. To date, teacher professional development has not used all the benefits that technology has to offer. Leaders should understand the need for distance professional development and strive to provide it to their teachers. In doing so, leaders must account for different levels of technological mastery and varying access to technology, as one would take any specific context into account when planning and implementing learning opportunities on site.

Supportive Cultures Increase Efficacy

Ferguson (2006) designed the *Effective Professional Development Framework* that details how people are more likely to be ambitious and industrious when five conditions are satisfied. These five conditions are critical to support a culture that engenders professional development and learning. The five conditions are:

1. Success seems feasible on goals that are clearly defined;

2. The goals seem important;

3. The experience is enjoyable;

4. Supervisors are both encouraging and insistent;

5. Peers are supportive. (p. 52)

These conditions parallel what we know about effective professional development and center on the core of what people need to feel successful while they are learning.

Feasibility

Just like the traveler on a long journey, teachers want a clear road map to be able to arrive at the final destination. Although there are often bumps in the road, travelers with a map and compass arrive safely at the destination. Although professional development is learning and professionals never cease to learn, people need feedback along the way. Teachers want to know if they are making progress toward the end goal. They also need to feel that what they are being asked to do makes sense and that the work is doable—that they can achieve what they set out to do.

Important Goals

The work of teachers must have importance and value for the individual and for the organization. The goals of professional development need to be grounded in data to frame the important issues of teaching and learning within the context of the school. Teachers do not want to waste their time "sitting in a workshop" that has little relevance to their daily work. Teachers want professional development that helps them become better professionals, engages them intellectually in the topic, and has immediate application to the work they do with students. Effective professional development has a specific set of goals and learning objectives, activities that support the goals and objectives, and the results from ongoing formative and summative evaluation that extends, adds, or improves skills while simultaneously extending knowledge.

Supportive and Insistent Supervisors

Like students, teachers want supervisors who are supportive of the work they do and the challenges they face; however, teachers need and want leaders who are insistent about leading with a vision focused on learning and development. Teachers will not thrive in an environment where learning—student's and adult's—is not the top priority. It is my belief that teachers do not want to survive in an environment that merely maintains the status quo—teachers want to exceed that benchmark in their own learning and the learning of their students.

Supportive Peers

Equally important to teachers are their peers. Schools that evolve as a learning community create an ethos of care for the individual and for the collective. Teachers want opportunities to learn alongside each other. They crave conversations and opportunities to engage in practices that will give them more data to make informed decisions about the work they are doing with students. Inquiry, reflection, and conversations need to be the staples of professional learning opportunities for teachers. Golja and Schaverien (2007) cite Clark's (2001) work related to the value of conversations as professional development:

> Conversation feels more like an exploratory, wandering walk around a mutually interesting place than a direct journey from one point to another....As a genre for learning and professional development, conversation groups have the wonderful quality of being controlled by the participants. (p. 2)

Collaboration is a key norm that supports and sustains a learning community (DuFour & Eaker, 1998). DuFour (2004b) poses four questions for principals to ask as they move forward with planning and designing professional development at the site. These four questions can serve as a guide in the work of the principal.

1. Does the professional development increase the staff's collective capacity to achieve the school's vision and goals?

2. Does the school's approach to staff development challenge staff members to act in new ways?

3. Does the school's approach to staff development focus on results rather than activities?

4. Does the school's approach to staff development demonstrate a sustained commitment to achieving important goals? (p. 6)

Professional Development Supports Teacher Voice

Teachers need to have a tremendous voice—they need to be heard and supported in their learning endeavors. Professional development must be grounded in a carefully conceived and clearly stated sense of purpose and be embedded in core beliefs that are under constant scrutiny by the members of the learning community. The core beliefs and sense of purpose will allow teachers to listen as their voices guide them in creating learning opportunities for themselves, their students, and the school. In *The Courage to Teach* (1998), Palmer writes: "The only way to get out of trouble is to go in deeper. We must enter, not evade, the tangles of teaching so we can understand them better and negotiate them with more grace…to serve our children well" (p. 2).

The principal's role is to assist teachers in finding their "learning" voices. Without continuous growth for adults, students are shortchanged: "What teachers know and can do is the most important influence on what students learn" (National Commission on Teaching and America's Future, 1996, p. iv). The National Commission on Teaching and America's Future's report concludes "…schools that have found ways to educate all students well have done so by providing ongoing learning for teachers and staff" (p. 9).

Professional Development Is Based on Data

Data are important in the framing of professional development. Data sources for framing professional development goals need to come from the site. Data could include:

♦ Student work samples;

♦ The results of quizzes, tests, standardized tests;

♦ The results of action research; or

♦ Information gathered from formal and informal classroom observations or walkthroughs made by peer coaches, administrators, and other school leaders.

The possibilities for collecting, analyzing, and interpreting data are endless. In subsequent chapters, data sources and approaches are examined. Chapter 6 includes an extended case study on what one school does with analyzing student data—and this type of learning is embedded within the workday and serves to assist the school leaders frame professional development.

Teachers Are Central to Leadership and Decision Making

Borko (2004) states that professional development is "woefully inadequate…fragmented, intellectually superficial, and do[es] not take into account what we know about how teachers learn" (p. 3). Principals do not have to repeat this history. Although budgets continue to tighten, and in many states professional development funds are among the first to be allocated to other needs, principals have one key resource—teachers. Katzenmeyer and Moller (2001) assert "leadership among teachers thrives when they are involved in planning and delivering professional development" (p. 5). The credibility of professional development at the site will yield results that are more positive if principals involve teachers in the planning of professional development (Youngs & King, 2002). Faculty involvement in decision making is essential because "collective decision making results in increased morale, ownership, understanding about the direction and processes of change, shared responsibility for student learning, and a sense of professionalism, all of which help to sustain improvement efforts" (McRel, 2003, p. 1).

Supporting Student and Teacher Learning

Professional development is about learning—learning for students, teachers, and other professionals who support children. Professional development is needed because "in the end, the quality of education that will be available in our public schools will depend on the quality of professional learning opportunities available to teachers" (Randi & Zeichner, 2004, p. 221). Learning to teach is a lifelong pursuit and Danielson (1996) indicates that "continuing development is the mark of a true professional, an ongoing effort that is never completed. Educators committed to attaining and remaining at the top of their profession invest much energy in staying informed and increasing their skills" (p. 115).

Student Learning Is a Primary Focus of Professional Development

The message across the literature and research is that a major factor in improving students' achievement is teacher performance and development (Darling-Hammond, 2003; Marzano, 2003; Randi & Zeichner, 2004). Focusing more on teacher performance is the relationship of teacher knowledge coupled with the ability to differentiate instructional methods to deliver this knowledge (content) (Borko, 2004; Guskey, 2003; Kent, 2004; Marzano, 2003).

It is Darling-Hammond's belief that student learning can be positively enhanced in schools and systems that "provide professional learning opportunities for teachers that build their capacity to teach ways that are congruent with contemporary understandings about learning, use sophisticated assessments to inform teaching, and meet differing needs" (2004, p. 1081). The lynchpin to improving teacher quality and seeing gains in student achievement rests, in part, to the overall professional development made available to teachers.

A caveat is offered here. It is not just the professional development offered to teachers. The everyday work of teachers should focus on assisting teachers to learn from

- ◆ the work they do,
- ◆ the work students do, and
- ◆ the work teachers do with other teachers.

Professional development must support and connect to these aspects of learning. Teachers need

- ◆ follow-up support to ensure that lessons learned in formal and informal professional development are being transferred into practice;
- ◆ the opportunity to learn from their actual work through job-embedded learning opportunities; and
- ◆ a learning community structure that is marked by trust, care, and concern for the members of the community.

Connecting to the Research Base on Professional Development and Student Learning

In 2005, the American Educational Research Association published a policy and research brief entitled, *Teaching Teachers: Professional Development to Improve Student Achievement*. The framers of this report succinctly state:

> It is suggested that professional development can influence teachers' classroom practices significantly and lead to improved student achievement when it focuses on (1) how students learn particular subject matter; (2) instructional practices that are specifically related to the subject matter and how students understand it; and (3) strengthening teachers' knowledge of specific subject-matter content. Close alignment of professional development with actual classroom conditions also is key. (pp. 1–2)

Although optimistic about the gains we have made in understanding learning over the past 20 years, Borko (2004) provides caveats about the impact of professional development on learning. Borko (2004) offers, "we have evidence that professional development can lead to improvements in instructional practices and student learning. We are only beginning to learn, however, about the impact of teacher change on student outcomes" (p. 3).

Earlier, Garet, Porter, Desimone, Birman, and Yoon (2001) shared the same concern about the paucity of research related to the "effects of professional development on improvements in teaching or on student outcomes" (p. 917). Both Borko (2004) and Garet et al. (2001) report that the results of professional development have not been large scale enough to generalize, and Birman, Desimone, Porter, and Garet (2000) report that historically, "evidence supporting the effectiveness of professional development is often anecdotal" (p. 28). However, the small-scale nature of many professional development studies have paved the way for the emergence of numerous "best practices" (Borko, 2004; Birman et al., 2000; Garet et al., 2001).

Borko (2004) identifies three phases in which the research on professional development has unfolded:

- ♦ Phase I: Research at the site with one facilitator;
- ♦ Phase II: Research at the site with multiple facilitators;
- ♦ Phase III: Research comparing "multiple professional development programs, each enacted at multiple sites" (p. 4).

Borko further elaborates that to conduct sound research on professional development researchers must attend to studying

- ♦ the professional development program;
- ♦ the teachers, who are the learners in the system;

♦ the facilitator, who guides teachers as they construct new knowledge and practices; and

♦ the context in which the professional development occurs (Borko, 2004, p. 4).

The base of research points to a strong correlation between effective professional development and gains in student achievement, particularly in the areas of math and science. Much of the research in math and science has been related to large-scale reform efforts. The research has been to scale including a larger number of participants (teachers) and the results of larger numbers of students whose teachers have participated in professional development (Birman et al., 2000; Garet et al., 2001).

Lessons Learned from the Research on Professional Development

Professional development can take many forms such as action research, lesson study, critical friends, and peer coaching—all covered in this book. A research base supports what we know about effective professional development. Throughout this text the word *effective* is used to describe practices that are research-based, tied to standards, and present a coherent structure for teachers who work in an environment in which the work of teaching is rooted in learning. To this end, professional development is not an add-on, and is not a series of discreet activities.

What Does Research Tell Us About Effective Professional Development?

Regardless of its form, professional development is effective if it is ongoing, long-term, and related to the teacher's content area (AERA, 2005; Garet et al., 2001; Learning Forward, 2011). Moreover, effective professional development becomes a part of the workday steeped in the work of teachers. This type of professional development creates opportunities for job-embedded learning. The research is clear:

Professional development leads to better instruction and improved student learning when it connects to the curriculum materials that teachers use, the district and state academic standards that guide their work, and the assessment and accountability measures that evaluate their success. (AERA, 2005, p. 2)

Figure 1.1 details the lessons learned from key research on professional development.

Figure 1.1. Lessons Learned from Key Research on Professional Development (Lessons and Practices Research)

Lessons and Practices	Research
Professional development extends over time	Garet et al., 2001; Loucks-Horsley, Hewson, Love, & Stiles, 1998; Porter, Garet, Desimone, Yoon, & Birman, 2000
Professional development includes planned followup	Corcoran, 1995; Garet et al., 2001; Joyce & Showers, 1995
Professional development is job-embedded connecting to the work of teaching (relevance)	AERA, 2005; Ancess, 2000; Borko, 2004; Wood & Killian, 1998; Wood & McQuarrie, 1999
Professional development is content-specific and related to subject matter	Birman, Desimone, Porter, & Garet, 2000; Corcoran,1995; Garet et al., 2001; Porter et al., 2003
Professional development promotes reflection and inquiry	Guskey, 1999; Loucks-Horsley et al., 1998
Professional development includes multiple modalities of learning— active engagement	Joyce & Showers, 1995; Garet et al., 2001; Porter et al., 2003
Professional development is site-based and includes teachers from the same grade level and subject area	Corcoran, 1995; Garet et al., 2001; Porter et al., 2000
Professional development is based on student performance data	Kazemi & Franke, 2003; McDonald, 2001; Sparks, 1995

Corcoran (1995) offers *Guiding Principles* built on the research of others. Corcoran reports that effective professional development

♦ stimulates and supports site-based initiatives. Professional development is likely to have greater impact on practice if it is closely linked to school initiatives to improve practice.

♦ supports teacher initiatives as well as school or district initiatives. These initiatives could promote the professionalization of teaching and may be cost-effective ways to engage more teachers in serious professional development activities.

- is grounded in knowledge about teaching. Good professional development should encompass expectations educators hold for students, child-development theory, curriculum content and design, instructional and assessment strategies for instilling higher-order competencies, school culture, and shared decision making.

- models constructivist teaching. Teachers need opportunities to explore, question and debate in order to integrate new ideas into their repertoires and their classroom practice.

- offers intellectual, social and emotional engagement with ideas, materials, and colleagues. If teachers are to teach for deep understanding, they must be intellectually engaged in their disciplines and work regularly with others in their field.

- demonstrates respect for teachers as professionals and as adult learners. Professional development should draw on the expertise of teachers and take differing degrees of teacher experience into account.

- provides for sufficient time and followup support for teachers to master new content and strategies and to integrate them into their practice.

- is accessible and inclusive. Professional development should be viewed as an integral part of teachers' work rather than as a privilege granted to "favorites" by administrators. (p. 12)

Linking Professionalism and Teacher Quality to Professional Development

The development of profession and professionalism is a complex process aligned to the dynamic nature of the workforce (Cervero, 1988). Teacher professionalism is examined here and throughout the text from a very narrow point-of-view—teachers increase their professionalism *when* they increase their capacity to lead, teach, and learn from the professional work they engage in during the workday. It is difficult to separate professionalism, teacher quality, and student achievement. Haycock (1998) asserts that "if education leaders want to close the achievement gap, they must focus, first and foremost, on developing qualified teachers" (p. 12). The relationship between student achievement, teacher quality, and professional development is interdependent (Darling-Hammond, 1999, 2004; Haycock, 1998; Randi & Zeichner, 2004). To achieve highly qualified teaching and learning, it falls to school leaders to "provide professional learning opportunities for teachers that build their capacity to teach in ways that are congruent with contemporary understandings about learning, use sophisticated assessments to inform teaching, and meet differing needs" (Darling-Hammond, 2004, p. 1081).

Teacher quality and teacher professionalism have been on the forefront of the national agenda since the release of *A Nation at Risk: The Imperative for Educational Reform*, from the National Commission on Excellence in Education (1983). Soon after this publication, the National Board for Professional Teaching Standards (NBPTS) was established (Danielson, 1996). Moving forward, the federal policy, the *No Child Left Behind Act of 2001* (NCLB), became law that, in part, addressed "highly qualified" teaching and also provided leverage for research-based professional development. NCLB focuses on four areas for recruiting and retaining highly qualified teachers. Those areas are teacher certification, recruitment, compensation for teachers, and professional development.

NCLB is the first time that professional development in federal legislation has been enacted. Darling-Hammond (2004) suggests that student achievement could be realized in school systems that "provide professional learning opportunities for teachers that build their capacity to teach ways that are congruent with contemporary understandings about learning, use sophisticated assessments to inform teaching, and meet differing needs" (p. 1081).

The topic *professionalism* could fill an entire book, but as an overview, teacher professionalism has focused on

- ◆ teacher certification (Cochran-Smith & Fries, 2001);
- ◆ levels of education (Cochran-Smith & Fries, 2001; Darling-Hammond, 1997a);
- ◆ comparisons of the teaching profession to other professions such as medicine and law (Sullivan, 1995);
- ◆ the relationship between teachers and community, parents, and students (Fenstermacher, 1990); and,
- ◆ decision-making patterns of National Board Certified teachers (Schulz, 2008).

What Is a Professional?

First, a professional must possess

- ◆ knowledge and competence acquired from highly specialized training and formal education;
- ◆ the respect and trust of community and peers that leads to a degree of autonomy and self-direction, and;

♦ a set of values, moral and ethical, that allow the performance of the job to become more service-oriented rather than profit-oriented (Darling-Hammond & Goodwin, 1993; Sullivan, 1995).

The next few sections lead the reader through examining professionalism, teacher quality, and the relationship to professional development.

Professionalism and Professions

The scope of time when theorists tried to define and analyze professionalization is quite short (barely 100 years). There are three major approaches to defining professions: static, process, and socioeconomic (Cervero, 1988).

Static Approach

The origins of static approaches go back to the 1915 work of Flexner (mentioned on page 1), which attempted to answer the question of whether social work could be called a profession. Even though the answer to the initial question was "no," this work became a cornerstone of attempts to define professions. Flexner's approach was very traditional; in its very core it was a dual definition with only two possible results: the occupation *is* a profession or *it is not*. The problem to solve was to find out whether the occupation is a profession inherently or not. This approach is very straightforward and does not account for societal, cultural, or any other changes, and, therefore, is limited. Cervero (1988) also pointed out that "[t]he major problem with this approach is the persistent lack of consensus about the criteria that should be used to define professions" (p. 6).

The process approach was initially suggested in the early 1960s (Cervero, 1988). Because static approach was often criticized for its "is or is not" classification, the process approach countered this belief with the statement that all occupations could be located in the realm of professionalism.

Process Approach

The process approach recognizes changes that are happening in the society as well as the influence these changes have on the professions. In addition, this approach views profession as a *process,* and analyzes the occupation in its development, overlooking how long the profession existed. Thus, under this definition the number of professions increases as new and younger occupations and "handicrafts" are added to the occupations that existed for centuries and were recognized as professions by proponents of static approach. Among the positive ones were alignment to the dynamic nature of modern world and association of profession and society; the downsides of this approach were ignoring of social inequities and neglect of history behind the profession (Cervero, 1988).

Buchner and Strauss (1961) claimed that process approach is a common-sense approach and is focused "upon diversity and conflict of interest within a profession and their implications for change" (p. 325). In addition, Buchner and Strauss (1961) claimed that segments differ or even conflict for the following aspect of profession: the sense of mission, work activities, methodology and techniques, clients, colleagueship, interests and associations, and unity and public relations. Because these segments are in movement and the changes are accounted for, the approach is defined as dynamic.

Socioeconomic Approach

Cervero (1988) summarized the studies from Great Britain and the United States that supported a socioeconomic approach and highlighted that these studies show that socioeconomic events classify professions. This approach recognizes a vast array of professions, omitting, perhaps, writers, artists, and athletes.

Larson (1977), a proponent of socioeconomic approach, based his definition on the origins of professions, and stated that historically, "professions were and are means of earning an income on the basis of transacted services" (p. 9). Thus, with new services and procedures introduced in the society, the list of professions increases as people find new ways of providing services and earning incomes.

In addition, Larson (1977) compared and contrasted community-oriented and market-oriented societies and singled out three distinctive characteristics of modern societies that impact the professions:

1. "…for a professional market to exist in a modern sense, a distinctive 'commodity' has to be produced" (p. 14);

2. "…in the formative period, most of the markets for professional services had to be created" (p. 14);

3. "…because the standardization of professional services is bound to the production of producers […,] it depends upon inducing new recruits to accept the economic and social sacrifices of training" (pp. 14–15).

Regardless of the approach, teaching is a profession and teachers should be treated as continually developing professionals.

Professionalism and Teaching

Studies indicate that teachers need not only content knowledge but also pedagogical knowledge (Darling-Hammond, 1997a; Darling-Hammond & Goodwin, 1993); consequently, acquisition of a broad body of knowledge becomes a key component in achieving professional status in education. These notions are often at odds with the typical bureaucratic system found in many schools. Bureaucratic systems lack the ability to treat teachers as highly skilled and trained professionals (Darling-Hammond, 1989) and little time is devoted to teacher induction, further learning, or opportunities for collaborative and collegial discussion about the work of teaching and learning from the work of teaching. Darling-Hammond (2004, p. 1079) states, "schools and districts need to provide systematic supports for ongoing teacher learning."

New policies and procedures will need to be implemented to align professional development activities with school improvement goals (Darling-Hammond, 2004; *No Child Left Behind Act of 2001*).

Professionalism and Decision Making

Policies prescribed by political agencies hinder the ability for teachers to make decisions that are in the students' best interests (Darling-Hammond, 1997a; Schulz, 2008). Darling-Hammond (1997b) states, "teachers who most faithfully follow rationalistic curriculum schemes are least likely to teach for understanding" (p. 72). Laursen (1996) also reiterates the need for a more reflective approach to instruction as opposed to the rationalistic curriculum as not only a means for gaining professional status but for increasing the "teachers' awareness of the learning of students and the creativity of teaching" (p. 54).

Schulz' (2008) examination of National Board Certified Teachers and their coverage of curriculum and decision making shows an unintended consequence—teachers did not believe they could make decisions about students and their progress and what was taught, and that at key times during the year, the curriculum was narrowed. In other words, for these teachers, their professional knowledge about the curriculum and the learners they taught was muted.

Standards

Well-trained professionals improve the quality of the profession as a whole through self-evaluation and continual refinement of best practices (Vinson, 2006). A key study by Clarke et al. (2003) reports the lack of capacity as one of the largest barriers for teachers when implementing standards, particularly in low performing schools. They recommend that states invest in quality professional development and training, especially in the area of classroom assessment techniques. The premise is that for students to show progress, teachers must be knowledgeable in interpreting tests results and monitoring and diagnosing student progress, and be familiar with effective strategies for fostering a motivation of student learning.

Learning Forward—The Standard-Bearer
for Professional Development

Although examined in detail in Chapter 4, the work of Learning Forward—formerly the National Staff Development Council (NSDC)[1]—has

---

1 In 2010, the National Staff Development Council (NSDC) formally changed its name to Learning Forward. This footnote is to acknowledge that change. To retain the meaning of the text of this book, all references to the National Staff Development Council will be retained unless it makes sense to reference Learning Forward.

proven to be the national leader in the work of professional development. Learning Forward (2011) emphasizes that "every educator engages in professional learning every day so every student achieves" (www.learningforward. org/index.cfm). This belief is emphasized throughout the new *Standards for Professional Learning* (Learning Forward, 2011). Sparks and Hirsch's early work (1997) underscored the paradigm shifts in staff development from:

- Individual development to individual development and organizational development;

- Fragmented, piecemeal improvement efforts to staff development driven by a clear, coherent strategic plan for the school district, each school, and the departments that serve schools;

- District-focused to school-focused approaches to staff development;

- A focus on adult needs and satisfaction to a focus on student needs and learning outcomes, and changes in on-the-job training;

- Training conducted away from the job as the primary delivery system for staff development to multiple forms of job-embedded learning;

- An orientation toward the transmission of knowledge and skills to teachers by "experts" to the study by teachers of the teaching and learning processes;

- Focus on generic instructional skills to a combination of generic and content-specific skills;

- Staff developers who function primarily as trainers to those who provide consultation, planning, and facilitation services as well as training;

- Staff development provided by one or two departments to staff development as a critical function and major responsibility performed by all administrators and teacher-leaders;

- Staff development directed toward teachers as the primary recipients to continuous improvement in performance for everyone who affects student learning; and,

- Staff development as a "frill" that can be cut during difficult financial times to staff development as an indispensable process without which schools cannot hope to prepare young people for citizenship and productive employment. (pp. 12–16)

These paradigm shifts in professional development have continued to evolve based on research and lessons learned from practice. Our journey will continue in Chapter 4, where the standards for professional learning are examined in greater detail.

Suggested Readings

Guskey, T. R. (2003). Analyzing lists of the characteristics of effective professional development to promote visionary leaders. *National Association of Secondary School Principals, NASSP Bulletin, 87*(637), 4–20. doi: 10.1177/019263650308763702

Lambert, L. (2003). *Leadership capacity for lasting school improvement.* Alexandria, VA: Association for Supervision and Curriculum Development.

Learning Forward. (2011). *Standards for professional learning.* Oxford, OH: Author.

Sparks, D. (2007). *Leading for results: Transforming teaching, learning, and relationships in schools* (2nd ed.). Thousand Oaks, CA: Corwin Press.

Sparks, D., & Hirsh, S. (1997). *A new vision for staff development.* Alexandria, VA: Association for Supervision and Curriculum Development.

2

Evaluating and Assessing Professional Development

With the end in mind, evaluating the impact of professional development must be at the forefront of planning efforts. Professional development, even in times of budgetary constraints, is a big ticket item with average expenditures ranging from "about 1 percent of operating budgets to more than 8 percent" (Miles, Odden, Fermanich, & Archibald, 2004, p. 1). Noyce (2006) reports similar patterns of spending and states that "we spend $5 billion to $12 billion on professional development each year" (p. 3). In the five school systems that Miles et al. studied, they reported that approximately $4,000 per year was spent on professional development for each teacher in those systems.

Expenditures include paying for substitutes to release teachers to attend professional development, purchasing materials, paying for registration fees, and allocating time for coaches to support teachers after learning new skills.

However, assessing impact and evaluating professional development goes beyond focusing on costs. The efforts involved in evaluating the impact of professional development are now front and center with the provisions related to *No Child Left Behind* (NCLB) and the push for research-based accountability (Guskey, 2000, 2003; Killion, 2002a, 2003; Sanders & Sullins, 2005).

A key element of any human endeavor is assessment. Doctors assess the physical or mental condition of their patients. Actors' performances are reviewed by critics. Figure skaters are evaluated by a panel of judges. Pencil-and-paper tests are administered to students across the country to evaluate how much they have learned. Education initiatives are evaluated to determine a measure of their effectiveness. Whether objective or subjective in nature, assessment is an attempt to measure value. The achievement of value is an important indicator of success.

In professional development, "value" is based on progress toward goals agreed on during planning (see Chapter 4). The success of professional development is based on the extent to which *change* occurs. Goals can be written to initiate change within many different areas: student achievement, implementation of new teaching strategies based on subject-matter standards, technology integration, and team building within the faculty. But there are at least two fundamental questions to ask:

- How does the leader know when transfer of a new practice has occurred?

- How does the leader know whether or not student achievement has increased?

Without systematic evaluation of efforts based on hard data, it is almost impossible to determine if lasting change has occurred.

Guskey (2000) offers four very important reasons why professional development efforts and programs should be evaluated:

1. Educators have gained a better understanding of the dynamic nature of professional development.

2. Professional development today is increasingly recognized as an intentional process.

3. There is a need for better information to guide reforms in professional development.

4. There is increased pressure at all levels of education for greater accountability. (p. 7)

No doubt, all schools and systems experience the press for accountability. Schools and districts launch programs intended to resolve problems, improve conditions, and get results. Sometimes programs are "judged" to be ineffective and scrapped. All too often such judgments are based on perceptions alone rather than on systematically collected evidence, examined in relation to specific, intended goals. Program evaluation is critical to assess professional development, and Killion (2002a) indicates, "Evaluation is a systemic, purposeful process of studying, reviewing, and analyzing data gathered from multiple sources in order to make informed decisions about a program" (p. 42). Informed decisions are based on data. Educators and policy makers need to make good decisions. To make intelligent choices, educators and policy makers need good information.

Royse, Thyer, and Padgett (2010) defined program evaluation as an "aspect of professional training aimed at helping you to integrate research and practice skills, using the former to enhance the latter" (p. 1). Ponticell and Olivarez (2000) suggest that the results of program evaluation can help to answer the following ten questions:

1. What programs are working?

2. Which are not working well and why?

3. What intended results have been realized? Which have not?

4. Which parts of programs have been contributing more than others?

5. Which parts are not contributing and why?

6. What professional development is needed?

7. What changes in supervision are needed?

8. What monitoring is needed?

9. In what areas do programs need to be improved?

10. Are there parts of programs or entire programs that should be discontinued?

Finding answers to questions such as these and more is the task of *program evaluation, the task of judging the worth or merit of a program* (Scriven, 1967).

You Can Do It!

There is only so much that a chapter on evaluating professional development can include. Thank goodness there are several books and resources to provide more in-depth coverage of this critically important topic. A pattern in this book is to offer Suggested Readings at the conclusion of each chapter. I deviate here and offer four books whose contents provide high-quality and in-depth coverage of program evaluation related to professional development. In alphabetical order, these books are:

◆ Guskey, T. R. (2000). *Evaluating professional development*. Thousand Oaks, CA: Corwin Press.

◆ Killion, J. (2002a). *Assessing impact: Evaluating staff development*. Oxford, OH: National Staff Development Council.

- Royse, D., Thyer, B. A., & Padgett, D. K. (2010). *Program evaluation: An introduction* (5th ed.). Belmont, CA: Wadsworth.

- Sanders, J.R., & Sullins, C.D. (2005). *Evaluating school programs: An educator's guide* (3rd ed.). Thousand Oaks, CA: Corwin Press.

Throughout this chapter, readers are led through the major concepts associated with program evaluation. Every attempt is made to show the connection between program evaluation and professional development. The primary message is that although there are a variety of program evaluation models, processes, and approaches, this book champions a collaborative, action-oriented approach to program evaluation (Aubel, 1999; Frechtling, 2002; Patton, 1996). According to Frechtling (2002), "evaluation should be conducted for action-related reasons, and the information provided should facilitate deciding a course of action" (p. 3). This approach aligns with the contents of this book and the insistence that professional development that makes a difference empowers teachers, administrators, and other stakeholders to make critical judgments based on the needs of the schoolhouse. As you engage in the process, remember that program evaluation "is a practical endeavor, not an academic exercise" (Royse, Thyer, & Padgett, 2010, p. 2).

Chapter 4 delves into planning for professional development . Following the back-mapping approach advocated by Guskey (2000) and the wisdom of Killion (2002a), the evaluation of professional development, regardless of the scope, content, or process, must be at the forefront of efforts. Killion expresses the "well-conceived" nature of professional development, and she underscores the integral manner in which program evaluation permeates the process. According to Killion (2002a), a well-conceived staff development plan

- results in an evaluation with more integrity, greater usefulness, and more value;

- ensures that the program's goals and objectives are clearly defined;

- has a clear, logical theory of change;

- guides the collection of relevant performance data;

- increases the likelihood of producing results for students. (p. 2)

As a leader, program evaluation undertaken as a participatory, collaborative approach engages those closest to learning in the process of taking a proactive action stance. Aubel (1999) reports that program evaluation undertaken as a participatory approach reaps key benefits:

- Hands-on, practical, experiential training in monitoring and evaluation techniques.

- Contributes to the institutionalization and use of information for project improvement by local actors.

- Promotes the development of "lessons learned," which can be applied in the future.

As described by Aubel (1999), the participatory approach to evaluation mirrors professional development practices that support job-embedded learning:

> A participatory evaluation is based on the assumption that the stakeholders' involvement will help ensure that the evaluation addresses the appropriate issues and will give them a sense of ownership over the evaluation results. It has been shown that stakeholder involvement also leads to greater use of evaluation results by program decision makers and implementers.
>
> In addition, the participatory approach constitutes a learning experience for the program stakeholders who are involved. It reinforces their skills in program evaluation. In addition, it increases their understanding of their own program strategy, its strengths and weaknesses. Another benefit of the participatory evaluation is that the interactive evaluation process itself can contribute to improved communication between program actors who are working at different levels of program implementation. (pp. 11–12)

With these insights and purposes, the evaluation of professional development becomes the responsibility of the learning community to own. As leader, it falls to you to support an environment where evaluation can be embraced to support and nurture learning. Evaluation is not a punitive, "thumbs up or thumbs down" proposition (Frechtling, 2002), but rather a way to figure out what's working, what's not, why, and where to make purposeful zigzags in the journey to get to the destination. That destination is purposeful learning.

What Is Evaluation?

Gredler (1996) defines evaluation as "the systematic collection of information to assist in decision making" (p. 3). Evaluation is a process in which data are collected and analyzed for the purpose of rendering a qualitative or quantitative (or a combination of both) judgment on the quality of a given initiative. Fullan (1982) warns of the difficulty in this process:

> The collection of evaluation data presents additional difficulties. The field of educational evaluation has burgeoned over the past decade, and in the same period has come the recognition that it is a very complicated business. There are three major interrelated problem areas that seem to plague…any program evaluation: *what information to collect, how to gather it,* and above all, *how to use it.* (p. 247, emphasis in the original)

McNamara (2007) offers a streamlined and practical definition of program evaluation that includes a common-sense approach. Essentially, Mc-

Namara's message is twofold: (a) keep it simple, and (b) focus on what you want to learn:

> Program evaluation is carefully collecting information about a program or some aspect of a program in order to make necessary decisions about the program. Program evaluation can include any or a variety of at least 35 different types of evaluation for needs assessments, accreditation, cost/benefit analysis, effectiveness, efficiency, formative, summative, goal-based, process, outcomes, etc. The type of evaluation you undertake to improve your programs depends on what you want to learn about the program. Don't worry about what type of evaluation you need or are doing—worry about what you need to know to make the program decisions you need to make, and worry about how you can accurately collect and understand that information. (p. 6)

Program evaluation is an iterative process. Program evaluation related to professional development in particular, requires examination of program goals, duration of professional development activities, levels of implementation, change in beliefs and practices, and myriad factors including the professional developer, that are examined throughout this chapter and essentially throughout this book. Because professional development includes teachers attending workshops and other specialized types of training sessions, it is important to track which teachers attended what types of professional development, the followup support provided after the professional development, and what teachers are doing to extend what was learned in these types of professional learning opportunities. In the end, the results of program evaluation serve two primary purposes—to decrease uncertainty while simultaneously increasing understanding.

As a leader, it is important to decide upfront what "it" is that needs to be evaluated. Mizell (2003) indicates there are several items to consider about evaluating professional development:

- ♦ Evaluate the delivery of professional development.
- ♦ Evaluate what educators learn as a result of staff development.
- ♦ Evaluate whether and how educators apply what they learn.
- ♦ Evaluate whether and how students benefit as a result of the educators applying what they learn through professional development. (p. 12)

It is clear from Mizell's list of items that evaluation must go beyond evaluating staff development seminars and workshops as a sole indicator of worth and value.

Myths About Evaluation

The thought of engaging in evaluating the impact of professional development can be daunting. This type of thinking is understandable, but the evaluation of professional development or any other program does not have to be fraught with burdensome complexities. Although the evaluation of professional development is more than rating a "facilitator" by giving "glow" statements at the end of a session, the process of evaluating specific aspects of professional development can prove to be an engaging process in which stakeholders partake in the process of not only collecting information about impact but also and more importantly providing meaning about the results.

The meanings about results stand to have more impact and the likelihood to influence classroom practices. Figure 2.1 (page 24) summarizes three myths about program evaluation.

Program Evaluation and Change

The objectives of evaluation in education are to measure change and to assess results.

- ◆ Have teacher or administrator behaviors changed as a result of professional development?

- ◆ Are these changes consistent with the original goals of the professional development?

- ◆ If not, why have they strayed from the original intent?

Answering these questions is the central aim of educational evaluation related to professional development. Moreover, change is related to professional development in fundamental ways. An end-result of professional development is learning and learning is change. To this end, it is important to understand change and the dynamics of change related to learning. These dynamics can influence professional development.

Figure 2.1. Myths About Evaluation

Evaluation Myth Number 1

Many people believe evaluation is a useless activity that generates lots of boring data with useless conclusions. This was a problem with evaluations in the past when program evaluation methods were chosen largely on the basis of achieving complete scientific accuracy, reliability, and validity. This approach often generated extensive data from which very carefully chosen conclusions were drawn. Generalizations and recommendations were avoided. As a result, evaluation reports tended to reiterate the obvious and left program administrators disappointed and skeptical about the value of evaluation in general. More recently (especially as a result of Michael Patton's development of utilization-focused evaluation), evaluation has focused on utility, relevance, and practicality at least as much as scientific validity.

Evaluation Myth Number 2

Many people believe that evaluation is about proving the success or failure of a program. This myth assumes that success is implementing the perfect program and never having to hear from employees, customers, or clients again—the program will now run itself perfectly. This doesn't happen in real life. Success is remaining open to continuing feedback and adjusting the program accordingly. Evaluation gives you this continuing feedback.

Evaluation Myth Number 3

Many believe that evaluation is a highly unique and complex process that occurs at a certain time in a certain way, and almost always includes the use of outside experts. Many people believe they must completely understand terms such as validity and reliability. They don't have to. They do have to consider what information they need in order to make current decisions about program issues or needs. And they have to be willing to commit to understanding what is really going on. Note that many people regularly undertake some nature of program evaluation—they just don't do it in a formal fashion so they don't get the most out of their efforts or they make conclusions that are inaccurate (some evaluators would disagree that this is program evaluation if not done methodically). Consequently, they miss precious opportunities to make more of difference for their customer and clients, or to get a bigger bang for their buck.

Source: Carter McNamara, MBA, PhD, Authenticity Consulting, LLC. (2007). *Basic guide to program evaluation.* Available at: www.managementhelp.org/evaluatn/fnl_eval.htm. Used with Permission.

Characteristics of Change

Hord, Rutherford, Huling-Austin, and Hall (1987) identify six important characteristics of change, and these characteristics mirror best practices related to professional development. Their research concludes that change is

♦ *a process:* meaningful change is a process that occurs over a period of several years, and is not a single event;

♦ *accomplished by individuals:* change is not effected by groups of people or programs, but through the efforts of individuals;

♦ *a highly personal experience:* because each person is a unique individual, each person reacts to change in a unique way;

♦ *incremental:* as individuals involved in change begin to trust and respect the new practice, they begin to grow in their ability to use it;

♦ *understood best in terms of one's own practice:* a teacher tends to react to change in terms of what impact it will have on the teacher's classroom, students, planning, and time, for example; and,

♦ *focused on the individuals involved in implementation:* first and foremost, change must focus on the people who will implement it, not on the materials to be used; materials do not effect change, people do. (pp. 5–7)

Change and the Evaluation of Professional Development

The evaluation of professional development is concerned with examining teachers' practices—the heart of professional development. Heller, Daehler, and Shinohara (2003) report a "cascade of influences" that needs to be considered when planning program evaluation related to professional development.

Program evaluation starts with the end or outcomes identified. For the program evaluation that Heller et al. (2003) describe, the following questions were aligned to outcomes to measure change and/or impact of professional development efforts:

♦ Do the staff development sessions have the features they were intended to have?

♦ Do participating teachers demonstrate shifts in thinking, knowledge, beliefs, and teaching practices consistent with the project's philosophy and objectives, and with the process and content of the actual sessions?

♦ Are such shifts accompanied by corresponding changes in these teachers' classrooms, with new and better opportunities for students to learn?

♦ Are these classroom changes accompanied by corresponding changes in what students know and can do? (p. 37)

Later in this chapter, data collection techniques and approaches, as well as tips and cues, are examined.

Types of Change

Schlechty (1997) identifies three different types of change: procedural change, technological change, and systemic change. *Procedural change* is an alteration in the order in which events occur, the pace at which they occur, or the configuration of events. An example is changing the sequence of procedures for enrolling new students. These changes are usually of little consequence. *Technological change* occurs because of an advancement in technology. The use of computers instead of typewriters, for example. The job has not changed; only the tools used to complete the job have. *Systemic change* is a modification in the nature of the work being done. This involves changes in beliefs, values, rules, relationships, and orientation. Systemic change challenges the very roots of the organization. It should be no surprise that of the three types of change, systemic change is the least understood and the most difficult to achieve.

Difficulties Inherent in Change

Change, because of its very nature, is a difficult concept for people in all walks of life. First, change means a loss of control (Marshak, 1996; Milstein, 1993). Nearly everyone wants some control over such aspects of life as health, happiness, and professional stability. If any of these are threatened, change is severely impeded. A second reason why change is difficult is that it is multidimensional. One dimension of change is the use of new materials. Another dimension is the implementation of new strategies. Also, change involves acceptance of new beliefs (Fullan, 2001, 2007).

In teaching, change can be as minor as using a new brand of chalk or as major as adopting a new textbook with a radically different perspective from the former one. For many teachers, the use of new approaches can be unnerving. Some teachers have fallen into the trap of using the same teaching strategies and questioning techniques day after day. The suggestion or mandate to implement new practice can be interpreted as an attack on one's competence as a teacher or, worse, on one's competence as a person. This apprehension can trigger defense mechanisms.

Perhaps the most personal dimension of change is the alteration of beliefs. At the very foundation of each person's psyche exists a paradigm "or frame of reference. In the more general sense, it's the way we 'see' the world... a simple way to understand paradigms is to see them as maps..." (Covey, 1989, p. 23). Frazier (1997) describes paradigms as "powerful expressions of how each of us perceives, understands and interprets our environments and our relationships with individuals and organizations" (p. 31). Challenges to our understanding tend to create fear which leads to resistance to change.

Resistance to Change

Resistance leads to barriers to proposed change. Basom and Crandall (1991) identify these barriers to change in schools:

- *Interrupted sequence of leadership:* frequent changes in key leadership positions prohibit the creation of a climate for change;

- *Change is viewed as unmanageable:* too many educators do not believe that meaningful change is possible;

- *Poor preparation:* teachers and principals are frequently ill-prepared for the complex nature of change; conflict management and organizational behaviors represent new and forbidding territory to many;

- *Underrepresentation in the decision-making process:* teachers or administrators who are disenfranchised from the decision-making process have no ownership stake in change; therefore, they do not "buy in" to the process;

- *Tradition:* some teachers and administrators become so deeply attached to the way that they believe school ought to be that any change can be a very painful experience;

- *Competing needs and visions:* administrators and teaching faculty at times have difficulty agreeing on what changes are needed and how resources should be allocated; and,

- *Insufficient resources:* too many times, a lack of time and/or money derail the change process before it starts. (p. 74)

Once the barriers to change have been removed, beliefs and practices can be more readily open to change. These are the fruits of quality professional development. Once barriers are erected, how can they be removed? The answer to this question is to understand the concerns of the individuals involved.

Understanding Personal Concerns

The approach throughout this book is on the highly collaborative nature of professional development and the belief that professional development occurs on the job—all day long, not just at predetermined times "set aside" at key times of the year. Although collaboration is highly desirable, changes in practice are highly personal. Because each person has an individual belief system or paradigm, people will react differently to change. These reactions are outgrowths of their own personal concerns. Hord et al. (1987) organized these concerns into a hierarchy called *Stages of Concern*, which is an integral part of the Concerns-Based Adoption Model (CBAM). In addition to

Stages of Concern, CBAM also employs Levels of Use and Innovation Configurations to assist in better understanding personal concerns in relation to change. Within CBAM, there are seven stages of concern (Figure 2.2). These stages are not set in stone, and people can drift in and out of stages while experiencing change.

Figure 2.2. CBAM Stages of Concern

- Stage 0: Awareness—no concern about this innovation at all;
- Stage 1: Informational—desire to know more about this innovation;
- Stage 2: Personal—"in what ways will implementation of this innovation affect me?";
- Stage 3: Management—preparation for the innovation monopolizes my time;
- Stage 4: Consequence—in what ways is the innovation affecting my students;
- Stage 5: Collaboration—how can this innovation work in concert with what other instructors are doing?;
- Stage 6: Refocusing—knowledge of another innovation which could work even better (Hord et al., 1987, p. 31).

Stages 0 to 2 are referred to as self concerns, stage 3 is a task concern, and stages 4 to 6 are referred to as impact concerns. *Personal concerns* are prevalent when a possible innovation is first announced. Teachers want to know how their practice, status, and job responsibilities will be affected. The management stage is characterized by intense preparation during the final days prior to the implementation of some innovation. Time management is a major concern at this stage. Impact stages are reached when a teacher becomes concerned about the effects of the innovation on students, rather than on himself/herself. Some teachers never reach the upper end of this hierarchy (Hord et al., 1987).

Also important in CBAM is the assessment of the level of use of the innovation. Hord et al. (1987) identified eight levels of use, which are summarized in Figure 2.3. CBAM provides tools for monitoring progress during the implementation of change. It is intended to assist school leaders (e.g., administrators, teachers, district coordinators, and others) in the facilitation and assessment of educational programs. CBAM also demonstrates, perhaps, the most crucial tenet of educational evaluation: participants in change progress through innovations at an individual pace. Given the highly human response to change, it is logical to examine the two primary types of evaluation: formative and summative evaluation.

Figure 2.3. CBAM—Levels of Use

- Level 0: Nonuse—no involvement in the innovation and no moving in becoming involved;

- Level 1: Orientation—information on innovation has been acquired quite recently and teacher is exploring the possibility of implementing it;

- Level 2: Preparation—preparation for the first use of the innovation is underway;

- Level 3: Mechanical Use—energy is focused on day-to-day use of innovation with modification just beginning;

- Level 4A: Routine—stability in use is now apparent and little preparation for use is needed;

- Level 4B: Refinement—use of innovation is varied in order to increase impact on students;

- Level 5: Integration—innovation now used in concert with colleague's strategies; and,

- Level 6: Renewal—teacher reexamines innovation to determine if major modifications are needed to continue to have impact on students. (Hord et al., 1987, p. 55)

Formative and Summative Approaches Needed to Evaluate Professional Development

Both formative and summative evaluation are important. Results from formative evaluation help to make decisions to improve or enhance efforts during the day-to-day, weekly, or monthly operations of professional learning, and this data helps to strengthen and improve efforts. Decisions are also needed to judge the final worth of a particular effort such as whether to continue funneling money and release time for teams of teachers to attend online training or to purchase polycam cameras for online book study or to determine its continuation, revision, or termination. Summative evaluation is conducted at the end of an initiative for the purpose of addressing questions of major changes or accountability (Sanders & Sullins, 2005). It is not uncommon for program evaluation to have both formative and summative components.

Formative Evaluation

The focus of formative evaluation, usually conducted internally, is to ascertain the need for revisions or midcourse corrections. For example, in the implementation of cooperative learning techniques in algebra class, the teacher recognizes that some of the students have limited experience in working in a team. The midcourse correction could take the form of team building exercises for the class followed by reteaching fundamentals of cooperative learning. Nan (2003) offers the key roles of formative evaluation (Figure 2.4).

Figure 2.4. Key Roles for Formative Evaluation

Formative evaluation encourages a process of reflective practice.

- ◆ Rapid feedback. Primarily, formative evaluation provides *rapid feedback*. While a project is in progress, a formative evaluation process provides feedback on how the work is going.

- ◆ Documentation. A formative evaluation process can *document* how professional learning is proceeding, what techniques are used, what problems are encountered, and what impacts are made in early and middle stages of work. Such documentation may be useful.

- ◆ Planning. Formative evaluations assist with *planning* and allow for revision of or recommitment to plans. Formative evaluation involves a comparison of program implementation with program plans. It also allows for a reconsideration of program goals and plans. When a formative evaluation reveals that a program has diverged from previous plans, those involved in the work can choose to revise plans to take advantage of new opportunities or return to previous plans in order to respond to current realities. Information from formative evaluation can provide input to future planning and implementation, thus forming the project's future.

Adapted from Nan, S. A. (2003). Formative evaluation. In G. Burgess & H. Burgess (Eds.), *Beyond intractability*. Conflict Research Consortium, University of Colorado, Boulder. Retrieved from www.beyondintractability.org/essay/formative_evaluation/

Summative Evaluation

Summative evaluation of professional development could provide decision makers and consumers with judgments about the worth or merit, particularly in relation to intended results. For example, suppose a higher-order thinking skills (HOTS) approach was intended to improve students' performance in mathematics on standardized achievement tests. A summative evaluation might compare current students' performance in mathematics on a state or district standardized test to trends in performance of previous students before the implementation of the HOTS approach. If the professional development and learning opportunities for teachers are having the intended effect on students' mathematics performance, the scores of current students should be higher than the trend in the scores of previous students. If the professional development is having no effect, the mathematics scores of current students should be approximately the same as the trend in the scores of previous students.

It is always best to start with the overall goals of the professional development, the training, the materials used to support teachers in learning new skills, and the types of support teachers are receiving as they implement new teaching practices. If half of the math teachers were involved in peer coaching and their students were doing better than those of the math teachers who did not participate in peer coaching, then the system could examine enlarging the participation of all math teachers in peer coaching and mentoring.

Differences Between Formative and Summative Evaluation

The important differences between formative and summative evaluation lie in the purposes and audiences for which they are conducted. In formative evaluation, the audience is the teachers, staff, and administrators responsible for the day-to-day implementation of professional learning. Formative evaluation leads to decisions about timely modification and improvement, and identifies learning needs. In summative evaluation, the audience is also teachers, staff, and administrators, but expands to decision makers and consumers. Summative evaluation leads to decisions about the continuation, revision, or termination of professional development activities.

General Guidelines for Evaluating Professional Development

Professional development evaluation, like professional development, is a basic organizational process (Duke & Corno, 1981). Effective evaluation programs should have both long- and short-term objectives (Rutherford, 1989). Short-term objectives usually target changes in teacher behaviors, in the school, or in the curriculum, whereas long-term objectives focus on improvements in student achievement or behavior. Professional development can be justified only if its ultimate goal is to improve education for students (Rutherford, 1989). Harris (2002a) reports that principals who are most successful in implementing improvements in practice communicate clearly their expectations, provide appropriate technical assistance, and monitor results.

Duke and Corno (1981) suggested four components of effective professional development evaluation. First, the evaluation model must provide information about the overall status of the educational environment created to enhance professional growth. The evaluation component must also provide information concerning the adequacy of the procedure used to initiate, manage, and maintain the organization. In addition, the evaluation model must supply data regarding the effects of training on participants, the school, and the students. Finally, all repercussions (positive and negative) on the participants and the organization must be reported through the evaluation process.

Overview of Program Evaluation Models Appropriate to Assess Professional Development

There are numerous program evaluation models, and each model supports approaches and procedures. Often, the procedures and approaches inherent in these models have many similarities. For the purposes of this chapter, Kirkpatrick's Model, Guskey's Model, and Killion's Model are highlighted. The next section examines overall processes and procedures inherent in program evaluation.

Kirkpatrick

Kirkpatrick and Guskey's evaluation models contain levels. Figure 2.5 highlights Kirkpatrick and Kirkpatrick's Model (1994).

Guskey

Figure 2.6 highlights Guskey's Levels of Evaluation (2000). Guskey contextualized Kirkpatrick's model to the realm of education, and he added the fifth level, Student Learning Outcomes.

In an interview with *The Evaluation Exchange*, Guskey (2005/2006) shared an insight from his work in the field related to Level 5, Student Learning Outcomes:

> Many educators are now finding how useful it can be to reverse these five levels in professional development planning. In other words, the first thing people need to do when they plan professional development is to specify what impact they want to have on student learning.

Figure 2.5. Kirkpatrick and Kirkpatrick's Model of Evaluation

Level	Description
Level 1: Evaluation— Reactions	Measures participants reaction to training. This is a perceptual level that collects data on whether participants liked the training and to determine if the participants believed the training was relevant to their work settings.
Level 2: Evaluation— Learning	Attempts to measure the learning that has occurred related to training (Level 1). Seeks to assess whether or not participants have increased knowledge, skills, and attitudes. Pretesting and posttesting measures are used in addition to perceptual reporting of training participants.

Level	Description
Level 3: Evaluation— Transfer	Seeks to measure/determine if what was learned in a training program (knowledge, skills) has been transferred to the work setting.
Level 4: Evaluation— Results	Seeks to measure/determine if there have been any results based on changed practices implemented in the work setting (e.g., increased production, decreased costs, etc.).

Figure 2.6. Guskey's Levels of Evaluation

Level	Description
Level 1: Participants' Reactions	Did participants find the experiences enjoyable and useful?
Level 2: Participants' Learning	Did they increase their knowledge or skill?
Level 3: Organizational Support and Change	With a shift from the individual learner toward larger organizational issues, were participants supported in order to implement their new learning?
Level 4: Participants' Use of New Knowledge and Skills	Are participants implementing new skills and knowledge?
Level 5: Student Learning Outcomes	Did the learning have an impact on or affect student achievement?

They begin planning by asking, "What improvements in student learning do we want to attain and what evidence best reflects those improvements?" Then they step back and ask, "If that's the impact we want, what new policies or practices must be implemented to gain that impact?" Next, they consider what types of organizational support or change are needed to facilitate that implementation, and so forth. This planning process compels educators to plan not in terms of what they are going to do but in terms of what they want to accomplish with their students. All other decisions are then based on that fundamental premise. (p. 5)

Killion

Figure 2.7 presents Killion's Eight-Step Evaluation Model. Killion (2002a) believes that both "planning and conducting evaluations is linear work in which the steps are highly interrelated. The success of one step depends on the success of the previous step" (p. 44).

Figure 2.7. Killion's Eight-Step Evaluation Model

Step	Description
1. Assess evaluability	To determine clarity, feasibility, and worth of the program, evaluator(s) examine the program's design—goals and objectives, etc. If the program is deemed evaluable, move to Step 2. If the program is not deemed to be evaluable, the evaluator suggests revisions in the program.
2. Formulate evaluation questions	Focus on developing formative and summative questions with an eye on short and long-term goals and objectives. Focus on: 1. results. 2. impact vs. program delivery.
3. Construct the evaluation framework	Determine: 1. what data/evidence to collect. 2. whom to collect data/evidence. 3. sources to find evidence Important to collect data/evidence and how data/evidence will be analyzed.
4. Collect data	Evaluators use the data collection methods determined in Step 3 to collect evidence to answer the evaluation questions.
5. Organize and analyze data	Organize and analyze collected data and display in formats (see Step 6).
6. Interpret data	Evaluators and stakeholders work collaboratively to interpret the data and to formulate recommendations.
7. Report findings	Evaluators report findings using multiple formats that make sense for the different audiences. Recommendations are offered as are different types of reports to meet the needs of the site.

Step	Description
8. Evaluate the evaluation	The evaluator assesses the evaluation cycle, reflecting on the process and the products of the evaluation.

Getting Down to Brass Tacks

Like many human endeavors, there is no uniquely correct method for evaluating educational programs. Professional development is no different. However, there are some generally accepted evaluation processes that are particularly applicable to educational programs: selecting a focus, establishing an evaluation agreement, collecting data, organizing and analyzing the data, and reporting the results to stakeholders.

Selecting a Focus

If an evaluation effort is to be beneficial to a school, precisely what is being evaluated needs to be defined. For any given professional development initiative, many aspects can be evaluated. Sanders and Sullins (2005) suggest examining:

♦ *Program needs:* establishing program goals and objectives;

♦ *Individual needs:* providing for instructional needs of individual learners;

♦ *Processes or strategies used:* deciding what was effective, and why;

♦ *Outcomes of instruction:* determining, to what extent, students are achieving predetermined goals; and,

♦ *Site/district goals:* ascertaining whether or not site and/or district goals are being met. (p. 5)

Establishing an Evaluation Agreement

Regardless of whether an external or internal evaluator is used, there has to be an agreement on what will be evaluated and by whom. It is helpful to have a written agreement that delineates the process (Ashur, Babayco, Fullerton, Jackson, & Smith, 1991). The agreement should establish, in writing

♦ *the focus(foci) of the evaluation:* exactly what is and is not to be evaluated;

♦ *who will be in charge:* who will have final authority over form and content of the evaluation;

- *how will the evaluation be conducted:* how and what types of data will be collected, when and by whom; also, how will the data be analyzed; and,

- *who is responsible for distributing the results:* who is responsible for ensuring that all stakeholders are fully informed of the results of the evaluation.

With a written agreement, everyone involved feels a sense of ownership of the evaluation process. Written agreements also help reduce the fear often associated with program evaluation.

Collecting Data

Program evaluations are designed to answer questions. Questions direct the evaluation. Questions can come from many sources. Probably, the most important sources are the program's participants and the audiences for the evaluation report. Common sources of questions, insights, perceptions, hopes, or concerns are

- policy makers (e.g., school board members);

- administrators and/or program managers;

- practitioners who deliver the program;

- consumers (e.g., students, parents); and,

- audiences (e.g., citizens, community groups).

To ascertain evaluation questions, evaluators most commonly interview these sources to determine

- their general perceptions of the program;

- their concerns;

- what they see as the major goals and results of the program;

- what program activities they see leading to these goals and results;

- what activities they see as critical to achieving these goals and results;

- what program activities they see as negatively affecting the attainment of these goals and results; and,

- what they would do with the program evaluation findings.

Worthen, Sanders, and Fitzpatrick (1997) suggest several criteria for determining which questions suggested by the evaluators' sources would be appropriate to guide the evaluation:

- Will the question be of interest to key audiences?

- Will the answer reduce uncertainty? Does the answer already exist?

- Would the answer yield important information?

- Is the question merely of passing interest to one individual, or is it of lasting interest to many?

- If the question were dropped, would the comprehensiveness of the evaluation be limited?

- Will the answer have an impact on decision making?

- Can the question be answered within available financial and human resources, time, methods, and technology?

An important consideration in data collection is deciding when the collection activities will occur. Sanders and Sullins (2005) identify three concerns in the timing of data collection:

- *Due date:* use the due date of the evaluation to schedule backwards to when the collection should occur;

- *Availability:* determine when the data will be available; and,

- *Convenience:* collect data when it is convenient for participants; avoid rush times such as the beginning or end of the school year, exam periods, or holidays.

A final consideration when collecting data is deciding who will do the collecting. Will teachers and site-level administrators collect data? Are these people available at the time the data collection needs to be done? The principal might want to develop an evaluation team comprised of teachers and other interested parties. If this is the case, then release time, along with other types of support, will be needed. The principal might consider seeking assistance from faculty members from the local college or university.

Organizing and Analyzing the Data

Evaluation questions guide what information is needed to answer each question. Evaluators should involve those requesting the evaluation in determining what information would best answer each evaluation question. Figure 2.8 provides an overview of the major methods used for collecting and analyzing data during evaluations.

Figure 2.8. **Overview of Methods to Collect Data**

Method	Overall Purpose	Advantages	Challenges
Question-naires, surveys, checklists	When need to quickly and/or easily get lots of information from people in a nonthreatening way	◆ Can complete anonymously ◆ Inexpensive to administer ◆ Easy to compare and analyze ◆ Administer to many people ◆ Can get lots of data ◆ Many sample questionnaires already exist	◆ Might not get careful feedback ◆ Wording can bias client's responses ◆ Are impersonal ◆ In surveys, may need sampling expert ◆ Doesn't get full story
Interviews	When want to fully understand someone's impressions or experiences, or learn more about their answers to questionnaires	◆ Get full range and depth of information ◆ Develops relationship with client ◆ Can be flexible with client	◆ Can take much time ◆ Can be hard to analyze and compare ◆ Can be costly ◆ Interviewer can bias client's responses
Documenta-tion review	When want impression of how program operates without interrupting the program; is from review of applications, finances, memos, minutes, etc.	◆ Get comprehensive and historical information ◆ Doesn't interrupt program or client's routine in program ◆ Information already exists ◆ Few biases about information	◆ Often takes much time ◆ Info may be incomplete ◆ Need to be quite clear about what looking for ◆ Not flexible means to get data; data restricted to what already exists

Method	Overall Purpose	Advantages	Challenges
Observation	To gather accurate information about how a program actually operates, particularly about processes	♦ View operations of a program as they are actually occurring ♦ Can adapt to events as they occur	♦ Can be difficult to interpret seen behaviors ♦ Can be complex to categorize observations ♦ Can influence behaviors of program participants ♦ Can be expensive
Focus groups	Explore a topic in depth through group discussion, e.g., about reactions to an experience or suggestion, understanding common complaints, etc.; useful in evaluation and marketing	♦ Quickly and reliably get common impressions ♦ Can be efficient way to get much range and depth of information in short time ♦ Can convey key information about programs	♦ Can be hard to analyze responses ♦ Need good facilitator for safety and closure ♦ Difficult to schedule 6–8 people together
Case studies	To fully understand or depict client's experiences in a program, and conduct comprehensive examination through cross comparison of cases	♦ Fully depicts client's experience in program input, process and results ♦ Powerful means to portray program to outsiders	♦ Usually quite time consuming to collect, organize and describe ♦ Represents depth of information, rather than breadth

Source: McNamara, C. (2007). *Basic guide to program evaluation*. Authenticity Consulting, LLC. Retrieved from: www.managementhelp.org/evaluatn/fnl_eval.htm. Used with Permission.

Figure 2.9 presents a useful matrix for planning which information sources to use for which evaluation questions, data to be collected, personnel responsible, data analysis methods, and audiences for the findings. Wolf (1990) identifies three major steps in the analysis of data. First, data must be organized. Because a large number of variables are usually associated with an education study, data must be organized by variable. Because they are analyzed differently, quantitative variables need to be separated from those that are qualitative. The second step is the actual analysis of the variables. Last is the presentation of the data.

Organization of data is an important step in the process of identifying cause and effect relationships. Separation of data by variables allows the evaluators to view each variable's individual effects on the focus of the evaluation. For example, data from peer-coaching sessions need to be analyzed separately from data collected during a followup training session for conclusions to be drawn concerning the effects of each treatment on a given practice.

Figure 2.9. Evaluation Planning Matrix

Evaluation Question	Information Source	Data Collection Method and Due Date	Personnel Responsible	Data Analysis Method and Due Date	Audience for Findings

Source: Ponticell, J. A., & Olivarez, A. (2000). Evaluating the block schedule. In S. Zepeda and R. S. Mayers (Eds.), *Supervision and staff development in the block* (pp. 197–225). Larchmont, NY: Eye On Education. Used with Permission.

Qualitative data may also be organized according to subject or by question if a written instrument is used. This allows the evaluator to assess the effects of an initiative on different areas within a new practice.

Reporting Results to Stakeholders

This is a crucial step in the evaluation process. How well results are communicated has a direct impact on the ability of decision makers to respond properly. Smith and Beno (1993) suggest these components for the evaluation report:

- ◆ Goals that were established and why;
- ◆ Activities implemented to meet the goals;
- ◆ Persons who participated;
- ◆ Resources used;
- ◆ Satisfaction of participants;

♦ Impact on participants, specific programs, and the institution; and,

♦ Recommendations for changes in the program.

Sanders and Sullins (2005) divide the reporting process into three stages:

1. Identify the audience;

2. Choose an appropriate method for reporting; and,

3. Follow up to ensure evaluation is translated into a plan of action.

Identify the Audience

Guba and Lincoln (1981) developed a set of questions to assist the evaluator in identifying potential audiences:

♦ Which audience is involved in supporting or developing the program to be evaluated?

♦ Which audience potentially benefits from the program?

♦ Which audience may see the program as a disadvantage?

Common audiences for an evaluation report include

♦ the developer(s) of the program;

♦ the funder(s) of the program;

♦ boards/agencies who approved the program;

♦ administrators, teachers, and staff managing and/or delivering the program;

♦ consumers of the program;

♦ groups perceiving negative effects of the program; and,

♦ general school publics/community.

All audiences are not interested in the same information. Some common uses for the evaluation report are

♦ to make policy;

♦ to make continuation or termination decisions;

♦ to make operational decisions;

♦ to provide input into the evaluation;

♦ to react to the evaluation report; and,

♦ to receive general information about the program.

Worthen and Sanders (1987) remind us that any one evaluation would generally not have all the audiences listed, nor serve all the uses for the evaluation report. However, it is important for evaluators to talk with key personnel representing various audiences to learn what they perceive as the purpose of the program to be evaluated, how well they think it works, concerns they have about it, what they have heard about the evaluation, what they hope to learn from the evaluation, and concerns they have about the evaluation. Important audiences might be involved in an evaluation advisory group, in data collection and interpretation of results, or as information sources. Some audiences will have little or no interest in participating in the evaluation process itself.

Choose an Appropriate Method for Reporting

The basic function of the evaluation report is to inform appropriate audiences of the findings and conclusions resulting from the collection, analysis, and interpretation of information gathered to answer the evaluation questions. Evaluation reports can serve many purposes, depending upon the role that the evaluation is intended to play. Brinkerhoff, Brethower, Hluchyj, and Nowakowski (1983) list nine purposes that can be served by evaluation reports (Figure 2.10).

Figure 2.10. **What Evaluation Reports Can Do**

- Demonstrate accountability
- Convince
- Educate
- Explore and investigate
- Document
- Involve
- Gain support
- Promote understanding
- Promote public relations

Worthen et al. (1997) indicate that there are some important items that should be included in almost every evaluation report. They offer a generic table of contents (pp. 414–415) that has been modified in Figure 2.11 (page 43). One critical feature of the evaluation report is balanced reporting. The Joint Committee on Standards for Educational Evaluation (1994) states, "The evaluation should be complete and fair in its presentation and recording of strengths and weaknesses of the program being evaluated, so that strengths can be built upon and problem areas addressed" (p. 105).

Another critical feature of the evaluation report is clear communication. Worthen et al. (1997) suggest several "rules" for clear communication in evaluation reports:

- Avoid jargon;
- Use simple, direct language appropriate to the audience;

Figure 2.11. Evaluation Report Outline

I. Executive summary (usually between two and six pages in length, the summary should contain a very brief description of the evaluation's purpose and data collection methods used, followed by a presentation of the most important findings, judgments, and recommendations with reference pages to the full report)

II. Introduction to the report

    A. Purpose of the evaluation (Why was the evaluation conducted? What was the evaluation intended to accomplish? What questions was it intended to answer?)

    B. Audiences for the evaluation report

    C. Limitations of the evaluation and explanation of disclaimers, if any (What conditions or events affected the collection, analysis, or interpretation of information? What is the evaluation? What is it not?)

    D. Overview of report contents

III. Focus of the evaluation

    A. Description of the program: the rationale for initiating the program, its goals and objectives, its participants, its structure and characteristics, strategies used for implementation of the program, its operating context, and/or resource requirements

    B. Evaluative questions or objectives used to focus the evaluation study

    C. Information used to complete the evaluation

IV. Brief overview of the evaluation plan and procedures (a brief summary of where the information came from and how it was obtained)

V. Presentation of evaluation results

    A. Summary of evaluation findings, using tables, displays, or quotations as appropriate

    B. Interpretation of evaluation findings

VI. Conclusions and recommendations

    A. Criteria and standards used to judge the program

    B. Judgments about the program (strengths and limitations)

    C. Recommendations

VII. Appendices

    A. Description of the evaluation plan/design, instruments, and data analysis and interpretation

B. Detailed tabulations or analyses of quantitative data, and transcripts or summaries of qualitative data

- Use examples, anecdotes, illustrations;

- Use correct spelling, grammar, and punctuation;

- Avoid cluttering the narrative with reference notes; and,

- Use language that is interesting, not dull.

Follow Up to Ensure Evaluation Is Translated into a Plan of Action

As an action-oriented process, program evaluation supports further action by participants or consumers of the evaluation report. For professional development, program evaluation can provide information that "...systematically [determines] the quality of a school program and how the program can be improved" (Sanders & Sullins, 2005, p. 5). Professional development needs ongoing evaluation to ensure that goals are being achieved, needs are being met, and that resources are being used wisely.

Given the iterative nature of program evaluation, the next logical step is for program refinements to be enacted based on the results of program evaluation.

Implications for Principals

Educational programs are inherently incomplete without a proper evaluation mechanism in place. It seems self-evident that the value and quality of a program remains a mystery if no one questions it. As professional developers, principals need to

- empower teachers to be evaluators of their own professional development; and,

- be active evaluators of their own learning.

For principals to expect teachers to take responsibility for their learning, teachers need to

- have a sense of ownership for individual initiatives;

- feel "safe" to take risks in their learning; and,

- be actively involved in the day-to-day evaluation of professional learning and the implications for efforts toward increasing student achievement.

Teachers need to be empowered to be evaluators of their own learning and, more specifically, of their professional development. Teachers, who are disenfranchised from leadership roles in planning and designing professional development, will be reticent concerning its evaluation. Fear or perceived fear of retribution for honest evaluation of professional development will inhibit any meaningful teacher participation in that process.

As with any other phase of professional development, the most effective way for principals to show leadership in evaluation is through modeling. When teachers see principals evaluating their own learning, as well as participating in the evaluation of the school's learning, they are much more apt to be active in evaluation themselves.

Conclusion

Nearly every human enterprise is evaluated to find an answer to the question "Is it working?" In other words, is the outcome of the initiative worth the human and fiscal resources that have been invested? Change is a difficult, yet critical process. It is critical because properly selected and implemented change is the catalyst for individual and organizational growth. Principals are held accountable for the allocation of resources at the local site. Proper evaluation of all programs helps ensure proper use of all resources, and can assist the principal in making the case for further funding. Given that we have started with the end, program evaluation, we continue with our journey with planning for professional development. Take a few minutes to stretch your legs as the journey continues with Chapter 3.

Suggested Readings

Fitzpatrick, J. L., Sanders, J. R., & Worthen, B. R. (2004). *Program evaluation: Alternative approaches and practical guidelines* (3rd ed.). Boston: Pearson Education, Inc.

Guskey, T. R. (2000). *Evaluating professional development*. Thousand Oaks, CA: Corwin Press.

Killion, J. (2002). *Assessing impact: Evaluating staff development*. Oxford, OH: National Staff Development Council.

Royse, D., Thyer, B. A., & Padgett, D. K. (2010). *Program evaluation: An introduction* (5th ed.). Belmont, CA: Wadsworth.

Sanders, J. R., & Sullins, C. D. (2005). *Evaluating school programs: An educator's guide* (3rd ed.). Thousand Oaks, CA: Corwin Press.

3

Focusing on Adult Learning: Releasing the Conditions for Professional Growth

In This Chapter…

♦ The Principles of Adult Learning

♦ Setting the Tempo for Professional Development and the Adult Learner

♦ Looking Across the Teacher Career-Stage Continuum

♦ Motivation and Adult Learning

♦ Principals Draw Out the Very Best Efforts in Teachers by…

The cornerstone of successful professional development is the way in which adults are engaged in learning. Adults need and want to grow professionally; they desire ongoing learning opportunities in a place nestled within their own schools so that they can improve practice.

Reflect on the ways in which traditional professional development unfolds in most schools and systems. Typically, activities are launched in flurries at the beginning of the year, or they are offered as a means for teachers to earn "points" toward requirements for district accountability measures. Disconnected from site or district initiatives, professional development activities scheduled as one-shot events have little lasting impact on adults and their learning, and even more negligible effect on student learning, a tightly coupled goal of professional development. Providing learning opportunities for teachers and staff to grow—professionally and personally—is the fundamental goal of professional development. For the principal to assist teachers with their growth, they need to explore the attributes of adult learning. These attributes should be incorporated into all professional development initiatives, regardless of the format, process, or content.

The Principles of Adult Learning

Over the last three decades, multiple theories attempted to explain how adults learn. Merriam (2001) suggested andragogy and self-directed learning as two pillars of adult learning theory. Adult learning theory integrates action learning, experiential learning, self-directed, and project-based learning (Conlan, Grabowski, & Smith, 2003). To be effective, adult learning should be built on ownership, appropriateness, structure, collaboration, internalization, reflection, and motivation (Langer & Applebee, 1986). Knowles (1990, 1992) asserted that adults are autonomous learners who are goals-oriented, relevancy-oriented, practical people with knowledge and experience behind them that they have learned from. In addition, Knowles asserted that adults need to be shown respect and be motivated to learn. Success, volition, value, and enjoyment are major motivator factors for adults (Knowles, Holton, & Swanson, 2005).

Andragogy, an important concept in planning for professional development, has been defined as "the art and science of helping adults learn" (Knowles, 1970, p. 38). Understanding how adults learn enhances professional development. Honoring the needs of adult learners not only helps teachers to grow professionally and personally but also helps the school move closer to becoming a community of learners.

Principals, more often than not, come from the rank and file of the classroom. As former teachers, principals might have difficulty shifting their view of learning—they are no longer classroom teachers responsible for the learning activities of children. The principal now shifts his or her attention to the ways in which adults learn. This shift might be tumultuous in that principals often find their doorways littered with the problem children, who absorb a great deal of their time and energy. Absent too frequently are discussions with adults about instruction, curriculum, and professional learning. Before exploring the principles of adult learning, consider a perspective offered by Merriam, Caffarella, and Baumgartner (2007):

> Just as there is no single theory that explains all of human learning, there is no single theory of adult learning. What we do have is a number of frameworks or models, each of which contributes something to our understanding of adults as learners. (p. 103)

The Differences Between How Children and Adults Learn

Drawing from the early framers in the field of adult learning, Dalellew and Martinez (1988) provide an overview of the principles of adult learning, and Roberts and Pruitt (2003) offer strategies to engage adult learners more appropriately in professional development. Figure 3.1 examines this overview of the principles of adult learning and the strategies that will more than likely yield richer learning experiences for the adult learner.

Figure 3.1. The Principles of Adult Learning and Strategies to Engage Adult Learners

Principles of Adult Learning	Strategies to Engage Adult Learners
◆ Adult-learning is more "self-directed" and...the impetus for learning is to share information, to generate one's own need for learning; ◆ Adults seek knowledge that applies to their current life situation; they want to know how this new information will help them in their development; ◆ Life experiences...shape their readiness for learning; ◆ Adults have differing levels of readiness to learn; and, ◆ Staff who voluntarily attend in-services, workshops, and seminars usually are those who have determined that they want to learn more.	◆ Make learning both an active and an interactive process. ◆ Provide hands-on, concrete experiences and real-life experiences. ◆ Employ novelty, but also connect to the adult learner's prior experiences and knowledge. ◆ Give them opportunities to apply the new knowledge to what they already know or have experienced. ◆ Be aware of the diversity in an adult group. Use a variety of approaches to accommodate different learning styles and experiences and use examples that reflect the diversity in the group composition. ◆ Use small-group activities through which learners have the opportunity to reflect, analyze, and practice what they have learned. ◆ Provide coaching, technical assistance, feedback, or other followup support as part of the training. ◆ Give adult learners as much control as possible over what they learn, how they learn, and other aspects of the learning experience.
Dalellew and Martinez (1988, pp. 28–29)	Roberts and Pruitt (2003, p. 61)

The Social Aspects of Adult Learning

It is important to consider the social aspects of adult learning. Although adults can learn "on their own," learning in the company of others is a more powerful design for professional development that supports the adult learner. Later, Chapters 7 to 12 explore professional development models and designs that are highly interactive—coaching, peer coaching, critical friends, lesson study, study groups, book studies, whole-faculty study groups, learning circles, and action research. Schools that embrace the adult learner purposefully find opportunities for teachers to learn from one another (Bransford, Brown, & Cocking, 1999; Garrison, 1997). Garrison (1997) stresses, "The individual does not construct meaning in isolation from the shared world" (p. 18). Professional learning opportunities that are embedded in the workday support teachers in learning about their own practices and the interactions with other teachers. The work of the principal in nurturing this type of environment is important, and according to Garrison (1997), "Just like the effective teacher, the effective principal understands the needs of learners, and, in the case of the principal, teachers as learners" (p. 18).

Teacher as Learner

To support teachers as learners, the principal needs to ensure that there are professional development opportunities that are developmentally appropriate and differentiated based on the very characteristics of the teachers at the site. Moreover, professional development that honors the adult learner has followup to ensure transfer of new knowledge into the land of practice. What the teacher does with new knowledge and skills is more important than the professional development activity that the teacher attended. Speck (1996) reports that to facilitate learning, "Coaching and other kinds of followup support are needed to help adult learners transfer learning into daily practice so that it is sustained" (p. 38). Followup support includes coaching (Chapter 7) and embedding learning opportunities within the workday (Chapter 6). Job-embedded learning opportunities, for example, include such work accomplished through study groups, book studies, and whole-faculty study groups (Chapter 8), critical friends (Chapter 9), lesson study (Chapter 10), and action research (Chapter 12).

The National Commission on Teaching and America's Future (1996) recommends that learning for adults needs to be

- connected to teacher's work with their students;

- linked to concrete tasks of teaching;

- organized around problem solving;

- informed by research; and,

- sustained over time by ongoing conversations and coaching. (p. 43)

Like children, no two adults learn in the same manner or at the same rate (Burden, 1982a, 1982b). To understand the ways in which adults learn, principals need to understand who is on their faculty and the experiences, expertise, and skills that each member of the learning community brings. Adults as learners have different learning needs. The ability of the principal to understand and apply the principles of adult learning will determine, largely, the success of learning opportunities (Burden, 1982b). Teachers need ongoing and sustained support in their efforts to learn because teachers

...have been asked to assume new responsibilities and adopt new practices that are substantially different from traditional notions about what it means to be a teacher. Under these circumstances, teachers need time to be learners themselves—a truth that is rarely factored...

and is quite likely an important variable in the dismal track record of educational change efforts over the past 30 years. (Adelman, 1997, p. 2)

With the teacher as the center of learning, ongoing administrative support needs to be embedded in learning goals to create momentum for growth. When organizational and individual learning goals are coupled, professional development has the capacity to transform the school into a learning community.

Time to Reflect on the Vision for What Learning Can Become for Adults

Take a few minutes to list the learning opportunities available to the teachers and staff at your school. List the types of programs and opportunities that adults engage in to enhance their teaching and student learning. Here are a few questions to help you reflect about how these programs engage the adult learner:

1. What roles do the teachers have in planning and delivering these opportunities?

2. What types of activities occur during these opportunities? What are the adults doing while they are learning?

3. What types of followup support do teachers have between formal learning opportunities?

Develop a brief vision statement that details the principles of adult learning you hope to nurture as a leader. Think through how a leader can support these principles in the types of learning opportunities offered to faculty and staff. This activity is well-suited for faculty to complete and the results used to foster school-wide discussion. Time at grade-level meetings, department meetings, subject-area meetings, and faculty meetings is an excellent use of time.

Fostering a unified vision for what professional learning can become, the principal must be in a position to include the community—teachers, professional staff, support staff, students, and parents. When all are engaged as learners, the organization is more capable of growth.

Setting the Tempo for Professional Development and the Adult Learner

Adult learning is supported through the tempo set by the principal, and the relationships that are built and nurtured between teachers, professional staff, and the administration. Figure 3.2 shows the iterative nature of how adults can and should be involved in the professional development processes. Professional development that supports teachers as active learners holds, "Learning is not a spectator sport."

Figure 3.2. Adult Learners and Professional Development

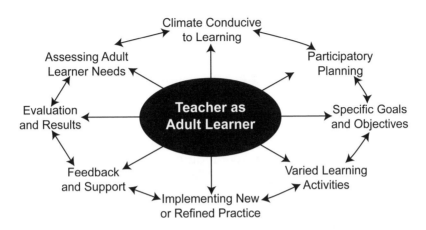

Seeing the relationship to the processes of professional development as depicted in Figure 3.2 can assist principals in providing meaningful learning opportunities. In a content analysis of professional development and school improvement plans in several states, Youngs (2001) offers conclusions about effective professional development:

1. Professional development activities should promote collaboration among teachers from same school;

2. Teachers should be involved in establishing shared goals;

3. High-stakes assessment systems cause a narrowing of focus of professional development and thus weaken professional community and capacity;

4. Professional development must achieve a balance between promoting coherence within and providing autonomy to individual schools. (pp. 296–298)

Effective Professional Development Does Not "Fix" Teachers

Professional development needs to be situated within the school as a proactive process, not as a "fix-it" intervention merely to remediate perceived weaknesses in teacher performance. Often, professional development is viewed from a "deficit" perspective (Ponticell, 1995), or as a "rehabilitation model…[where] an instructional specialist may make several follow-up visits and suggest a variety of specialized programs *for* the teacher…" (Dalellew

& Martinez, 1988, p. 29, emphasis added). Another view is that professional development provides "relief" "…to meet an immediate need within the organization" (Dalellew & Martinez, 1988, p. 29). When these views are assumed by those who initiate professional development opportunities, it is unlikely that teachers will experience growth. The cycle of deficit thinking replete with knee-jerk interventions to "fix" the teacher perpetuates the commonly held view that much of professional development deals with fads that recycle every decade.

Brookfield's (1995) view of the adult learner provides a more optimistic outlook related to the ways in which professional development is approached at the site:

> Viewing teachers as adult learners means that we focus on how they learn to make critically reflective judgments in the midst of action and how they change subsequent actions to take account of these insights. From the perspective of the adult learning tradition, assisting this uniquely adult form of learning becomes an important focus for any professional development activity. (p. 222)

Professional Development and Highly Qualified Teachers

With the advent of the *No Child Left Behind Act of 2001* (NCLB) and its provisions for highly qualified teachers, a larger view of professional development is warranted. History was made with the NCLB legislation because this was the first act to include very specific language about professional development and the nexus between highly qualified teachers who have the skills and knowledge to provide effective instruction and student achievement. The relationship between student achievement and teacher quality has been examined throughout the literature (Darling-Hammond, 1999; Harris, 2002b; Haycock, 1998; Kent, 2004; Randi & Zeichner, 2004). Although the NCLB legislation defines highly qualified in relation to certification and preparation and focuses on the provisions for receiving federal funding to support professional development, principals and others "must do more" to support teachers (Zepeda, 2006).

There is also clear and compelling research that professional development supports teacher quality (Darling-Hammond, 2004; Fullan, 2001; Kent, 2004; Strahan, 2003), and that professional development for in-service teachers supports continuous improvement of teaching (Killion, 2002b). If school systems are to meet the needs of students, there is urgency to "provide professional learning opportunities for teachers that build their capacity to teach ways that are congruent with contemporary understandings about learning, use sophisticated assessments to inform teaching, and meet differing needs" (Darling-Hammond, 2004, p. 1081).

Research About Professional Development and Teachers

There is a relationship between high-quality professional development, teacher quality, and adult learning. Consider these findings:

♦ Professional development should provide for different learning styles, include hands-on activities, and allow for individual teacher goals and self-directed activities (Glickman, Gordon, & Ross-Gordon, 2009);

♦ Professional growth must meet the needs of the individual teacher as well as the needs of students (Fenwick, 2004);

♦ Participation in ongoing professional development increases improved teacher pedagogy (Levin, 2003; Printy & Marks, 2004);

♦ Teacher development is the center of professional development (Gordon, 2004);

♦ Teachers who participate in professional development related to their content field improve their teaching strategies (Frome, Lasater, & Cooney, 2005; Smith, Desimone, & Ueno, 2005);

♦ Learning that is job-embedded at the site, ongoing, and involves group and peer participation is more effective than professional development that is held offsite (Garet, Porter, Desimone, Birman, & Yoon, 2001);

♦ The longer the duration of professional development activities in terms of time and contact hours increases the effectiveness of the activity in terms of teacher learning (Garet et al., 2001);

♦ In schools in which the entire staff engages in professional development and then focuses collaboration on school improvement, the success rate is higher (Murphy & Lick, 2004; Printy & Marks, 2004);

♦ Collaboration at the school site allows for teachers to problem solve among themselves (Randi & Zeichner, 2004);

♦ Teacher learning is more effective when professional development activities are learning-centered, knowledge-centered, assessment-centered, and community-centered (Bransford, Brown, & Cocking, 1999); and,

♦ Professional development that supports learning communities has the potential to meet teacher needs (Bransford et al., 1999).

Prior Experience and Adult Learning

Prior experiences are powerful sources of knowledge and need to be considered as a map to future learning opportunities for teachers. Knowles (1992, as cited in Brookfield, 1995) indicates that "in any situation in which adults' experience is ignored or devalued, they perceive this as not just rejecting their experience, but rejecting them as persons" (p. 223). A major adult-learning principle is for new knowledge and skills to be related to prior learning and experience.

Whether you are a new leader or have held the position for an extended time, it might be useful to profile the adult learners in your building. Figure 3.3 can help guide developing a profile of the faculty. With careful analysis of the information about prior education, professional development, specialized training, and travel, for example, the principal gains insights about the type of professional development activities (content and process) that might make more sense to meet current individual and organizational goals. This type of information also adds information about faculty expertise, and opens windows for teachers to share their expertise with other members of the faculty.

Figure 3.3. Faculty Profile

Teacher	Years of Experience	Highest Degree	Specialized Training
Adams	7	BS (Mathematics)	Cooperative learning applied to math; active in NCTM at the state and national levels
Bailey	15	MA + 15 Spanish & French	Spent 3 months in Spain; Nationally Board Certified

The information collected in Figure 3.3 can be examined more closely by department, grade level, or subject area. Such a profile could give the principal insight on who has what areas of expertise or who has had what types of training.

Next, the principal can *broadly* profile a school's faculty by gathering statistical information about its members. This statistical profile can help the principal reflect on the adult learning needs of the faculty. A faculty sign-in sheet offers a tool to help track and tally information. Figure 3.4 (page 55) offers a worksheet to help collect data about the overall characteristics of the faculty.

The patterns discovered about a faculty can provide a basis for understanding the overall learning needs of teachers. The information gleaned from such a profile is very broad; in a sense, it relates to all but to none.

Such a profile can highlight experience and education; however, this type of profile does very little to provide insights about the developmental and professional stages of the faculty. This is a dilemma because adult needs can change over time as a result of experiences, professional development activities, and personal life events. Similar to young children, adults fluctuate in what they need, at any given time, in order to learn. However, if principals

Figure 3.4. **Characteristics of a Faculty**

1. Number of teachers: _____ Male _____ Female

2. For each teacher, indicate the number of years in teaching and then total the number of years of experience. Then, calculate the average years of faculty experience.

3. Number of teachers whose experience falls years in the ranges:

   a. 1 to 3 years _____ b. 4 to 7 years _____ c. 8 to 11 years _____

   d. 12 to 15 years _____ e. 16 to 19 years _____ f. 20+ years _____

4. Number of first-year teachers _____

5. Number of teachers who will retire at the end of the year _____

6. Wild cards:

   First-year teachers with experience _____

   Alternatively certified teachers _____

   Teachers returning to work after an extended leave _____

   Other _____

7. What overall patterns do you notice?

establish trusting relationships and build confidence, their teachers will reveal what they need. As a result, principals are in a better position to assist teachers meet their own learning needs and to build capacity for the school's collective ability to make improvements to meet the learning needs of their students. Examining career stages gets us closer to knowing more about teachers as learners.

Looking Across the Teacher Career-Stage Continuum

Burden (1982a) found in his research that changes occur over time in teachers'

- ♦ *job skills, knowledge, and behaviors*—in areas such as teaching methods, discipline strategies and curriculum planning;

- ♦ *attitudes and outlooks*—in areas such as images of teaching, professional confidence and maturity, willingness to try new teaching methods, and concerns; and,

- ♦ *job events*—in areas such as changes in grade level, school, or district; involvement in additional professional responsibilities; and age of entry and retirement. (pp. 1–2)

Burden's (1982a, 1982b) research further reveals that teachers go through three distinct stages: survival stage (first year of teaching), adjustment stage (years two through four), and mature stage (years five and beyond).

Earlier, Feiman and Floden (1980) discussed teacher growth in terms of career and developmental stages. Figure 3.5 depicts dominant ideas about teacher stages and career development. You are encouraged to think about your teachers while reviewing this figure. What you surmise from such an analysis might shed some insight on the staff development needs of teachers.

Figure 3.5. Career Stages and Developmental Needs

Stage Name	Approximate Years in Field	Developmental Theory and Needs
1 Preservice	0 Years	Training and preparation for a profession.
2 Formative	1–2 Years	Survival Stage (Burden, 1982a; Feiman & Floden, 1980). Seeks safety and desires to learn the day-to-day operations of the school and the complexities of facing new situations in the classroom. (Ponticell & Zepeda, 1996).
3 Building	3–5 Years	Striving to develop professionally
4 Striving to Develop Professionally	5–8 Years	Confidence in work mounts as does understanding. Building the multifaceted role of teaching.
5 Crisis	Varies	Actively seeks out professional development and other opportunities for professional growth; high job satisfaction (Burke, Christensen, & Fessler, 1984, p. 15).
6 Complacency	Varies	Teacher burnout (Burke, Christensen, & Fessler 1984, p. 15).
7 Career Wind Down	Varies	Complacency sets in; innovation is low.
8 Career Exit	Varies	"Kahuna" status lets the teacher get by without exerting much effort. Retirement.

Based on the work of Burden (1982a); Burke, Christensen, and Fessler (1984); Christensen, Burke, Fessler, and Hagstrom (1983); Feiman and Floden (1980); Newman, Dornburg, Dubois, and Kranz (1980); and Ponticell and Zepeda (1996).

Uncovering Career Stages—Know Your People

To uncover career and/or developmental needs, the principal can engage teachers in charting their own career stages (Newman, Burden, & Applegate, 1980). A caveat is offered, however: identifying the stages of teacher development is tricky business in that there are no absolutes. The activity described in Figure 3.6, developed by Newman et al. (1980), can help take the guesswork out of this process by having teachers self-identify where they think they are in their own career stage.

Figure 3.6. **Assessing Teacher Career Stages**

Process

1. Have teachers draw a horizontal line across the blank page. This represents the time line of their teaching careers.

Beginning Teacher   **Midcareer Teacher**   **Veteran Teacher**

2. Say, "Careers may be marked by different stages, experiences, changes. If you were to divide your teaching career into several parts, what would mark your divisions? Mark them down on the line. Jot down the special characteristics of each part" (p. 8).

3. After teachers have identified where they are in their careers, the principal needs to provide a forum for sharing this "private" information.

Source: Newman, Burden, & Applegate, 1980.

Setting Professional Development Goals

The process of determining placement along the continuum of career stages and development (Figure 3.6) would be incomplete without followup activities. Goal setting is a natural followup activity. (See Figure 3.7, page 58.) The goals identified by the teacher—influenced by life experiences, prior knowledge, and present needs—can frame a more tailored, differentiated, and developmentally appropriate professional development plan for and by teachers. Working together, the teacher and the principal can determine what types of professional development and learning opportunities will help the teacher achieve these goals.

To extend the credibility of setting individual goals, the principal should build in a mechanism for teachers to evaluate their progress. Some supervisors might prefer to hold a midyear meeting with each teacher. Others might prefer to ask teachers to identify markers of meeting their goals and track progress on their own. In any case, the principal and the teacher should come together at the end of the year to assess growth and learning.

Figure 3.7. Professional Development Goals Worksheet

Cupp Elementary School

Teacher's Name _____ Academic Year _____

PROFESSIONAL DEVELOPMENT GOAL 1:

1. Objectives for Goal:

2. Support Needed to Accomplish Professional Development Goal 1:

3. Relationship of This Goal to:

    a. Team:

    b. School Improvement Goals:

    c. Goals Set in Prior Years:

4. Markers of Goal Completion:

PROFESSIONAL DEVELOPMENT GOAL 2:

1. Objectives for Goal:

2. Support Needed to Accomplish Professional Development Goal 2:

3. Relationship of This Goal to:

    a. Team:

    b. School Improvement Goals:

    c. Goals Set in Prior Years:

4. Markers of Goal Completion:

    Midyear Meeting Date: _____

    Signature _____ Date_____

Progress toward goals need not stop at year's end. Often teachers take the summer to reflect on their year, attend workshops, reconfigure curriculum materials, and refine their instructional approaches. Therefore, the beginning of the school year is an opportune time for teachers to set goals, which in turn can frame the principal's work with teachers throughout the year.

Motivation and Adult Learning

Maslow's (1954) hierarchy of needs might inform a principal's effort to provide learning opportunities based on the needs of the learner. A critical component of effective learning is that teachers become more satisfied, gain self-confidence, and derive value from work and working with others. Adult learners are motivated by success, volition, value, and enjoyment (Knowles, Holton, & Swanson, 2005).

Competence at lower levels of development lays the foundation for working toward higher levels of growth and learning. Motivation theory and career stage theory support the assumption that teachers who focus on survival as they learn the day-to-day tasks of teaching cannot be expected to fulfill their potential for intellectual achievement, aesthetic appreciation, and self-actualization. The principal who knows how individual teachers perceive their own unmet needs can respond appropriately to specific, rather than global needs. Figure 3.8 (Hlavaty, 2001) correlates Maslow's hierarchy of needs to broadly accepted teacher career stages.

Figure 3.8. A Comparison of Maslow's Hierarchy of Needs and Teacher Career Stages

Maslow's Stages	Teaching Stages
◆ Self-actualization	◆ Realizes that teaching is not just a job—teaching is a profession.
◆ Aesthetic appreciation	◆ Enjoys teaching. Seeks additional knowledge and derives satisfaction from the seeking.
◆ Intellectual achievement	◆ Learns things that are applicable. Shares with others.
◆ Self-esteem	◆ Is recognized by coworkers for efforts. Feels appreciated by students and parents.
◆ Belonging and love needs	◆ Getting to know coworkers. Feels comfortable about asking questions.
◆ Emotional and physical safety	◆ Classroom routines established. Keeping up with the workload.
◆ Basic survival	◆ Beginning career. Getting through each day.

Regardless of the stage of career development, all teachers have needs. Their needs and potential for growth can be met only when the overall principles of adult learning and development are considered. The following principles can serve as points of departure in working with teachers.

Principals Draw Out the Very Best Efforts in Teachers by...

If applied, the following six principles for working with adult learners can guide the principal in drawing out the very best in teachers while providing learning opportunities aimed at deepening their knowledge of the teaching craft.

Making Learning Authentic for the Adult Learner

Adults want authentic learning experiences with immediate application in their real worlds of teaching. Langer and Applebee's (1986) research in the area of reading and writing instruction offers a construct for making learning authentic for adults. Authentic learning embraces ownership, appropriateness, structure, collaboration, internalization, reflection, and motivation.

- *Ownership*—When teachers own their learning pursuits, they are more intrinsically motivated to face the thorny issues of teaching and self-learning.

- *Appropriateness*—The maxim *no two learners are the same* also applies to adult learners. The one-size-fits-all learning approach gives way to differentiated approaches, based on teachers' levels of experience (number of years in the school, experience with subject and grade level), career stages, and developmental levels (e.g., a first-year teacher at a new site who has nine years' experience elsewhere).

- *Structure*—Mechanisms are in place to support teacher choices about learning such as peer coaches and study group members.

- *Collaboration*—Opportunities exist for teachers to talk about their learning and for learning to occur in the company of others. For adults, this means that the talk about learning goes beyond casual exchanges in the hallways or at the photocopier. Teachers need to be involved in "animated conversations about important intellectual issues" (Prawat, 1992, p. 13).

- *Internalization*—For teachers to extend their classroom practices, they need to practice and experiment with new methods, receive supportive feedback, and then refine practices gained through the insights that result.

- *Reflection*—Reflection supports teachers to "learn by actively constructing knowledge, weighing new information against their previous understandings, thinking about working through discrepancies (on their own and with others), and coming to new understanding" (O'Neil, 1998, p. 51).

♦ *Motivation*—Adults often seek new knowledge in response to a need. Cross (1992) indicates that adults are motivated by the need to

- achieve practical goals;

- achieve personal satisfaction and other inner-directed goals;

- gain new knowledge; and,

- socialize with others.

Knowing What Motivates the Adult Learner

The changes that mark various stages of life can either motivate or demotivate the adult learner. Adult learning is not static; what motivated an adult in previous years might not do so now. Prior learning experiences affect adults and their current beliefs, self-confidence, levels of self-esteem, and overall drive to succeed at learning. Thompson (1996) points to three very broad assumptions about motivation:

1. Motivation involves the behavior of *individuals,* and this has important implications for principals trying to motivate others. *Principals create conditions* in the workplace that enhance the ability of other individuals to motivate themselves.

2. Individual motivation is driven by something, whether it is goals, needs, or desires, and principals who wish to be successful in creating conditions for motivation must be cognizant of the particular goals, needs, and desires which drive staff members to behave in certain ways.

3. Motivation entails not only initiating, but also maintaining and directing behavior. Therefore, the principal's creating conditions to enhance the motivation of others is not a "one-shot" effort. (pp. 4–5, emphasis in the original)

Empowering Transformational Learning

The primary objective of transformational learning is "to help learners learn what they want to learn and at the same time acquire more developmentally advanced meaning perspective" (Mezirow, 1991, p. 199). Baumgartner (2001) explains that transformational learning differs from informational learning in that it concerns "how" we learn, not "what" we learn (p. 16) and because of this, principals challenge the status quo by empowering teachers to

♦ make critical judgments;

♦ ask critical questions of their practice; and,

♦ revise methods based on active inquiry over time.

Supporting Active Construction of Knowledge

Adults want to study their practices and then through these explorations and conversations, they want to construct new knowledge based on what they have learned. Constructing new knowledge about practice might cause disequilibrium as teachers struggle with new concepts, ideas, beliefs, and values about past practices. Teachers need to be supported as they take risks. Astute principals cast a safety net by supporting a culture for risk taking.

Establishing a Climate Conducive to Adult Learning

An environment of open discussion fosters adult learning. McCall (1997) states, "Underlying all others is a basic assumption that adult learning is best achieved in dialogue" (p. 32). Wheatley (as cited in Lambert, 1995), believes that "individuals generate information in their interactions with each other, information then becomes a feedback spiral enriching and creating additional information" (p. 32).

A relationship of mutual trust and respect between teachers and the principal enhances the likelihood of professional and personal growth. Adult learners are more motivated to take risks if they feel support from their administrators and colleagues, and they are more likely to try new skills if there is no threat of retribution should they falter.

Conclusion

The literature on career stages and adult learning shows that adults have unique learning needs; no one model can be applied across all adult populations. The only constant is that professional development and growth must be ongoing and sustained. An understanding of adult learning constructs and career stage theories can help principals and teachers develop a long-term program of growth aligned with current and future developmental learning needs.

Darling-Hammond and Goodwin (1993) state: "The strength and legitimacy of any profession depends on the continued growth and development of its members.... Professional organizations must have effective mechanisms that provide opportunity for consultation, reflection, self-assessment, and continued improvement" (p. 42).

There is no more powerful method for principals to communicate this axiom to teachers than by modeling a proactive learning posture. Principals who are active learners have taken the first step in creating a community of learners.

Suggested Readings

Knowles, M., Holton, E. F., & Swanson, R. (2005). *The adult learner: The definite classic in adult education and human resource development* (6th ed.). New York: Elsevier.

Merriam, S. B., Caffarella, R. S., & Baumgartner, L. M. (2007). *Learning in adulthood: A comprehensive guide* (3rd ed.). San Francisco: John Wiley & Sons.

Printy, S. M., & Marks, H. M. (2004). Communities of practice and teacher quality. In W. K. Hoy & C. G. Miskel (Ed.), *Educational administration, policy, and reform; Research and measurement,* (pp. 91–122). Greenwich, CT: Information Age Publishing.

Roberts, S. M., & Pruitt, E. Z. (2003). *Schools as professional learning communities: Collaborative activities and strategies for professional development*. Thousand Oaks, CA: Corwin Press.

Releasing the Conditions
for Professional Growth

4

Framing Professional Development Efforts

In This Chapter. . .

♦ Standards for Professional Development

♦ Planning for Professional Development

♦ Identifying Professional Development Needs

♦ Job-Embedded Learning—Finding Time for Professional Development

♦ Planning for Professional Development—Pulling the Pieces Together

♦ Connecting Classroom Observations and Professional Development

---

The structures to support teachers include supervision, professional development, and teacher evaluation. However, some schools, and perhaps by extension the systems in which they reside, fail to connect these support structures to create seamless learning opportunities for teachers. For professional development to make a difference, there is a need to bundle multiple learning opportunities to work in complementary ways. The defining features of such efforts would include learning opportunities embedded in the workday replete with opportunities for reflection, dialogue, and collaboration. Without a school culture that supports collaboration, these efforts will yield few lasting results. However, professional development that informs and inspires individual teachers is not enough. Professional development that matters is systemic.

Professional development cannot be left to chance. Professional development must be planned purposefully and deliberately as part of the workday. Professional development is never the end but rather the beginning of the journey toward learning. Systemically, professional development needs to be integrated with the other learning systems, such as curriculum, assessment, and instruction. In this book, professional development—its many designs and forms—is being "pulled out" for the purpose of learning more about, for example, lesson study, critical friends, whole-faculty study groups, and learning circles.

As teachers and school personnel begin to implement and learn from the professional learning gained from their "professional development," leaders will need to keep an eye on other school systems and programs to redirect attention and to realign these parts of the school system. Because professional development is learning and learning is change, it makes sense that systems—policies, procedures, curriculum, and instruction—within the school will be affected. Professional development should cause shifts.

Teacher professional development should be a continuous process aimed at building professional capacity in teachers (Morey, Satchwell, & Loepp, 2006). To be effective, professional development should be systemic. The six principles offered by Little (1994) illustrate the systemic nature of professional development, and these principles serve to underscore how and under what conditions professional development can be a reform strategy for schools and their people. The six principles (available at www.ed.gov/pubs/EdReformStudies/SysReforms/little1.html) are:

1. Professional development offers meaningful intellectual, social, and emotional engagement with ideas, with materials, and with colleagues both in and out of teaching.

2. Professional development takes explicit account of the contexts of teaching and the experience of teachers.

3. Professional development offers support for informed dissent.

4. Professional development places classroom practice in the larger contexts of school practice and the educational careers of children.

5. Professional development prepares teachers (as well as students and their parents) to employ the techniques and perspectives of inquiry.

6. The governance of professional development ensures bureaucratic restraint and a balance between the interests of individuals and the interests of institutions.

This chapter examines some ideas about professional development, national perspectives and standards for professional development, the process of planning for professional development, and approaches to framing professional development within the context of the school.

Standards for Professional Development

There is a relationship between accountability, improved teaching, and support that teachers need from those who supervise the instructional program. Accountability systems have essentially created a ripple effect between what students and teachers do. Recognizing this effect, the National Association of Elementary School Principals (NAESP) reports:

We've learned that it's meaningless to set high expectations for student performance unless we also set high expectations for the performance of adults. We know that if we are going to improve learning, we must also improve teaching. And we must improve the environment in which teaching and learning occurs. (2001, p. 2)

In its publication, *Professional Learning Communities: Strategies That Improve Instruction* (n.d.), the Annenberg Institute for School Reform (AISR) reports:

Effective professional development to improve classroom teaching also concentrates on high learning standards and on evidence of students' learning. It mirrors the kinds of teaching and learning expected in classrooms. It is driven fundamentally by the needs and interests of participants themselves, enabling adult learners to expand on content knowledge and practice that is directly connected with the work of their students in the classroom. (p.1)

AISR also asserts that "research findings have repeatedly confirmed that a significant factor in raising academic achievement is the improvement of instructional capacity in the classroom" (p. 1) and that professional development that achieves these ends has four "critical factors." Professional development is:

♦ Ongoing

♦ Embedded within context-specific needs of a particular setting

♦ Aligned with reform initiatives

♦ Grounded in a collaborative, inquiry-based approach to learning (p.1).

Wiggins and McTighe (2006) provide insight about learning that can be applied to professional development. Figure 4.1 (page 67) details these insights. There are standards for professional development. In 1995, the U.S. Department of Education published a report, *Building Bridges: The Mission and Principles of Professional Development.* This report provides a broad-based set of principles for effective professional development practices (Figure 4.2, page 67).

In 1995, the National Staff Development Council (NSDC) (renamed in 2010 to Learning Forward) developed the *Standards for Staff Development* and revised them in 2001 to reflect changes in the field. The 12 NSDC *Standards for Staff Development* developed in 2001 are available for review at www. learningforward.org/index.cfm.

In July 2011, reflecting research and the collective perspectives of a task force that vetted feedback from national organizations and policy makers at the state, national, and federal levels, Learning Forward unveiled its latest set of standards. The 2011 *Standards for Professional Learning* contain some major shifts that uniquely situate professional learning as the core mission of the standards. In brief, the 2011 *Standards for Professional Learning*:

1. Have fewer standards;

2. Embrace a holistic view in which the standards work in tandem with one another;

3. Combine the content standards to embrace student learning outcomes and educator performance objectives; and,

4. Have a revised introductory stem, "Professional learning that increases educator effectiveness and results for all students...."

(excerpted from p. 19, *Standards for Professional Learning*)

The *Standards for Professional Learning* (2011) are organized into three major categories: context, process, and content.

Figure 4.3 (page 68) presents the 2011 *Standards for Professional Learning*.

Figure 4.1. Insights about Professional Development that Supports Adult Learning

Learning promotes. . .

♦ fluency and flexible transfer to immediate and long-term situations;

♦ value and worth in the application of knowledge;

♦ transfer of skills;

♦ the power of ideas in the work to be accomplished;

♦ practical applications;

♦ clear priorities;

♦ multiple opportunities for continuous feedback;

♦ opportunities for reflection, self-assessment, and opportunities to apply and reapply prior knowledge to new situations; and,

♦ personalization for the learner.

Adapted from G. Wiggins and J. McTighe (2006). Examining the Teaching Life. *Educational Leadership, 63*(6), 26–29.

Figure 4.2. Mission and Principles of Professional Development

Professional development. . .

♦ Focuses on teachers as central to student learning, yet includes all members of the school community.

♦ Focuses on individual, collegial, and organizational improvement.

♦ Respects and nurtures the intellectual and leadership capacity of teachers, principals, and others in the school community.

♦ Reflects the best available research and practice in teaching, learning, and leadership.

♦ Enables teachers to develop further expertise in subject content, teaching strategies, uses of technologies, and other essential elements of teaching to high standards.

- Promotes continuous inquiry and improvement embedded in the daily life of schools.

- Is planned collaboratively by those who will participate in and facilitate that development.

- Requires substantial time and resources.

- Is driven by a coherent long-term plan.

- Is evaluated ultimately on the basis of its effects on teacher instruction and student learning, and uses this assessment to guide subsequent professional development efforts.

Source: U.S. Department of Education (1995). Building bridges: The mission and principles of professional development. Retrieved from www.ed. gov/G2K/bridge.html

Figure 4.3. The Learning Forward 2011 *Standards for Professional Learning*

Context Standards

Learning Communities: Professional learning that increases educator effectiveness and results for all students occurs within learning communities committed to continuous improvement, collective responsibility, and goal alignment.

- Engage in Continuous Improvement
- Develop Collective Responsibility
- Create Alignment and Accountability

Leadership: Professional learning that increases educator effectiveness and results for all students requires skillful leaders who develop capacity, advocate and create support systems for professional learning.

- Develop Capacity for Learning and Leading
- Advocate for Professional Learning
- Create Support Systems and Structures

Resources: Professional learning that increases educator effectiveness and results for all students requires prioritizing, monitoring, and coordinating resources for educator learning.

- Prioritize Human, Fiscal, Material, Technology, and Time Resources
- Monitor Resources
- Coordinate Resources

Process Standards

Data: Professional learning that increases educator effectiveness and results for all students uses a variety of sources and types of student, educator, and system data to plan assess, and evaluate professional learning.

- Analyze Student, Educator, and System Data
- Assess Progress
- Evaluate Professional Learning

Learning Designs: Professional learning that increases educator effectiveness and results for all students integrates theories, research, and models of human learning to achieve its intended outcomes.

- Apply Learning Theories, Research, and Models
- Select Learning Designs
- Promote Active Engagement

Implementation: Professional learning that increases educator effectiveness and results for all students applies research on change and sustains support for implementation of professional learning for long-term change.

- Apply Change Research
- Sustain Implementation
- Provide Constructive Feedback

Outcome Standard

Professional learning that increases educator effectiveness and results for all students aligns its outcomes with educator performance and student curriculum standards.

- Meet Performance Standards
- Address Learning Outcomes
- Build Coherence

Source: Learning Forward. (2011). *Standards for Professional Learning.* Oxford, OH: Author.

Planning for Professional Development

Instructional leaders who are visible in classrooms and in other settings in which teachers meet (grade level or department meetings) are in an advantageous position to identify professional development needs and to provide the followup support teachers need to implement new skills or to refine existing skills into their daily practices. The supervisor plans for professional development on two levels.

- The first level is planning for professional development to meet global or large-scale needs of the faculty related to school improvement plans.

- The second level is planning professional development that meets individual teacher needs as identified during classroom observations and working with teams of teachers (e.g., grade level, subject matter, departments).

In a perfect world, the first and second levels will meet. More often than not, however, large-scale needs for various reasons often take center stage to meet individual and targeted group needs. The leader can begin thinking about professional development by asking some general questions:

- What professional development is needed and by whom?

- What planning for professional development needs to be completed?

- What resources are needed to provide professional development?

- What followup activities are needed to support the application and extension of skills learned during formal professional development?

- How can the overall impact of professional development on student and teacher learning be evaluated?

The answers to these questions can serve as a guide for framing professional development.

Knowing and understanding the history of professional development in the school and the district is important, and consulting with the district professional development contact person will help to acquaint the principal with the district's vision of professional development. Examining artifacts such as descriptions of professional development offerings will help the principal discover when professional development is offered (during the year, summer), who offers professional development (outside consultants, district-wide personnel), and where professional development is conducted (at site buildings, central office, college/university campus).

At the site level, the principal needs to uncover:

- Who conducts professional development?

- Who decides what professional development should be made available?

- Does professional development align with site-level goals?

- Are there processes in place for teachers to request professional development?

The answers to these questions will help the principal understand the history of professional development at both the site and district levels and to gain insight how and if professional development between these two levels aligns.

Identifying Professional Development Needs

Methods of identifying professional development needs include *informal discussion* (e.g., during planning periods, over lunch), *formal discussions* (e.g., faculty meetings, department, team, or grade-level meetings), *faculty surveys*, and *classroom observations* (Zepeda, 1999). A tracking sheet (Figure 4.4) can assist in (a) tracking identified professional development needs, (b) making connections between identified needs, and (c) identifying strategies to meet those needs.

Figure 4.4. Tracking Professional Development Needs

Need	Teacher(s) Requesting/ Needing	In-House Resources	Strategies
Cooperative Learning	Temple, Vanderhoof, Witt	Ms. Patton	Two workshops, model teaching unit by Ms. Patton, and classroom observations
Classroom Management	All-district mandated	Assistant Principal Smith	Workshop on district classroom management policy; individual meetings with each grade level/ team/department member; classroom observations; followup meetings
Integrating Technology	Denton, Watson, Younger	Dr. Vardaman. (computer science teacher)	Workshop, modeling teaching unit by Dr. Vardaman; followup meetings with each teacher

Perhaps nothing is more hurried than the schedule of a Pre-K–12 teacher. Therefore, making every minute count becomes a necessity, and principals need to learn how to scan the environment, looking for opportunities for teachers to learn. However, before developing learning opportunities for adults, principals need to know *what needs to be learned and by whom.* Opportunities abound for principals to talk with teachers and include time during planning periods and lunch periods to engage teachers in discussion about teaching. In the relaxed atmosphere of the faculty lunchroom, teachers tend to be more comfortable participating in candid discussions about teaching. During informal discussions, the principal can work as a prospector, searching for hidden "nuggets" that can be further examined through more formal discussions in a department, grade level, or team meeting or become a focus in future classroom observations.

The principal can purposefully link supervision and professional development through classroom observations. Needs can also be identified through more formal means such as informal and formal classroom observations. This is the value of making classroom observations a priority. Through an analysis of data collected and the discussion that occurs during the pre- and postobservation conferences, the principal can assist teachers in identifying techniques that can help enhance strategies already in use in the classroom as well as help to identify new strategies or potential problem areas that need attention.

As much of the planning for professional development occurs before each school year begins, some schools distribute surveys so teachers can formally indicate what they want and need to learn. Ideally, there is alignment between site-level goals and the professional development offered at the site. Figure 4.5 offers a sample questionnaire.

Figure 4.5. **Professional Development Questionnaire**

Developmentally Appropriate Middle School

Name: _____ Date: _____

1. Considering our school goals in the areas of assessment, technological applications, and integrated learning, are there specific areas within these goals that you would like to explore next year and for which you feel you would benefit from involvement in professional development activities?

2. What kinds of activities (workshops, collaborative meetings, planning time, in-the-classroom support, formal coursework, etc.) do you feel would most benefit you in your support of the school goals?

3. Are there other areas in which you are interested—classroom management, specific projects, curriculum materials, idea exchanges, discussion groups, etc.?

4. Are there areas in which you have been working and in which you have developed proficiency to be a leader and resource for other teachers in the school or district?

Teacher Expertise—A Rich Resource for Learning

As professional development needs are identified, strategies to meet those needs should be taking form. Often, district and site professional developers look immediately to outside facilitators to support their professional development programs. In the process, resources within the district or site are overlooked. At the beginning of the school year, principals are encouraged to "solicit" volunteers to assist with in-house professional development. Think of the potential in any given school. For the most part, teachers are lifelong learners, and they continually attend workshops, graduate school courses, and other specialized training opportunities to add to their repertoire of skills.

Teachers attend to their own learning during the school year and during the summer. Teachers return to the schoolhouse with new knowledge and new skills eager to implement in their classrooms. However, followup support and encouragement from those who plan professional development is often missing. Here are some sobering facts about learning and transfer of skills. Hirsh and Ponder (1991) conclude that on the strength of a workshop alone, only approximately 10% of teachers are able to transfer newly learned skills into daily practice, and according to McBride, Reed, and Dollar (1994), only 12.6% of teachers reported any meaningful followup to determine if skills learned in professional development workshops were being implemented in the classroom. Chapter 7 continues the discussion about transfer of skills and coaching.

One irony in the work lives of teachers is that they often do not have the opportunity to share with others what they have learned. Effective principals find opportunities for teachers to share their expertise with others. The first step in the process is to identify expertise among teachers, and this can be achieved by *asking* teachers to self-identify their expertise and willingness to share knowledge with others. Two strategies include

♦ developing a self-reporting faculty expertise survey distributed at the beginning of the school year (Figure 4.6); and,

♦ tracking professional development, workshops, and university courses that teachers attend throughout the year (Figure 4.7).

Another way to track teacher expertise is to keep a record of what professional development teachers attend throughout the school year and summer. Often, school systems pay teachers to attend professional development during the year and summer, and teachers need to request funds and substitute teachers to attend workshops and seminars. Teachers by their very nature are lifelong learners and many pursue advanced degrees, add-on certificates (e.g., ESOL, Gifted and Talented, Special Education), and prepare for National Board Certification. A database can assist with tracking this information.

Figure 4.6. **Faculty Expertise Survey**

Dear Colleagues:

Every year we update our Teacher Expertise Pool. Please take a few minutes to review the following areas and check those in which you have expertise and are willing to share your knowledge with others. Looking forward to hearing from you,

Paula

1. Peer Coaching _____

2. Phonics _____

3. Literacy _____

4. Math Our Way Series _____

5. Writing Across the Curriculum _____

6. Big Book Lesson Planning _____

7. Authentic Assessment and Rubrics _____

8. Technology Applications _____

9. Portfolio Development _____

10. At-Risk Children _____

11. Reluctant Learners _____

12. Outdoor Education _____

13. Science Fair _____

14. Music and Art Therapy _____

15. Conflict Resolution _____

16. Other: _____

Name: _____ (optional)

Figure 4.7. Database—Teacher Professional Development

Teacher	Conference or Workshop	Dates	Date of Followup Presentation Made to the Faculty (Meeting Date)	Resources Needed for Followup
Arnold	Cooperative Learning for Special Needs Students	10/23/07	11/09/07	Preview video series on cooperative learning; purchase workbooks for teachers; possible full day in-service for staff—check with central office for funding
Asher	Managing Aggression in Students	03/24–27/07	04/11/07; 04/14/07 (PTA presentation)	Schedule a meeting with counselors and social workers in the school cluster; books recommended by Asher

Job-Embedded Learning—Finding Time for Professional Development

The notion of job-embedded learning is critical to professional development; Chapter 6 fully discusses job-embedded learning. Chapters 7 through 13 detail job-embedded forms of professional development. For now, the discussion of job-embedded learning is purposefully briefly related to time and overall benefits to the professional development efforts.

Job-embedded learning occurs in the context of the job setting and is related to what people share about what they learn from their teaching experiences, reflecting on specific work experiences to uncover new understanding. Job-embedded learning occurs through the ongoing discussions where colleagues listen and learn from each other as they share what does and does not work in a particular setting. Job-embedded learning is about sharing best practices discovered while trying out new programs, planning new programs and practices, and implementing revisions based on the lessons learned from practice (Sparks & Hirsh, 1997; Wood & Killian, 1998; Wood & McQuarrie, 1999).

Sparks and Hirsh (1997) share:

> Job-embedded learning...links learning to the immediate and real-life problems faced by teachers and administrators. It is based on the assumption that the most powerful learning is that which occurs in response to challenges currently being faced by the learner and that allows for immediate application, experimentation, and adaptation on the job. (p. 52)

It is clear that job-embedded learning is about learning from everyday practice as people learn by doing, reflecting on the experience, and making modifications based on the experience, the talk, and the action of doing. Figure 4.8 highlights the attributes and strengths of job-embedded learning. Speck (2002) states that job embedded learning should be a "part of every school's institutional priorities" (p. 20).

Figure 4.8. Attributes and Strengths of Job-Embedded Learning

Job-embedded learning...

- does not require participants to set aside a separate time to learn.

- promotes immediate application of what is learned.

- can be formal or informal.

- links current information to previously learned information.

- supports the generation of new ideas.

Job-Embedded Learning and Time

Time for learning regularly built into the routine of the school day is needed. The principal can consider two strategies for extending learning time into the regular school day by:

- *Rearranging existing time:* planning time for teachers is rearranged to create extended time for teacher learning and planning; and,

- *Creating additional time:* planning time, in addition to the traditional daily planning period, is provided for collaborative learning.

In the best of all worlds, teachers would have extended periods for collaborative planning and learning without having to sacrifice any of their traditional planning time. In the elementary arena, some principals have discovered that by multiplying the school site's workers through innovative use of outside volunteers, this dream can be realized. The varied and complex nature of the curriculum in the secondary arena creates an ideal setting for enlisting the assistance of outside experts. Because both district and state attendance mandates and curricular requirements confine the frequency with which students may be released, schools can multiply their workers through volunteers to provide time for teacher learning. The key is the recruitment of enough volunteers to make release of the teaching faculty for a half-day or full day of learning and planning possible. Volunteers to support this effort could come from parents, patrons of the district, and local business and professional people, especially those who look to the local school district to produce the best possible workforce.

Most schools hold faculty meetings—some weekly, some biweekly, some monthly. Regardless of the faculty-meeting configuration, faculty meetings provide opportunities for staff development opportunities and the promotion of staff collaboration. Much of the typical information that is shared during faculty meetings can be easily distributed by memo, e-mail, or in a faculty bulletin. Principals are encouraged to work with their teachers to design and implement strategies for using faculty meeting time for providing learning opportunities for teachers.

The faculty meeting can become a powerful forum for professional development when teachers who attend workshops and seminars paid for by the school system "present" what was learned. Again, this goes back to the notion that teachers are the most important resource—they bring expertise to their work. The following suggestions can assist framing faculty meetings as a learning opportunity.

- Introduce the teacher and the name of the conference or seminar the teacher attended.

- Publicize the topic and presenters in the weekly memo, send an all-school e-mail, or use the meeting agenda.

- Allow sufficient time by asking the teacher to project how much time is needed.

- Include time for teachers to ask questions, to discuss implications, or to work in small groups.

- Videotape the presentation and keep a copy of the presentation in the library. By the end of the year, there should be a sizeable collection of learning materials. These materials will be helpful for newcomers to the staff in subsequent years.

- Assist teachers with developing a handout about the content of the seminar (or be ready to provide secretarial support to reproduce materials from the seminar) before the faculty meeting.

♦ Followup after the faculty meeting with a summary of the discussion. Seek additional learning materials for faculty based on needs or interest generated during the faculty meeting. Consult with district staff to obtain additional resources.

One way to transform faculty meetings into learning opportunities is to develop a planning committee that would help to shape the focus of faculty meetings throughout the year. The professional development planning committee could meet a few weeks before the school year begins to plan. The committee could include the lead teacher, the instructional coordinator, or one or two grade-level leaders or department chairs in addition to either the principal or the assistant principal. Much of the configuration of the committee will depend on the level—elementary, middle, or high school.

The names of the individuals on the planning committee could be published in a staff bulletin or memo, so that all of the teachers can give their ideas to one of the individuals on the professional development planning committee. The key is to get teachers talking about their professional development needs.

After professional development needs have been identified, a yearlong agenda with a time line based on the consensus of the teachers' professional development needs can be developed. Once the agenda of topics is identified, leadership among the members of the professional development committee can be shared—lining up teachers to present or conduct the professional development with the principal or a teacher (or both) acting as facilitator, timekeeper, or recorder during faculty meetings or in-service days. The agenda and focus of the professional development can be varied. For instance, some topics may deal with faculty interests, while others may relate more to district initiatives or school goals. Sometimes, simply sharing a specific teaching technique makes for a stimulating professional development topic. Figure 4.9 (page 79) offers a summary form of in-house professional development human resources.

This form will expand as expertise and willingness to share expertise grow. In addition to potential workshop facilitators, the process of identifying "in-house" professional development expertise might also assist principals to locate faculty members with expertise and interest in various professional development and supervision models such as peer coaching, action research, reflection, and portfolio development. Other sources of professional development support include regional service centers, area universities, and state departments of education.

Identifying professional developers inside and outside of the district or site is just the first step in planning for professional development. Because workshops alone do not adequately support teacher growth, a comprehensive plan that promotes continuous learning is needed. Although no "magical formula" for planning and conducting professional development exists, some general strategies that help to promote ongoing learning include estab-

Figure 4.9. In-House Professional Development Resources

Teacher	Subject(s) Taught	Areas of Expertise/ Interest
Allison	Mathematics	Integrating Technology in Instruction
Clay	Mathematics	Classroom Management
Jay	Science	Modifying Instruction for Diverse Learners
Patton	Social Studies	Cooperative Learning; Socratic Seminars
Rascoe	English	Calling Patterns as a Classroom Management Tool

lishing the initiative, developing a followup plan, and creating a method for assessing the initiative.

Planning for Professional Development—Pulling the Pieces Together

There are numerous processes and steps to be taken in the planning for professional development, and the scope of this book does not allow for full coverage of each process. Figure 4.10 (page 80) offers planning considerations for large-scale site professional development. By working through these questions and processes with others (such as a planning committee discussed earlier), the principal will be in a solid position to plan and to deliver professional development that is responsive to the needs of the teachers at the site.

Connecting Classroom Observations and Professional Development

Earlier in this chapter, the second level of planning for professional development that meets individual teacher needs as identified during classroom observations and working with teams of teachers (e.g., grade level, subject matter, departments) was identified as a goal. The informal and formal classroom observations and the discussions during pre- and postobservation conferences provide windows of opportunities to connect that work to professional development. Through the purposeful interactions, the supervisor can seek to discover

♦ skills teachers are implementing in practice;

♦ skills that teachers are struggling to implement;

♦ what is working in practice—how, why, or why not;

♦ the ongoing support and resources that teachers need;

♦ followup activities needed to support implementation; and,

♦ teachers who would be willing to let others observe their teaching.

Through peer coaching, action research, and the use of the portfolio, classroom observations can be extended to include teachers working with teachers in addition to the principal. Professional development can be personalized for each teacher and be based on the data collected during classroom observations and teachers' sense of what is most important to examine. The value of connecting classroom observations and professional development represents the tailored nature of learning for adults.

Figure 4.10. **Planning Considerations for Professional Development**

1. Identify the objectives and goals of the plan.

2. Identify the target population (e.g., first-year teachers, fifth grade math teachers, high school English teachers).

3. What are the needs of the teachers and staff who will be the benefactors of the professional development?

4. How were needs determined?

5. Who will be involved in the planning of the program?

6. How will these people be involved in planning?

7. What resources are needed? What are the costs of thee resources?

8. Detail the workings of the plan: What will be involved? What will teachers be doing (hopefully, more than just listening to someone)? What activities are planned for teachers? Identify the types of learning activities that will be embedded in the day-to-day work of teachers and how these activities will be embedded.

9. What types of ongoing support will be provided for teachers? How will this support be given and by whom?

10. How will the plan be monitored?

Conclusion

To provide appropriate learning opportunities, the principal understands the career stages of teachers, the principles of adult learning, the vital importance of sustained "teacher talk" over time, and coaching. In addition to professional development conducted outside of school hours, teachers need learning opportunities that are a part of their daily work. Fulfilling this need requires time during the day. Through job-embedded learning techniques such as peer coaching, study groups, and action research, the principal situates the teacher as the "doer" in their own learning. Planning for professional learning opportunities takes center stage in a school that is a learning community.

Suggested Readings

Easton, L. (2004). *Powerful designs for professional learning.* Oxford, OH: National Staff Development Council.

Ferguson, R. F. (2006). Five challenges to effective teacher professional development. *Journal of Staff Development, 27*(4), 48–52.

Gordon, S. P. (2004). *Professional development for school improvement: Empowering learning communities.* Boston: Allyn & Bacon.

Learning Forward. (2011). *Standards for professional learning.* Oxford, OH: Author.

Roy, P., & Hord, S. (2003). *Moving NSDC's staff development standards into practice: Innovation configurations, Volume I.* Oxford, OH: National Staff Development Council.

Zepeda, S. J. (2007). *The principal as instructional leader: A handbook for supervisors* (2nd ed.). Larchmont, NY: Eye On Education.

Zepeda, S. J. (2008). *The instructional leader's guide to informal classroom observations* (2nd ed.). Larchmont, NY: Eye On Education.

5

Learning Communities

In This Chapter…

♦ What We Know About Learning Communities

♦ Leadership Practices That Sustain Learning Communities

♦ Characteristics of Learning Communities

♦ Learning Communities Promote a Common Vision

♦ Learning Communities Use Data to Ensure Student Success

♦ Teacher Leadership In Learning Communities

Schools can become learning communities if the principal is willing to launch the potential of the people who reside in these communities. Thompson, Gregg, and Niska (2004) make a compelling call for schools to form as learning communities:

> Never before in the history of education has there been such a clarion call for leaders who can create a culture that fosters both adult and student learning and expands the definition of leadership to include all stakeholders in the school. (p. 4)

For learning communities to evolve and then to thrive, DuFour and Eaker (1998) believe that principals need to "create collaborative structures with a focus on teaching and learning" (p. 196). Further developing the ideas of DuFour and Eaker (1998), Polly and Hannafin (2010) note that professional learning communities "and computer-based assessments enable teachers to use student work samples and assessment data as to identify gaps in student learning, select learner-centered tasks that will address the gaps, and make instructional decisions based on evidence of student learning" (pp. 559–563).

Without ensuring that the "right set" of learning conditions is present, a learning community cannot exist, let alone flourish (Joyce, 2004). Schools will continue to be complex, and the press for accountability mounts pressure for people to perform. Because of these complexities and the work that teachers are called upon to accomplish, there is a need to reconfigure the ways in which adults work with one another. Teachers need a safety net to be able to thrive in their work.

A learning community is built by everyone. A learning community will only evolve if the leader actively nurtures and models growth-oriented practices and processes. As the leader of leaders in a learning community, the principal must possess a strong resolve to create and sustain the conditions and culture needed to build capacity in the individual and the organization. Finally, the role of the principal in a learning community needs to change from that of telling teachers how to teach and selling teachers on new fads to that of facilitating the processes by which teachers can discover knowledge about themselves and their practices. For the school, moving toward a learning community is "an adventure in shared leadership and authentic relationships" (Sergiovanni, 1994, p. 155).

What We Know About Learning Communities

A learning community is a group of individuals who share a similar vision of educational values (e.g., honesty, respect, trust, courage, and compassion) and beliefs (e.g., all children can learn). As a result of this shared vision, a community of learners can work toward common goals that enhance professional and personal development. In addition, a community of learners, whose work and activities are linked to the organization, helps the organization grow. Through collaborative efforts, a community of learners creates synergy, a synchronized energy where the power of the group is more profound than that of any one individual (Covey, 1992; Senge, 1990). Harris (2003) forwards that in the learning community structure, all "teachers participate in decision making and take joint responsibility for outcomes of their work" (p. 321), and according to Bolam et al. (2005):

> A professional learning community is an inclusive group of people, motivated by a shared learning vision, who support and work with each other, finding ways, inside and outside their immediate community, to enquire on their practice and together learn new and better approaches that will enhance all pupil's learning. (p. 2)

Whereas traditional professional development approaches to learning have focused on helping educators hone individual skills, the construct of the "professional learning community" as a schoolwide professional development effort involves the collective capacity of all people in the organization (Dufour & Eaker, 1998; DuFour, DuFour, Eaker, & Many, 2006).

Skerrett (2010) examined how academic departments strove to become learning communities and differentiated between a community of practice and a learning community. The major difference between the two exists in the focus of the work:

> Communities of practice initially develop around a shared work objective but they do not automatically operate as learning communi-

ties. Learning communities are those that continuously inquire into their practice, and, as a result, discover, create and negotiate new meanings that improve their practice. It takes sustained collaborative engagement in practice and the careful design of social infrastructures to enable a community of practice to develop into a *learning* community. (Skerrett, 2010, p. 648, emphasis in original)

In a learning community, both teachers and administrators work to provide leadership. To this end, learning community members must be ready to confront the fragmented way in which schools are organized (e.g., departments, grade levels, and specialty groups such as gifted and talented), and they must be committed to working alongside each other as a collective to provide support.

Leadership Practices That Sustain Learning Communities

A community needs a clear focus to sustain learning and to keep everyone moving in the same direction. The needs of individuals and the organization must be identified so that stakeholders can embrace learning itself for its intrinsic rewards. In learning communities, those closest to making the school successful need a voice in developing, implementing, and evaluating professional development (Zepeda, 1999). If the principal wants to transform instruction and learning, the principal should first examine core beliefs about professional development as a vehicle to improve "what's best for kids."

To start the discussion, engage the community in identifying core beliefs (Figure 5.1, page 85). This exploration cannot be done in isolation, and the members of the learning community need to be engaged in prolonged discussions about the core beliefs. This type of discussion can begin during a faculty meeting, but much more time will be needed to come to consensus and then formulating a plan to work toward supporting the shared core beliefs.

A major tenet in learning communities is that interconnectedness exists among members of the community. The interconnected nature of a professional learning community requires teachers to participate in

> reflective dialogue; observe and react to one another's teaching; jointly develop curriculum and assessment practices; work together to implement new programs and strategies; share lesson plans and materials; and collectively engage in problem solving, action research, and continuous improvement practices. (DuFour & Eaker, 1998, pp. 117–118)

To support this type of work, roles related to authority need to be examined.

Figure 5.1. **Identifying Core Beliefs**

As a faculty, we believe:

Students…

    1.

    2.

    3.

The role of community members in supporting these beliefs…

    1.

    2.

    3.

Parents can be engaged in helping us by…

    1.

    2.

    3.

The supports we need include…

    1.

    2.

    3.

The Changing Roles of Authority in Learning Communities

To provide the conditions that support learning communities, a broader picture of the school is needed. This broader picture includes examining the role of teachers and others, including the principal, and the ways in which decisions are made. Sergiovanni (1996) believes that leaders, "plant the seeds of community….They lead by following. They lead by service…[and] by involving others to share in the burdens of leadership" (p. xix). Similarly, Senge (1996) indicates that leaders who want to promote a learning organization are "seed carriers" who "connect people of like mind in diverse settings to each other's learning efforts" (pp. 55–56).

In schools that form as a learning community, "the principal becomes less [of] an inspector of teacher competence and more [of] a facilitator of teacher growth" (Marks & Printy, 2003, p. 374). Principals, according to Doyle (2004), would move from "sole decision makers" to "facilitators," teachers would move from "passive participants" to "key decision makers"; to engage in these shifts, and to assume this new work, teachers would need "encourage-ment, support, and professional development" (p. 197).

The learning community construct is about building the capacity of its members. The following perspectives about building capacity have been culled from the research and literature about learning communities:

- ♦ Building leadership capacity requires examination of hierarchical structures and the culture of a school (Harris, 2003);

- ♦ Empowering others to share in the responsibility of decision making (DuFour et al., 2006);

- ♦ Encouraging "mutual respect, shared purpose, allowance for individual expression" (Crowther, Kaagan, Ferguson, & Hann, 2002, p. 38); and,

- ♦ Promoting distributed leadership that supports leadership as a practice in which the work is dispersed through the interactions of school leaders and followers within the context of the school (Spillane, 2006; Spillane, Halverson, & Diamond, 2001, 2004).

Teacher Development: The Heart of a Learning Community

Learning communities can only be built by reconceptualizing how we think about teacher and organizational development through an examination of processes and practices that

- ♦ encourage teachers to reflect on their own practice;

- ♦ acknowledge that teachers develop at different rates, and that at any given time some teachers are more ready to learn new things than others;

- ♦ acknowledge that teachers have different talents and interests;

- ♦ give high priority to conversation…among teachers;

- ♦ provide for collaborative learning among teachers;

- ♦ emphasize caring relationships and felt interdependencies;

- ♦ call upon teachers to respond morally to their work; and,

- ♦ view teachers as supervisors of learning communities. (Sergiovanni, 1996, p. 142)

Releasing the Conditions for Growth

Sergiovanni's (1996) view of the teacher as learner promotes reflection and collaborative relationships that can help meet the needs of both the organization and its people—all the while building capacity:

All organizations learn, but not always for the better. An organization whose people can learn has an enhanced capacity to adapt and change. It is an organization in which learning processes are analyzed, monitored, developed, managed, and aligned with improvement and innovation goals. (Gephart, Marsick, Van Buren, & Spiro, 1996, p. 36)

From examining what we know about learning communities, it is clear that building one takes all the members of the organization working toward common values and goals. No longer is the administrator merely a leader, nor is the role of teacher solely that of follower. Each assumes these responsibilities equally (e.g., Doyle, 2004; Gephart et al., 1996; Senge, 1996; Sergiovanni, 1996).

Characteristics of Learning Communities

Significant study and research, especially that of DuFour (2004a); DuFour and Eaker (1998); Senge (1990, 1996), and Sergiovanni (1996), have contributed to the growing knowledge and understanding of learning communities. For the organization, profit is important, but so, too, is the professional enhancement of employees. In schools, profit is threefold:

- The development of teachers (refining existing skills, learning new skills, and keeping abreast with new and emerging knowledge within subject areas);

- The enhancement of student learning as a result of such efforts; and,

- The empowerment of teachers who can model lifelong learning to students. (Zepeda, 1999).

Learning Communities Are Characterized by Inclusive Environments

In a community of learners, the principal creates an inclusive environment for both students and teachers. Brookfield (1986) indicates that "when adults teach and learn in one another's company, they find themselves engaging in a challenging, passionate, and creative activity" (p. 1). An inclusive environment fosters ongoing dialogue among its participants. Teachers are free to discuss issues, regardless of the topic. Collective meaning is embraced daily through open discussion and reflection among the members of the community.

Learning Communities Support Change

The changes that schools have undergone throughout history are complex (Fullan, 2007). To develop a learning community, the principal must begin by examining the complexities associated with power. Leaders who want to create a learning organization give up power and assume a mindset that "no power is power" (Senge, Kleiner, Roberts, & Smith, 1994, p. 55). The structure of the organization and the leadership style of the principal needs to support the development of a learning community and the changes that will occur. Authentic change comes from individuals working toward a common goal.

Change from a personal perspective needs to be understood if the principal is to move the school toward forming as a learning community. With understanding, changes in the types of professional development, supervision, and other forms of collegial support can be made. Learning communities support optimism and hope for the future.

Learning Communities Are Collaborative

Through collaboration, the power to make a difference is shared by all the members of the community. Hargreaves (1997) reports:

> Cultures of collaboration among teachers seem to produce greater willingness to take risks, to learn from mistakes, and share successful strategies with colleagues that lead to teachers having positive senses of their own efficiency, beliefs that their children can learn, and improved outcomes…. (p. 68)

Collaboration is dependent on the feeling of interdependence (we are in this together) and opportunity. When teachers collaborate, they share ideas and problem-solve solutions to the thorny issues they face in the classroom.

Through collaboration, teachers are able to support growth and development while improving their practices. Collaboration includes such activities as coplanning and teaching lessons, brainstorming ideas, conducting action research, and interclassroom observations (peer coaching), and the reflection and dialogue that follows in postobservation conferences.

Teachers are willing to take risks in an environment that encourages (without facing retribution for less than satisfactory progress) efforts to improve teaching and learning. Through collaboration, the climate of a learning community moves from being a frozen tundra to a warm, supportive haven for the generation of new, diverse ideas and practices.

Learning Communities Support Autonomy and Foster Connectedness Among Members

There is a natural tension between autonomy and connectedness. People thrive in communities that nurture independence and free-thinking individuals who can join together to express values and beliefs. However, there is a need for people to feel bound by a common vision about learning. Effective principals reconcile the tensions between autonomy and interconnectedness by

♦ accepting people in a nonjudgmental manner;

- promoting a willingness in others to listen and share ideas; and,

- "lighting fires" by valuing growth and finding relevance in the work teachers do.

Learning Communities Hold That Reflection Is at the Core of All Adult Learning

Although reflection is discussed across several of the forms of job-embedded professional learning in later chapters, reflection is examined in this chapter in relation to its overall utility in learning communities. At the end of this chapter is a set of reflection tools adapted from the work of Huntress and Jones (2000) to support professionals.

Reflection is in a sense a form of professional development. Reflection is "thinking and [a] cognitive process," (Leitch & Day, 2000, p. 180) that is rooted in learning from experience (Dewey, 1933, 1938). When teachers work with others, the chances of doubling the amount of information they can learn increases, and I suspect even more learning occurs when teachers can also add reflection to the experiences of learning. Boud (2001) captures this idea:

> Reflection involves taking the unprocessed, raw material of experience and engaging with it in a way to make sense of what has occurred. It involves exploring often messy and confused events and focusing on the thoughts and emotions that accompany them. (p. 10)

An early pioneer on reflection, Schön (1983, 1987) developed two theories about reflection: *reflection-in-action* and *reflection-on-action*. Schön (1987) believed that individuals could engage in reflection-in-action while they were actually doing something, and that individuals engaged in reflection-on-action after the fact. Because important learning occurs on the job, reflection-in-action and reflection-on-action are forms of job-embedded learning. Supporting these types of reflection supports inquiry into making sense of practice. At the end of this chapter appear several reflective practice tools to promote reflection (page 116–122).

Learning Communities Thrive in a Positive School Culture and Climate

Healthy school cultures and climates thrive in environments built through collaboration, trust, and care for the members of the school, and Bogler and Somech (2004) believe it is critical for learning communities to develop "shared norms and values, a focus on student learning, reflective dialogue with colleagues, and peer collaboration" (p. 285).

According to Peterson (2002),

> [A] school culture is the set of norms, values and beliefs, rituals and ceremonies, symbols and stories that make up the "persona" of the

school. These unwritten expectations build up over time as teachers, administrators, parents, and students work together, solve problems, deal with challenges and, at times, cope with failures. (p. 10)

School climate includes the perceptions that people have of various aspects of the internal environment (safety, high expectations, relationships with teachers, students, parents, administrators). Moreover, school climate includes the aspects of the school that influence behavior—how people interact with one another. Freiberg (1998) reports:

The elements that make up school climate are complex, ranging from the quality of interactions in the teachers' lounge to the noise levels in hallways and cafeterias, from the physical structure of the building to the physical comfort levels (involving such factors as heating, cooling, and lighting) of the individuals and how safe they feel. Even the size of the school and the opportunities for students and teachers to interact in small groups both formally and informally add to or detract from the health of the learning environment. (p. 22)

A positive school culture can never be built through the sole efforts of the principal. Building a collaborative school culture and a positive school climate is dependent on several variables, including, most notably norms and workplace conditions. Norms and workplace conditions are interrelated and together they form both the culture and climate of the school.

Norms are unwritten rules of behavior that serve as a guide to the way people interact with one another (Chance & Chance, 2002). Saphier and King (1985) identify 12 norms of school culture, which, if strong, contribute to the instructional effectiveness of a school. The norms that "grow" strong school culture and climate include:

1. *Collegiality:* How people interact with one another, the openness members of the community have toward one another.

2. *Experimentation:* Risk taking.

3. *High expectations:* Do people have high expectations for themselves, for each other, and for students?

4. *Trust and confidence:* Do people trust one another?

5. *Tangible support:* Resources—time, support.

6. *Reaching out to the knowledge bases:* Information is available.

7. *Appreciation and recognition:* People feel important, respected, and part of the school. They feel that what they do is important and those colleagues, administrators, and the larger community hold the work they accomplish in high esteem.

8. *Caring, celebration and humor:* People thrive when they feel emotionally supported. Communities take the time to celebrate—the big and small accomplishments of each other and students.

9. *Involvement in decision making:* Decision making spans the school environment and is not just a function of the administration.

10. *Protection of what is important:* Principals and others identify what is important, and then protect time and secure resources to support priorities.

11. *Traditions:* Traditions shape the culture and traditions are upheld as part of the community.

12. *Honest, open communication:* People talk to one another; they share ideas openly without fear.

The principal is in a position to support the development of a healthy school culture through a variety of means that range from shared decision making, to implementing peer-coaching programs, and from supporting beginning teachers through formal and informal mentoring programs to providing time for teachers to meet. Professional development that matters cannot thrive in a culture that does not have trust as its center. Figure 5.2 (page 92) is offered as a way to do a reality check on the programs for teachers that shape the school culture.

Trust Is at the Center of a Learning Community

Trust is a prerequisite for building a positive school climate and culture. Without trust, efforts to build a collaborative culture marked by collegial interactions between teachers and administrators will be diminished. Without trust, relationships will flounder. Trust and respect build a strong foundation for the work and efforts of teachers.

Bryk and Schneider (2002) identify "relational trust" as the core ingredient for school improvement. Relational trust rests on a foundation of respect, competence, personal regard, and integrity. Building and maintaining trust evolves over time. Trust is built on history—the history of trust in the organization and the history of trust between teachers and administrators. A leader must ask several questions:

♦ Do teachers trust me?

♦ Do teachers have confidence in my actions?

♦ Do my words and actions align with each other?

♦ Do teachers believe I hold them in high regard?

♦ Do I exhibit integrity in the way I make decisions, communicate expectations, and allocate resources?

Figure 5.2. Programs for Teachers
That Shape the School Culture

Programs for Teachers

- ◆ What types of professional development activities are available for teachers?

- ◆ How many teachers participate in these activities?

- ◆ What types of programs would teachers like to see initiated?

- ◆ What types of leadership activities are available for teachers?

- ◆ How many teachers are involved in formal and informal leadership activities?

- ◆ What types of teacher recognition programs are in place?

Professional Development...

- ◆ Focuses on teachers as central to student learning, yet includes all members of the school community;

- ◆ Focuses on individual, collegial, and organizational improvement;

- ◆ Respects and nurtures the intellectual and leadership capacity of teachers, principals, and others in the school community;

- ◆ Reflects the best available research and practice in teaching, learning, and leadership;

- ◆ Enables teachers to develop further expertise in subject content, teaching strategies, uses of technologies, and other essential elements of teaching to high standards;

- ◆ Promotes continuous inquiry and improvement embedded in the daily life of schools;

- ◆ Is planned collaboratively by those who will participate in and facilitate that development;

- ◆ Requires substantial time and resources;

- ◆ Is driven by a coherent long-term plan; [and,]

- ◆ Is evaluated ultimately on the basis of its effects on teacher instruction and student learning, and uses this assessment to guide subsequent professional development efforts.

Source: U.S. Department of Education (1995). *Building bridges: The mission and principles of professional development*. Retrieved from www.ed.gov/G2K/bridge.html

The answers to those questions can serve as a guide to self-discovery about the patterns of trust and the work needed to build more trusting relationships with teachers. If any of these answers are negative, indicating that trust is an issue, then the principal needs to develop strategy to ensure that words and deeds point to developing and maintaining trust. Because of the change and risk involved in building learning communities, teachers need leadership from the principal that fosters trust. Without trust, positive relationships with teachers as well a willingness to take risks will not be forthcoming.

Caring Is a Trademark in a Learning Community

With the complex nature of schools, relationships that build interdependence with others are essential to build collaborative cultures. In schools with positive cultures, trust acts as the glue that helps teachers take risks needed to make changes—both in and out of the classroom—and to work together as teams (Peterson, 1999). Trust is built on relationships in which all members of the school are encouraged to contribute, to learn, and to be part of the discussion about school improvement. Trusting relationships thrive in a school culture that embraces two-way communication, feedback, and "care," which includes two primary goals: "promoting human development and responding to needs" (Beck, 1992, pp. 456–457).

Learning Communities
Promote a Common Vision

The school's vision serves to unify people and programs. The question in a learning community is, however, "Whose vision?" Lambert (2005) aptly answers this rhetorical question focusing on building capacity, a common thread in the learning community literature:

A principal's vision, standing alone, needs to be "sold" and "bought into." By contrast, a shared vision based upon the core values of participants and their hopes for the school ensures commitment to its realization. Realizing a shared purpose or vision is an energizing experience for participants, and a shared vision is the unifying force for participants working collaboratively. (p. 6).

Vision is powerful when the principal creates:

…ongoing processes in which people at every level of the organization, in every role, can speak from the heart about what really matters to them and be heard….The quality of this process…determines the quality and the power of the results. (Senge et al., 1994, p. 299)

To "hear" the voice of the community, the principal needs to involve all stakeholders—teachers, students, parents, staff (e.g., secretaries, maintenance persons, and cafeteria workers), central administrators, and members of the broader community the school serves (e.g., the neighborhood and the local business sector)—in the process of developing the school's vision. All views need to be considered in an apolitical forum.

Work With Teachers to Create the Vision

With the principal's active involvement, barriers that might undermine the vision can be identified. Teachers are creative problem solvers when they have an empowered voice. They can help the principal make changes within the operating structure of the school. Through ongoing refinement and removal of barriers, the right conditions bring the vision to life.

Provide Coordination Mechanisms

Most schools are large organizations where teachers work most of the day in isolation. Weekly faculty meetings are typically filled with agenda items that merely disseminate information. The effective principal uses this meeting time to facilitate discussion of important issues. Because it can be difficult to discuss critical issues in a large group setting, employ small groups but report all ideas to the collective group for expanded discussion to be processed by all members of the learning community.

The principal can use mechanisms such as cooperative learning to commit small group ideas to writing. Often roles such as recorder, researcher, and timer are developed within groups that utilize cooperative learning. The principal can be sensitive by not assigning such roles, but by encouraging group members to develop roles for themselves. With the assistance of the school secretary, artifacts of the vision-building process can be produced. With results distributed in a timely manner, the principal can help sustain the creative momentum of the community.

Maintain and Improve Interpersonal Skills

Developing a collective vision, based on the beliefs, attitudes, and prior history of the school, can create tensions for community members. Divergent points of view need to be communicated so that all can reflect upon the meanings of these views. If an atmosphere of openness is created among the members, then divergent points of view can be examined in a non-threatening manner. Interpersonal skills need to be nurtured to support a more responsive learning environment.

Recognize Political Allegiances

When all stakeholders are involved in the process of framing the school's vision, politics could enter into the process. Without making a value judgment, many members bring their own agendas to the community. Depending on the perceived power of community members, allegiances can form, causing interests to splinter the whole into parts and further reinforcing hidden agendas. A learning community is able to overcome "part" thinking and behavior when members can agree upon common purposes that assist in creating a vision that can be embraced and infused into the daily operations of the school.

Examine Motivation

Members must be motivated to develop a community vision that is relevant to individual and collective practices. Principals cannot force people to participate in the process. It is realistic to expect a third of the faculty to embrace the process, a third of the faculty to be initially neutral, and a third of the faculty to resist.

This point of view might appear to be overly pessimistic; however, people only work hard when they are motivated. Some people are motivated by external factors and others by internal factors. Herzberg (1968) developed the motivator-hygiene theory that can be blended with Maslow's hierarchy of needs theory. By examining Herzberg's and Maslow's work in relation to motivation, the principal is better able to understand what motivates people. From this understanding, the principal is in a better position to nurture an environment that is more responsive to the needs of the community. Figure 5.3 illustrates Herzberg's and Maslow's theories.

Figure 5.3. **Understanding Motivation**

	Herzberg Motivation Model	Maslow's Hierarchy of Needs
High-Order Needs		
Motivation	◆ Job Content ◆ Achievement ◆ Recognition ◆ Work Itself ◆ Responsibility ◆ Growth ◆ Advancement	Need for ◆ Knowledge ◆ Understanding ◆ Self-Actualization
Low-Order Needs		
Hygiene Factors	◆ Pay/Salary ◆ Fringe Benefits ◆ Type of Supervision ◆ Company Policies & Procedures ◆ Status ◆ Job Security ◆ Interpersonal Relations	◆ Survival Needs ◆ Security Needs ◆ Belonging Needs ◆ Esteem Needs

Adapted from Gage and Berliner, 1998; Razik and Swanson, 2001.

Intellectual stimulation occurs when meetings are productive and engage teachers in meaningful inquiry, discussion, and reflection. Work should begin with clearly defined goals. Thompson, Gregg, and Niska (2004) assert that "in professional learning communities the principal encourages teachers to pursue personal development as part of their job" (p. 5) by engaging in learning that promotes continuous reflection and inquiry. The core of the vision focuses on data to support and enhance student learning.

Learning Communities Use Data to Ensure Student Success

Learning communities exist to support and to nurture student learning. In 1970, the Apollo 13 space flight drama unfolded. After the famed line, "Houston, we have a problem," came the response similar to "Failure is not an option," which later became a book title for Gene Kranz. Part of the work of a learning community is to examine student learning using both formative and summative assessments and the data that these assessments yield. From the data, professional development can be tailored to help teachers support student learning so that truly, *failure is not an option!*

Data are important for professional development and according to the National Education Association (NEA) Foundation for the Improvement of Education (NFIE) (2003), data can be used in two complementary ways:

1. As the actual substance of professional development, as educators convene with each other to study student work and analyze the instructional practice that produced such results.

2. As a basis for making decisions about educators' on-the-job learning, including decisions pertaining to professional development resource allocation, content, and delivery. (p. 2)

For a review on how the examination of student work can help frame professional development, consult the section entitled "Focusing on Student Work as Professional Development" in Chapter 10 (page 233). In short, the use of data needs to be elevated because "when teachers analyze and discuss instructional practice and the resulting samples of student work, they experience some of the highest caliber professional development available" (NFIE, 2003, p. 2).

Chapter 2 examined the differences between formative and summative evaluation and assessment. Chapter 6 includes an in-depth case study of how teachers and administrators in one school use data to not only track student progress but also to frame professional development. Regardless of their forms, data are important. Data generated by teachers are important because "academic research produces general knowledge, practitioners seek just-in-time data that help them improve their work with students" (NFIE, 2003, p. 4).

This book supports a collaborative approach not only to professional development but to all the work of teachers. The power of data can be magnified through working toward understanding of the meaning of data. The Iowa Department of Education (n.d.) notes some pitfalls to avoid when working with data:

♦ Only a few administrators and teachers work with data.

♦ Staff receives summary data statements, and never studies actual district, building, and classroom data.

♦ School staff members cannot select professional development content directed at specific student learning needs because item analysis data are not studied. (p. 6)

Data-Driven Instruction

Much of the "just-in-time" data supports better decision making. Scott McLeod (2005) and his work with the CASTLE (Center for the Advanced Study of Technology Leadership in Education) group have been instrumental in forwarding the idea that teachers can be data leaders. According to McLeod, the five major elements of data-driven instruction are

♦ good baseline data,

♦ measurable instructional goals,

♦ frequent formative assessment,

♦ professional learning communities, and,

♦ focused instructional interventions.

Figure 5.4 illustrates the iterative nature of how data drives the analysis of instruction vis-à-vis frequent formative assessments and the like, as envisioned by McLeod (2005).

Figure 5.4. The Iterative Nature of Data-Driven Instruction

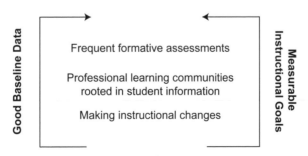

Source: McLeod, S. (2005). *Data-driven teachers.* Minneapolis, MN: University Center for the Advanced Study of Technology Leadership in Education (CASTLE). Used with permission.

McLeod (2005) believes that data-driven teachers and principals make better decisions about student learning. Figure 5.5 illustrates with more detail the data-driven principles that McLeod suggests in Figure 5.4.

Figure 5.5. Making "Better" Data-Driven Decisions—Teachers and Principals

Data-Driven Teachers Make Better Decisions Because They...	Data-Driven Principals Support Teachers Making Better Decisions Because They...
♦ understand the importance of utilizing multiple measures, and multiple indicators within measures, when assessing school and student success.	♦ create and implement a comprehensive, long-term professional development plan that is designed to ground teachers in the skills they need to be effective data-driven instructors.
♦ utilize data from yearly summative assessments to improve student learning.	♦ provide teachers with data that are accurate, timely, and in a format that can inform classroom instruction.
♦ select key indicators of success for their classrooms.	♦ work with district personnel to design and implement data systems that allow for exploration and reporting of raw data.
♦ are well-grounded in assessment literacy concepts so that they can appropriately interpret summative baseline data.	♦ provide access to data.
♦ set measurable year-end instructional goals, which serve as meaningful targets to guide their pedagogical strategies (SMART Goals).	♦ actively help teachers identify key indicators of classroom success, appropriately analyze their data, and then turn those data into strategic pedagogical interventions. ♦ help teachers "chunk" ambitious long-term objectives into short-term SMART goals.
♦ identify and work toward only a few key instructional goal areas each year.	♦ model the goal-setting process.

Data-Driven Teachers Make Better Decisions Because They...	Data-Driven Principals Support Teachers Making Better Decisions Because They...
♦ utilize their instructional expertise to identify key formative indicators of success that can be used to measure student progress during the school year.	♦ recognize that the driving engine behind substantial improvements in student learning outcomes is a strong system of formative assessment, coupled with the opportunity for teachers to collaboratively make sense and act upon the formative data they receive.
♦ use summative and formative assessment data together to implement strategic, targeted, focused instructional interventions to improve student learning. These interventions should be aligned with state standards and district curricula as well as content-specific, developmentally appropriate best practices.	♦ give teachers the necessary time to collaboratively analyze and act upon data, and train teachers in effective teaming and communication strategies.
♦ implement effective teaching practices and design and implement teacher-driven action research projects that investigate the effectiveness of specific pedagogical strategies	♦ help teachers identify and implement new research-based curricula and teaching practices. ♦ support teachers by connecting them with appropriate training opportunities and instructional experts. ♦ help teachers recognize what is working (and what is not) in their classrooms and vigorously support their faculty as they transform ineffective instructional practices into those that result in desired outcomes.

Figure continues on next page.

Data-Driven Teachers Make Better Decisions Because They...	Data-Driven Principals Support Teachers Making Better Decisions Because They...
◆ view data as feedback, not as indictments. ◆ use data to inform pedagogical modifications and actively seek out more data to judge the success of those changes; ineffective strategies are discarded, and successful strategies are tweaked or modified to achieve even larger learning gains. ◆ discuss their instructional strengths and weaknesses with peers to facilitate shared communities of practice focused on individual and organizational learning.	◆ facilitate school climates where it is professionally and emotionally safe to look at student data. ◆ never use data for evaluative or punitive purposes. ◆ use data to highlight faculty strengths and to structure professional development opportunities. ◆ conduct a needs assessment of their staff's concerns and fears and then work diligently to address those needs in collaboration with their faculty.
◆ seek out evidence about the success or failure of their pedagogy. ◆ challenge the status quo and continually strive for further improvement, even when already exhibiting high levels of success. ◆ are risk takers who understand that trying something new and different may be the only path to improved outcomes.	◆ help teachers connect with necessary resources to facilitate effective educational interventions. ◆ facilitate teachers' understanding that taking greater responsibility for student learning can result in improved student achievement.

The information in Figure 5.5 was excerpted from: McLeod, S. (2005). *Data-driven teachers*. Minneapolis, MN: University Center for the Advanced Study of Technology Leadership in Education (CASTLE). Used with permission.

Data-Driven Competencies Needed to Support Data Analysis

Figure 5.6 (page 101) illustrates the essential competencies needed for data-driven teachers to use data widely to change instruction based on data from multiple sources. Teachers need support (see Figure 5.5, page 98) in developing these competencies, and teachers need an environment that supports collaboration.

Figure 5.6. Essential Competencies for Data-Driven Teachers

Essential Concepts	Collecting and Analyzing Summative Data	Setting Measurable Goals
Understanding the conceptual differences between data-driven decision making and federal/state accountability	Understand the importance and impact on student learning of summative assessment practices	Understand the importance of establishing SMART goals for instructional success
Articulate what effective data-driven instruction	Get relevant summative data out of district DMA systems for analytical and reporting purposes	Understand the six key characteristics of SMART goals
Understand how the following elements interact to improve student learning: 1. summative baseline data, 2. measurable goals, 3. frequent formative assessment, 4. professional learning communities, and 5. making instructional and organizational changes based on formative and summative data	Select key summative indicators of success for their classrooms	Utilize summative data to get SMART goals for their classrooms
Understand the importance of utilizing multiple measures, and multiple indicators within measures, when assessing school and student success	Are familiar with relevant assessment literacy concepts and can appropriately interpret summative data	

Figure continues on next page.

Collecting and Analyzing Formative Data	Making Changes	Data Transparency and Safety	Alignment for Results
Understand the importance and impact on student learning of frequent formative assessment practices	Implement focused interventions in instruction to improve student learning	Facilitate the creation of school climates where data visibility is frequent and important	Understand the importance of results-driven practice and how that is different than previous practices
Select key formative indicators of success to measure school and student progress during the school year	Ensure that instructional interventions are aligned with state standards and district curricula	Ensure that relevant data are accessible to parents and students (i.e., no gate keeping)	Understand the importance and impact on student learning of continuous and progressive SMART goal-setting
Use appropriate technologies to collect, organize, analyze, and report student formative assessment data	Ensure that instructional interventions are aligned with content-specific instructional best practices	Facilitate the creation of school climates of data safety (i.e., data are used for feedback and/or information, not for evaluation)	Ensure that personal professional is aligned to student, school, and district needs
Meet regularly and frequently for collaborative, data-based discussion of student progress and identification of appropriate instructional interventions		Utilize print and electronic communication channels to disseminate status and progress information on key summative and formative assessment indicators to parents and students	Ensure that curricular design and delivery are aligned to student, school, and district needs

Collecting and Analyzing Formative Data	Making Changes	Data Transparency and Safety	Alignment for Results
Are familiar with relevant assessment literacy concepts and can appropriately interpret formative assessment data		Utilize data to celebrate instructional progress and successes, not just to identify continuing needs	
Identify emergent patterns from formative assessment data			
Engage in root cause analysis to identify appropriate interventions			

Source: McLeod, S. (2005). *Data-driven teachers*. Minneapolis, MN: University Center for the Advanced Study of Technology Leadership in Education (CASTLE). Used with permission.

Learning Communities Work Together to Analyze Instructional Practices

Learning community members focus a majority of their time working collaboratively to learn. Because examining data can be risky business, a team approach where learning permeates the business of meetings is suggested. With permission of Scott McLeod, the following PLC Team Meeting Agenda (Figure 5.7) is provided as a sample. This PLC Team Meeting Agenda provides illustration of how meetings can be structured around sharing instructional strategies and the insights gained from thinking about student learning from evidence of practice—data.

Figure 5.7. PLC Team Meeting Agenda—Focus on Instructional Strategies and Student Success

WOODLAND ELEMENTARY

OSSEO AREA SCHOOLS

PLC Team Meeting Agenda

Grade Level _____

Recorder _____

During your PLC time this month, please focus on the following questions, all relating to reading fluency. Please select a recorder who can write down comments, ideas, and/or decisions.

1. Please share one strategy that you have used in your classroom that has been especially effective at building students' reading fluency skills. (Please ask each team member to share at least one idea.)

2. What are the data telling you to date regarding your students' progress?

3. What percentage of your students is currently meeting our building improvement plan goal? What achievement differences, if any, are you seeing between white and minority students?

4. What changes have you made in your instructional practices based on the data that you have collected?

5. What kind of progress have your students identified as nonproficient made since your last meeting? What evidence do you have to show this?

6. Based on your analysis and discussion of your data as well as your ongoing observations of your students, what changes will you make in the future to help nonproficient students be successful?

7. Which solutions might be best for the team to focus on between now and next month? How will we get that done?

8. How can Linda support our efforts?

For more information about how the information from these PLC team meetings is used to drive instruction, contact Linda Perdaems, Principal, Woodland Elementary, Osseo Area Schools, (763) 315–6400, perdaemsl@district279.org

Source: Woodland Elementary PLC Questions. Used with permission of Scott McLeod.

Members of a Learning Community Collaboratively Plan for Instruction

Data are the driving force for examining student success, mastery, and competency. McLeod (2006) offers several forms for teachers, teams, grade levels, or any other grouping configuration to complete (Figures 5.8 through 5.13). These forms can assist teachers identifying not only students who are at risk but also identifying root causes, intervention strategies, and resources needed to help reach students. With permission, these forms are reproduced in this text.

Teacher Leadership in Learning Communities

Patterson and Patterson (2004) define teacher leaders as "teachers who work with colleagues for the purpose of improving teaching and learning whether in a formal or an informal capacity" (p. 74). Strong school cultures embrace teacher leaders as part of the tapestry of a learning community. Learning communities that support teacher leadership embrace:

1. *Developmental focus.* Teachers are supported in learning new skills. They are encouraged to help each other learn. Assistance and guidance are provided for them.

2. *Recognition.* Teachers are respected and recognized for professional roles that they take and the contributions made. There is mutual respect among teachers.

3. *Autonomy.* Teachers are encouraged to take initiative in improvement efforts. Barriers are removed and resources provided.

4. *Collegiality.* Teachers collaborate on instructional strategies, share materials, and observe each other.

5. *Participation.* Teachers are actively involved in making decisions and give input on important matters. Department/team leaders are selected with the participation of teachers.

6. *Open communication.* Teachers feel that they are informed and easily share opinions and ideas. There is honest communication.

7. *Positive environment.* There is a high level of job satisfaction. An environment of mutual respect with parents, students, administrators, and teachers. The school has effective administrative leaders. (Katzenmeyer & Moller, 2001, pp. 77–78)

(Text continues on page 113.)

Figure 5.8. **Creating an Intervention Plan**

Intervention plans should be systematic, timely, and directive.

Initially conceived of in the 1970s through the work of Deno and Mirkin (1977), response to intervention (RTI) provided a method for at-risk and special education students to receive remediation support outside of prescriptive and inadequate classroom strategies. Now in its new form, Response to Instruction and Intervention (RTI^2), this method continues to enable children to receive support and guidance around literacy and content with specific focus to change learner performance as a result of directly targeted instruction.

Fisher and Frey (2010) define the RTI^2 model as a way to:

> encourage teachers to vary instruction and time to create a constant level of learning. A core assumption of RTI is that all students can reach high levels of achievement if the system is willing (and able) to vary the amount of time students have to learn and the type of instruction they receive. (p. 15)

RTI^2 provides varied and differentiated instruction and time that lead to constant learning outcomes by using tiers of intervention that increase over time, intensity, and expertise. Initially, the student receives support through core instruction, followed by supplemental intervention, and finally through intensive intervention (Fisher & Frey, 2010).

The teacher plays an essential role in establishing authentic assessments and useful instruction that meet the objectives of a student's RTI^2 plan. Establishing a purpose and corresponding objectives for a student's RTI^2 is determined according to the student's language and content ability. The teacher and classroom support staff may use guided instruction, modeling, group work, and independent learning as a response to instruction and intervention.

Fisher and Frey (2010) believe:

1. We have to hold high expectation for student and ourselves.

2. We have to focus on high-quality core instruction, first and foremost.

3. We have to make sure that instruction and intervention are linked.

4. We have to manipulate a number of variables (time, assessment, expertise, and instruction) to intensify intervention.

5. We have to build in a feed-forward method so that RTI^2 results inform classroom instruction and programmatic improvements.

6. We have to keep the teacher and family at the center of communication. (pp. 140–141)

Ultimately, for RTI² to succeed, coordination, communication, and collaboration must be at the forefront of each RTI² committee, ensuring agreements are met, all appropriate support members are involved, and the student is strengthened.

As DuFour, DuFour, Eaker, and Karhanek (2004) in *Whatever It Takes: How Professional Learning Communities Respond When Kids Don't Learn* notes professional learning communities (PLCs) are action-oriented: "not only do they act, but they are unwilling to tolerate inaction" (p. 4). This packet is intended to help your teacher team walk through the steps necessary to begin answering the four important PLC questions:

1. What do we want each student to learn?

   - Have you mapped your curriculum to state standards?

   - Have you time-mapped your curriculum over the school year?

   - Have you identified critical skills that your students must learn?

2. How will we know when each student has learned it?

   - Have you identified appropriate assessments for critical skills?

3. How will we respond when students experience difficulty in learning?

   - Are you able to identify ongoing student learning needs that remain unmet?

   - Do you have an intervention plan for unsuccessful students that is systematic, timely, and directive?

   - How will we respond when students already have mastered essential knowledge and skills?

   - Do you have an intervention plan for successful students that is systematic, timely, and directive?

Use the charts and diagrams on the pages that follow to facilitate your team's conversations around these important questions. Duplicate the final three pages as needed for each learning need/critical skill.

If your team has difficulty completing these planning sheets, discuss how you will get the answers necessary to finish them in the future.

Source: McLeod, S. (2006). *Pyramid of Interventions Packet* (Draft; updated June 14, 2006). Used with permission.

Figure 5.9. **Learning Needs/Critical Skills**

What learning needs do our students have? *and/or*

What are the critical skills/concepts we want our students to learn?

Look over the standards for your course/subject/grade. As a team, brainstorm the critical skills/concepts/power standards that are absolutely *essential* for students to master.

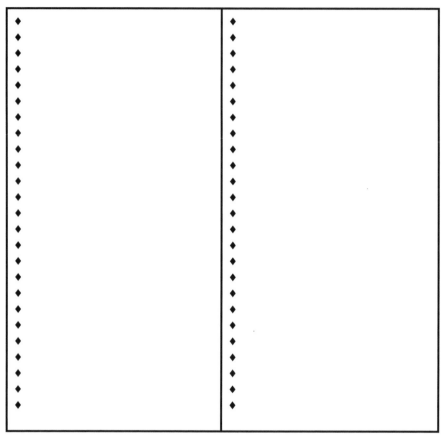

After you're done brainstorming, collaboratively check the top 4 to 6 (no more!). Circle these.

Source: McLeod, S. (2006). *Pyramid of Interventions Packet* (Draft; updated June 14, 2006). Used with permission.

Figure 5.10. **Possible Assessments**

How will we assess our students' mastery of these learning needs/critical skills?

Insert one of your team's essential skills/concepts here:

◆	◆
◆	◆
◆	◆
◆	◆
◆	◆
◆	◆
◆	◆
◆	◆
◆	◆
◆	◆
◆	◆
◆	◆
◆	◆
◆	◆
◆	◆
◆	◆
◆	◆
◆	◆
◆	◆
◆	◆
◆	◆
◆	◆
◆	◆
◆	◆

After you're done brainstorming, collaboratively decide on which one the team will do and circle it. Also decide how frequently this assessment will occur.

Source: McLeod, S. (2006). *Pyramid of Interventions Packet* (Draft; updated June 14, 2006). Used with permission.

Figure 5.11. Pyramid of Interventions—Nonsuccess

How will we respond when students are unsuccessful?

Learning Need / Critical Skill

As we focus on this, we will

For students who are unsuccessful, we will

For students who are still unsuccessful, we will

For students who are still unsuccessful, we will

Source: McLeod, S. (2006). *Pyramid of Interventions Packet* (Draft; updated June 14, 2006). Used with permission.

Figure 5.12. **Pyramid of Interventions—Success**

How will we respond when students are successful?

Learning Need / Critical Skill

As we focus on this, we will

For students who are successful, we will

For students who are still successful, we will

For students who are still successful, we will

Source: McLeod, S. (2006). *Pyramid of Interventions Packet* (Draft; updated June 14, 2006). Used with permission.

Figure 5.13. **Web of Resources**

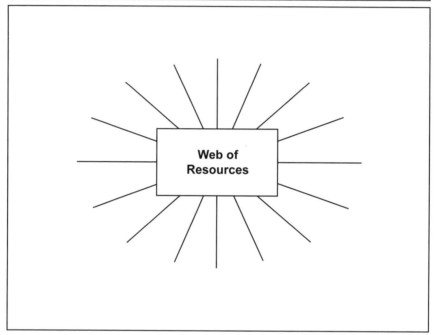

What resources do we have to help students with this learning need/critical skill?	
Learning Need / Critical Skill	**Assessment**

Source: McLeod, S. (2006). *Pyramid of Interventions Packet* (Draft; updated June 14, 2006). Used with permission.

Given opportunity, support, and affirmation, most teachers will respond to the call to leadership (Zepeda, Mayers, & Benson, 2003); they desire to emerge as leaders beyond the confines of the classrooms. Effective principals:

♦ Create opportunities for more teachers to share their expertise;

♦ Develop an ethos of support and care to nurture teacher leadership through mentoring teachers through the process of evolving as leaders; and,

♦ Embed leadership as learning opportunities in the day-to-day work of teachers.

How do principals accomplish this? Principals accomplish this by providing professional development and mentoring for teacher leaders while encouraging risk-taking.

Provide Professional Development and Mentoring for Teacher-Leaders

Teachers come to the profession with varying experiences and backgrounds, and they develop skills needed to organize instruction, assess learning, manage a room full of children, and communicate with children and parents. However, when teacher-leaders assume leadership, they are called on to exert different skills that go beyond the day-to-day work of the classroom. For example, teachers interact with students daily; however, teacher-leaders extend communication beyond the classroom, and they might need assistance learning how to communicate more effectively with other adults. Closely related to communication are group processing skills such as reaching consensus and conflict resolution. Using these skills with adults is much different than with children.

Principals recognize these needs, and they provide opportunities for teacher-leaders to participate in professional development aimed at enhancing leadership and the myriad skills that make good leaders better leaders. Professional development can include, for example, opportunities to:

♦ Shadow other teacher leaders over sustained time.

♦ Attend professional meetings, conferences, and workshops.

♦ Enroll in graduate school coursework in leadership.

♦ Get on a listserve of teacher leaders and engage in the talk of leadership with peers.

♦ Read professional journals, participate in professional reading and discussion groups, or join a group interested in solving a schoolwide problem. (Zepeda et al., 2003)

Teacher-leaders need opportunities for learning how to further leadership skills. Mentoring and induction to the culture of leadership are prerequisites to supporting new teacher leaders. Like beginning teachers, teacher leaders new to a position or role need assistance as they learn the work of teacher leadership, and effective principals provide the support necessary for teachers to take the risks associated with leadership.

Assuming Leadership Can Be Risky Business for the Newcomer to Leadership

According to Stone (1995), teachers who are risk takers "experience the freedom to take risks, which is important for growth and change" and, furthermore, "empowerment enlightens the teacher to the positive side of failure—learning what does not work and then trying again to find out what does" (p. 295). More broadly, teacher-leaders, according to Patterson and Patterson (2004), can greatly influence how the "dynamics of the school culture evolve" (p. 75). For teacher-leaders to take risks, they need the support and encouragement from the principal. Teacher-leaders can experience the positive side of failure and the growth and development from the insights gained through taking the risk needed to succeed.

New leaders need time to learn the work of teacher leadership, and they need guidance and support as they exert leadership. Time is well spent engaging the new teacher-leader in the "talk of leadership," leading the newcomer to make sense of her work. Making sense of experience includes not only talk (over extended time) but also multiple opportunities to reflect on the meanings of work. Dialogue, reflection, and a return to experience will assist the new teacher leader to make significant contributions to her work as a leader.

Conclusion

This chapter introduced the reader to the foundation on which successful professional development is built—a reflective, learning community. When a school works toward becoming a learning community, all stakeholders are valued, collaboration is the norm, learning occurs naturally, and reflection is fostered through collegial conversations.

Because learning communities value persons as individuals, change no longer needs to be viewed as a threat to any stakeholder's worth. The implication is clear: The transformation of the school into a learning community must begin with the principal. The principal sets the tone for learning by modeling active learning, investing time in the process, and by empowering teachers as leaders.

Suggested Readings

Bolam, R., McMahon, A., Stoll, L., Thomas, S., Wallace, M., Hawkey, K., & Greenwood, A. (2005). *Creating and sustaining effective professional learning communities*. Research Report RR637. University of Bristol. Retrieved from www.education.gov.uk/publications/standard/publicationDetail/Page1/RR637

Hord, S. M. (Ed.). (2004). *Learning together, leading together: Changing schools through professional learning communities.* New York: Teachers College Press.

Joyce, B. (2004). How are professional learning communities created? History has a few messages. *Phi Delta Kappan, 86*(1), 76–83.

Moller, G., & Pankake, A. (2006). *Lead with me: A principal's guide to teacher leadership.* Larchmont, NY: Eye On Education.

Wald, P. J., & Castleberry, M. S. (Eds.). (2000). *Educators as learners: Creating a professional learning community in your school.* Alexandria, VA: Association for Supervision and Curriculum Development.

York-Barr, J., Sommers, W. A., Ghere, G. S., & Montie, J. (2006). Schoolwide reflective practice. In *Reflective practice to improve schools: An action guide for educators* (2nd ed., pp.199–243). Thousand Oaks, CA: Corwin Press.

Zepeda. S. J., Mayers, R. S., & Benson, B. N. (2003). *The call to teacher leadership.* Larchmont, NY: Eye On Education.

Reflective Practice Tools[1]

Narrative

Teachers write specific incidents about classroom practices as narratives. These narratives can support independent or collaborative reflection. Reflection can lead to the refinement of practice. Critical incidents can be identified

- In class with teachers and their students
- With colleagues
- Through journaling

The critical incidents can serve as a means to support Guided Individual Reflection and Collaborative Reflection. Sources include:

- McEntee, G. Appleby, J., Dowd, J., Grant, Hole, S., & Silva, P. (2003). *At the heart of teaching: A guide to reflective practice.* New York, New York: Teachers College Press.

- Olson, M. R. (2000). Linking personal and professional knowledge of teaching practice through narrative inquiry. *The Teacher Educator, 35*(4), 109–127.

Portfolios

(Also see Chapter 13.)

Involves collecting evidences of practice, developing a framework of core competencies and professional values, document teacher growth and encourages collaborative learning. In a concrete, visible, tangible way it can bring about accomplishments and learning-related change. Other sources include:

- Atonek, J., McCormick, D. E., & Donato, R. (1997). The student teacher portfolio as autobiography: Developing a professional identity. *The Modern Language Journal, 81*(1), 15–27.

- Davies, M. A., & Willis, E. (2001), Through the looking glass… Preservice professional portfolios. *The Teacher Educator, 37*(1), 27–36.

- Seng, S., & Seng, T. (1996, November). *Reflective teaching and the portfolio approach in early childhood staff development.* Paper presented at the Joint conference of the Australian Association of Singapore and the Australian Association for research in Education, Singapore.

---

1 Adapted from Huntress, J., & Jones, L. (2000, April). *Reflective process tools.* A presentation made at the annual meeting of the Association for Supervision and Curriculum Development for the Instructional Supervision Network. New Orleans, LA.

- Tillema, M. A. (2001). Portfolios as developmental assessment tools. *International Journal of Training and Development, 5*(2), 126–135.

E-portfolios include using a variety of multimedia. The processes and development consider the same characteristics: Portfolio process includes:

♦ Decide and assess

♦ Decide and plan

♦ Decide and gather

♦ Implement

♦ Evaluate

Portfolio development includes:

♦ Collection

♦ Selection

♦ Reflection

♦ Projection

♦ Presentation

Source: Hill, D. (2003). E-Folio and teacher candidate development. *The Teacher Educator, 38*(4), 256–266.

Reflections bear striking similarities across both types of portfolios: "Process" and "Product." Though they were different in content, purpose, organization. Learning can be at the technical levels and not necessarily be at the interpretative and critical levels of reflection.

Source: Orland-Barak, L. (2005). Portfolios as evidence of reflective practice: What remains "untold." *Educational Research, 47*(1), 25–44.

Teacher as a Researcher

(Also see Chapter 12.)

Action Research

♦ Intentional and systematic inquiry by practitioners in their classrooms affords insights and knowledge generated in the process of their own work. Preferably done in collaboration rather than in isolation, action research promotes critical reflections.

Inquiry

♦ Uses response about experiences of students and/or teachers, responses to readings, group discussions, and reflection papers enable teachers to explore unexamined parts of personal and professional knowledge of teaching and link these in explicit ways.

Source: Olson, M. R. (2000). Linking personal and professional knowledge of teaching practice through narrative inquiry. *The Teacher Educator, 35*(4), 109–127.

- Response to experiences
- Response to readings
- Small- and large-group discussions

Mindfulness

Zen-like mindfulness helps by living in the present moment. Teachers' spontaneity relies on their intuition and emotions as they keep peace with student's understanding that arise during the lesson.

- Be present in the moment
- Teaching moves with the rhythm of the students
- Teachers rely on the discussion to determine the plan
- Does not rely on a scripted plan with discussion points well laid out
- Relies on intuition and emotion

    Source: Jay, J. K. (1999, February). *Untying the knots: Examining the complexities of reflective practice.* Paper presented at the Annual Meeting of the American Association of colleges for teacher education. Washington, D.C.

Journaling

Journal entries related to beliefs, knowledge, observations, actions and reflections enhance professional practice. *Response & Reflective Journals* are notebooks or folders to record personal reactions to, questions about, reflections on what they observe, do and think. It can be in various formats, guided by appropriate prompts given by a facilitator.

    Source: Good, J. M. (2002). Encouraging reflection in preservice teachers through response journals. *The Teacher Educator, 37*(4), 254–267.

- Begin with prompts and gradually move to own prompts
- Variety in topics
- Response in nontraditional format concept map, poetry, collage, chart
- Share with a "journal buddy" and reflect on each other's entries too

    Source: Spalding, E., & Wilson, A. (2002). Demystifying reflection: A study of pedagogical strategies that encourage reflective journal writing. *Teachers College Record, 104*(7), 1393–1421.

- Narrative vs. reflective writing
- Different types of reflective writing (e.g., in/on action, deliberative, critical)
- By e-mail or hard copy
- Peer sharing choice of topic on teaching-learning
- Use various genre (newspaper article, satire, poetry)

Source: Moon, J. A. (1999). *Reflection in learning and professional development. Sterling,* VA: Stylus Publishing.

♦ Alter point of view: write in the third person, or at a different stage of life

♦ Use a metaphor for the incident or the person

♦ Unsent letters

♦ Stepping stones: range of memories on a particular topic using a word or phrase in chronological order

Dialogue or Collaborative Journals are journals between two or more people, who take turns making an entry. While the dialogue journal is commonly done between teacher and student, collaborative is done by a group with some commonality.

Source: Alterio, M. (2004). Collaborative journaling as a professional development tool. *Journal of Further and Higher Education, 28*(3), 321–332.

♦ Conegotiate ground rules anonymity, confidentiality

♦ Common journal, rotates weekly

♦ Pose questions related to professional lives

♦ Discuss ideas

♦ Share stories

Case Studies

Detailed descriptions of real teaching episodes.

Source: Valli, L. (1997). Listening to other voices: A description of teacher reflection in the United States. *Peabody Journal of Education, 72*(1), 67–88.

♦ Fictionalized accounts of real incidents of a conflict or a problem

♦ School or classroom event

♦ Includes events in order, history, context, thoughts and feeling of participants

Online Dialogues

WebCT and online interviews through email create virtual discussion groups using thematic questions and use of conversational techniques.

Source: Heflich, D. A. (1997, March). *Online interviews: Research as a reflective dialogue.* Paper presented at the Annual Meeting of the American Educational Research Association. Chicago, IL.

♦ Develop interview protocol using thematic questions

♦ Use conversational technique

Source: Clarke, M., & Otaky, D. (2005). Reflection "on" and "in" teacher education in the United Arab Emirates. *International Journal of Educational Development, 26*(2006), 111–122.

♦ Discussion and reflection on teaching

Audio-Video Tapes

Video and audio tapes aid in accurate recapture of feelings and events for collaborative discussions and reflections with peers or a trained facilitator.

♦ Interpersonal process recall (IPR)

♦ Inquirer pause tapes during replay to ask open, nondirective questions to probe the experience

♦ Feelings, thoughts, impressions, recollection, expectations, others' effect on them are probed

Sources: Dawes, L. (1999). Enhancing reflection with audiovisual playback and trained inquirer. *Studies in Continuing Education, 21*(2), 197–215, and Hu, C., Sharpe, L., Crawford, L., Gopinathan, S., Khine, M. S., Moo, S. N., & Wong, A. (2000). Using lesson video clips via multipoint desktop video conferencing to facilitate reflective practice. *Journal of Information on Technology for Teacher Education, 9*(3), 377–388.

♦ Small groups

♦ Watch each other's and their own video clips three minutes per competency

♦ Individual chooses a competency to focus

♦ Video streaming group watches individually

♦ Predetermined guidelines for live conference

♦ Synchronous conference

Collaborative Work

Collaborative work with peers, mentor or instructor to inquire into practice through a research project, writing journals, watching or listening to audio or video tapes.

Source: Alterio, M. (2004). Collaborative journaling as a professional development tool. *Journal of Further and Higher Education, 28*(3), 321–332.

♦ Conegotiate ground rules anonymity, confidentiality

♦ Common journal, rotates weekly

♦ Pose questions related to professional lives

♦ Discuss ideas

♦ Share stories

Sources: Valli, L. (1997). Listening to other voices: A description of teacher reflection in the United States. *Peabody Journal of Education, 72*(1), 67–88, and Holloway, K., & Long, R. (1998). Teacher development and school improvement: the use of "shared practice groups" to improve teaching in primary schools. *Journal of Inservice Education, 24*(3), 535–545.

- Representatives of a minimum three schools

- Establish areas of shared interest related to classroom products

- Teachers volunteer to join groups that cater to their interest

- Maximum of 12 and a minimum of six in a group

- Needs a facilitator who has expertise in the area of interest

- Discussion on children's work or any record of classroom activity

  Sources: Moore, R. (1999). Preservice teachers engaged in reflective classroom research. *The Teacher Educator, 34*(4) 259–275, and Dawes, L. (1999). Enhancing reflection with audiovisual playback and trained inquirer. *Studies in Continuing Education, 21*(2), 197–215.

Critical Incidents Analysis

Analysis of an incident.

- Facilitator first describes an incident of her own that the participants analyze for assumptions in small groups.

- Individuals then write a vivid description of a recent incident that has had an impact on them.

- They analyze in triads, taking turns to listen to the others' incidents.

- At a time, two try to identify assumptions that are embedded in the description.

- They then reflect on it and come to understand what they have learned from it.

  Sources: Moon, J.A. (1999). *Reflection in learning and professional development.* VA: Stylus Publishing Inc., and McEntee, G., Appleby, J., Dowd, J., Grant, J., Hole, S., & Silva, P. (2003). *At the heart of teaching: A guide to reflective practice.* New York: Teachers College Press.

Critical Friends Groups (CFG)/Reflective Practice Groups (RPG)

(Also see Chapter 9.)

CFGs, RPGs, and "shared practice groups" are all groups of educators engaged in reflective discussions on teaching and learning. Whereas CFGs are made up of small groups of educators, RPGs are a mixed group of educators induction teachers, mentors, veteran teachers, administrators and teacher educator. All these groups engage in collaborative study to improve teacher efficacy and teacher practice which positively impact student learning. In CFG context, critical means "important," "key," "essential," or "urgent," such as in "critical care."

- Group discuss and develop norms about responses.

- Build trust and confidentiality among participants.

- It is continual.

- Time-managed protocols (strategies or formal structures) for examining student work or teacher work of one of the members.

- Give, receive feedback and reflect on the above work, address dilemmas, collaborate across disciplines, confronting assumptions, mindsets, and expectations, but never by blaming students or social conditions.

- Maintain reflective journal on a predetermined prompt.Request for peer observation.

- Text-based discussion of a topic of concern or interest to the group.

  Possible source: www.nsrfharmony.org

  Other sources: McEntee, G., Appleby, J., Dowd, J., Grant, J., Hole, S., & Silva, P. (2003). *At the heart of teaching: A guide to reflective practice.* New York: Teachers College Press, and Holloway, K., & Long, R. (1998). Teacher development and school improvement: the use of "shared practice groups" to improve teaching in primary schools. *Journal of Inservice Education, 24*(3), 535–545.

RPGs use a 10-step process.

- Convene the group.

- Each participant takes two to three minutes to share a personal situation at school setting that he/she did not know how to handle.

- The group chooses one episode for an in-depth discussion.

- The episode is retold in detail by the originator including facts and emotions. Others ask for further details.

- All participants write a brief independent hypotheses for the rationale behind the action the narrator took. The hypotheses are that include psychological, pedagogical, and institutional factors and may begin, "A teacher in such a situation might feel frustrated because…"

- The participants share the hypotheses that were written. This begins to suggest the teaching theory behind the episode.

- The narrator responds to the hypotheses and attempts to relate them to the experience that was described. The narrator begins to uncover some the internalized knowledge, practice, and self-awareness associated with the episode.

- Group discussion on "What did the students learn from this?"

- Group discussion on alternative approaches, benefits and reasons for the choice.

- The group summarizes and debriefs.

  Source: Chase, B., Germundsen, R., Brownstein, J. C., & Distad, L. S. (2001). Making the connection between increased student learning and reflective practice. *Educational Horizons, 79*(3), 143–147.nd

6

Job-Embedded Learning

In This Chapter ...

♦ The Teacher as Adult Learner

♦ Job-Embedded Learning

♦ The Conditions Needed to Support Job-Embedded Learning Opportunities

♦ Skills Needed to Support Job-Embedded Learning

♦ Research About Job-Embedded Learning in Action

♦ Implications for School Leaders and Staff Developers

The concept of job-embedded learning evolves from adult learning theory. Lindeman (1926) contributed to the development of adult learning theory when he wrote: "…the approach to adult education will be via the route of *situations* not subjects" (p. 8). Lindeman continues: "The situation approach to education means the learning process is at the outset given a setting of reality. Intelligence performs its [*sic*] function in relation to actualities, not abstractions" (p. 9).

In today's world of professional work, there is a growing awareness of the power of job-embedded learning. The concepts of job-embedded learning have been expressed in other terms including learning on the job, learning at work, and on the job training. IBM (2006) identifies embedded learning as learning that "involves learning on the job but emphasizes completing the task at hand successfully" (p. 3). Rae and O'Driscoll (2004) suggest that ease of access or proximity and relevancy are two key elements in embedded learning. Rae and O'Driscoll explain:

> the nature of work-embedded learning provides content in context— turning the whole learning paradigm on its head. Work-embedded learning considers the individual's job role and experience level and is accessed as the individual performs work. It does not ask, "What am I going to teach you?" but "What work do you do?" and "What do you need?" When an enterprise looks at a work process and the

individual's role, it can come up with ways to deliver learning embedded into the job, and actually increase the consumption of learning in the organization. (p. 5)

The efficiency and relevancy of job-embedded learning is successful because of how adults typically learn and what motivates them to learn.

The Teacher as Adult Learner

Although adult learning is explored in Chapter 5, it is important to look at the relationship between adult learning and job-embedded learning. Adult learners are motivated by success, volition, value, and enjoyment (Knowles, Holton, & Swanson, 2005). Generally, adults want to be successful learners who find pleasure and relevance in their learning. For adults, relevancy adds value to learning, and intrinsic motivation based on success, value, and enjoyment are significant motivating factors. Job-embedded learning can be achieved more readily if learning opportunities are efficient, relevant, and yield mastery of skills and increases in knowledge that can be applied immediate to the work of teaching.

Teachers know about pedagogy, the teaching of children. Because of this orientation, it is common practice to train and offer professional development using pedagogical models and approaches such as "sit and get" workshops dealing with the latest best practices. In this model, the trainer focuses on subject matter, content, or procedures that disengage the teacher as adult learner (Knowles, Holton, & Swanson, 2005). The one-way content approach to professional development does not support job-embedded learning because adults "learn new knowledge, understandings, skills, values, and attitudes most effectively when they are presented in the context of applications to real life situations" (Knowles, 1990, p. 61).

Job-embedded learning can be formal or informal. Active engagement through job-embedded learning opportunities can include consultation with other teachers and observations of other teachers (Ponticell, 1995); action research (Chapter 12); coaching and peer coaching (Chapter 7); membership in study groups, whole-faculty study groups, and book studies (Chapter 8); lesson study (Chapter 10); critical friends (Chapter 9); and learning circles (Chapter 11).

Job-Embedded Learning

Wood and Killian (1998) define job-embedded learning as "learning that occurs as teachers and administrators engage in their daily work activities" (p. 52). Job-embedded learning for teachers can result in a simple interaction between teachers that would constitute an informal sharing of information that results in teacher growth (Northeastern Nevada Regional Professional Development Program, 2009). Wood and Killian (1998) further observe, "Teachers and administrators often rely on job-embedded learning to improve instructional practice but don't recognize that that's what they are doing (p. 52). For powerful informal learning to occur, a school culture that supports high levels of collegiality, trust, and positive collaboration must exist. In other words, an established professional learning community can foster powerful informal job-embedded learning.

Opportunities for job-embedded learning are critical to professional development. Speck (2002) argues that professional development "...conducted on the fringes of the school year and day will never become an integral part of the school" (2002, p. 17). Sparks and Hirsh (1997) write that

> job-embedded learning...links learning to the immediate and real-life problems faced by teachers and administrators. It is based on the assumption that the most powerful learning is that which occurs in response to challenges currently being faced by the learner and that allows for immediate application, experimentation, and adaptation on the job. (p. 52)

Job-embedded learning means that professional development is a continuous thread that can be found throughout the culture of a school. There are three attributes of successful job-embedded learning: (a) it is relevant to the individual teacher; (b) feedback is built into the process; and (c) it facilitates the transfer of new skills into practice.

Relevance for the Individual Teacher

First, because job-embedded learning is a part of the teacher's daily work, it is, by its very nature, relevant to the learner. Job-embedded learning addresses professional development goals and concerns of the individual teacher. In addition, job-embedded learning occurs at the teacher's job site. Therefore, the teacher's learning becomes an integral part of the culture of the classroom and by extension the school.

Feedback Is Built into the Process

Second, through job-embedded learning, feedback is built in. Processes that can generate feedback include mentoring, peer coaching, reflection and dialogue, study groups, videotape analysis of teaching and discussion about the events on tape, and journaling. Teachers can use these tools to chronicle implementation of new instructional skills, to provide artifacts for assessing transition from one learning activity to the next, or to use as material to frame future initiatives.

Facilitates the Transfer of New Skills into Practice

Third, job-embedded professional development facilitates the transfer of new skills into practice. When ongoing support through the tools of job-embedded professional development is linked with instructional supervision, transfer of skills into practice becomes part of the job.

The Conditions Needed to Support Job-Embedded Learning Opportunities

There are four essential conditions to ensure successful implementation of job-embedded professional development.

♦ *Learning needs to be consistent with the principles of adult learning:* learning goals are realistic; learning is relevant to the teacher, and concrete opportunities for practice of skills being learned are afforded;

♦ *Trust in the process, in colleagues, and in the learner him-/herself:* For learning to occur on the job, teachers must be able to trust the process (e.g., peer coaching, videotape analysis), their colleagues, and themselves. Teachers need to know that feedback will be constructive, not personal;

♦ *Time within the regular school day needs to be made available for learning:* Traditionally, professional development takes place after hours, usually at some remote site. Job-embedded learning requires time to be available within the context of the normal working day at the teacher's school site; and,

♦ *Sufficient resources must be available to support learning:* Providing release time for teachers' professional development requires the creative use of human resources. In addition, outside facilitators are sometimes needed to assist teachers in learning new skills. Funding must be made available to meet these costs (Zepeda, 1999).

Skills Needed to Support Job-Embedded Learning

Those who study professional development have reported the rise in efficacy for teachers whose learning is embedded in the workday and tailored to individual needs. McLaughlin and Oberman (1996) indicate that administrators and others responsible for professional growth need to "recognize the importance of embedding teachers' learning in everyday activities" (p. x). This importance is derived, in part, through the skills that job-embedded learning supports. Professional development that embraces job-embedded learning:

♦ Enhances reflection;

♦ Promotes collegiality;

♦ Combats isolation;

♦ Makes learning more relevant to each teacher;

♦ Increases transfer of newly learned skills;

- Supports the ongoing refinement of practice; and,
- Fosters a common lexicon that facilitates dialogue and improvement.

Job-Embedded Professional Development Enhances Reflection

Reflection—serious thought about professional practice—thrives in an atmosphere where teachers are free to make decisions about their own learning based on the realities of their situations. Practices such as peer coaching, action research, book studies, study groups, and critical friends support active reflection, inquiry, and conversations with others.

Job-Embedded Professional Development Promotes Collegiality

Job-embedded professional development flattens traditional hierarchies, breaks down barriers between teachers and principals, and makes their work more collaborative. Professional development that brings teachers and principals together in the classroom promotes collegiality. The work of the school is accomplished most efficiently when all members of the learning community work together as a team.

Job-Embedded Professional Development Combats Isolation

Compartmentalized into their separate cubicles of classroom and office, educators too often feel distant from one another. Lortie (1975) identified isolation as one of the most common problems teachers face. Professional development practiced by and for teachers can transform a group of isolated individuals into a faculty of colleagues.

Job-Embedded Professional Development Makes Learning More Relevant to Each Teacher

Adults seek learning opportunities that are relevant to their current situation (Knowles et al., 2005). When professional development is a part of the teacher's daily practice, learning opportunities are tailored to the teacher's specific learning needs.

Job-Embedded Professional Development Increases Transfer of Newly Learned Skills

The traditional model of professional development places learning in workshops and courses removed from the work environment. When principals embed professional development in the workday, learning becomes integral to practice. Teachers implement new techniques as they acquire them.

Job-Embedded Professional Development Supports the Ongoing Refinement of Practice

Learning how to teach is an ongoing and iterative practice. Opportunities to refine practice embedded in the teacher's daily work along with feedback, places practice closest to where it occurs—classrooms.

Job-Embedded Professional Development Fosters a Common Lexicon

By infusing professional development throughout the day, learning becomes a daily routine. Through the routine of learning, refining, and collaborating, a common lexicon emerges so that teachers and administrators understand one another. This process enhances dialogue, promotes reflection, and paves the way for improving instructional practices.

The educator who understands the principles of professional development masters the practices inherent in myriad forms of professional development, and understands how these forms can help further refine classroom practices and teacher development. The stakes are high; the rewards, immense. Teachers and administrators embarking on this journey can expect pleasures and pitfalls, frustrations and fulfillment, learning and growth. The journey waits.

Research About Job-Embedded Learning in Action

The positive impact of providing job-embedded learning opportunities has been reported in the research and popular literature in education, business, and the medical professions. The following discussion highlights some of this research and popular literature in education.

Wood and McQuarrie

Realizing the potential of teachers and administrators learning on the job as they engage in daily work activities, Wood and McQuarrie (1999) pose that the interaction of individuals within schools can be a powerful professional development tool. Job-embedded learning is a result of individuals sharing and reflecting on strategies and activities within the context of the organization.

Wood and McQuarrie (1999) identify a number of formal structures that exist in schools that provide such learning opportunities for educators—study groups, action research teams, and reflective logs to name a few. As educators work to solve problems of practice and to learn new strategies, they increase their knowledge and develop new skills in areas such as team teaching, cooperative learning groups, and teaching disabled students. Furthermore, they learn about their individual strengths and weaknesses with delivering instruction, designing classroom management strategies, and working with students.

Finding the time to establish formal structures is often a challenge, but Wood and McQuarrie (1999) argue that more effort should be devoted to seeking informal job-embedded activities, for these too can be productive learning experiences. They support the use of curriculum planning groups as an opportunity to learn about such topics as strategies, content knowledge, and changes in instructional practice. Faculty meetings, which have long been used as opportunities to take care of "housekeeping" duties, can be creatively structured so that teachers share instructional ideas with colleagues.

Wood and McQuarrie (1999) point out that meaning must be brought to the learning that occurs in job-embedded activities if it is to be useful. Therefore, the reflection facet of the model is critical. Experience, reflection, analysis, sharing—this is the continuum to which educators must adhere if the learning is to have meaning.

Jolly and Evans

Jolly and Evans (2005) used job-embedded strategies to support paraprofessionals moving from doing clerical work for reading teachers as they assume more responsibility. Evans and Jolly introduced a learning and action cycle where a new teaching strategy is discussed, studied, and then practiced in the classroom. The impact of the strategy is then analyzed at the next team meeting. Team members record their thoughts in reflective logs. Teachers reported that paraprofessionals were increasingly willing to engage in collegial discussions and to observe new teaching strategies.

Wood and Killian

In an effort to identify practices that contribute to school improvement, Wood and Killian (1998) conducted a study involving five successful elementary schools. Surprisingly, teacher evaluation and instructional supervision had little impact on the accomplishments of these institutions. Rather, their achievement occurred as a result of professional development that was directly linked to school improvement goals and to job-embedded learning. Wood and Killian (1998) amplify discussion, peer coaching, informal peer observations, mentoring, study groups, action research, strategic planning, and curriculum alignment as examples of activities implemented in the schools in the study.

During interviews, teachers noted workshops and conferences as means of professional learning, but failed to recognize the aforementioned activities as such. Ironically, it was the instructional leader in each school—the principal, who was very much aware of the potential in these structured activities. In fact, school leaders had made a conscious effort to create such environments and opportunities so that job embedded learning could take place. Specifically, principals were responsible for connecting formal staff development and job related activities to school improvement goals. There was a focus on sharing of best practices, a transfer of learning into instructional practice, and more importantly, a climate of trust was established where teachers learned together and helped each other improve.

Wood and Killian (1998) suggest that more formal professional development should be provided to principals so that they learn to facilitate job-embedded learning. They also stress the importance of transferring learning from professional development workshops into daily practice—taking the formal and applying it to the workplace environment. Job-embedded learning opportunities according to Wood and Killian (1998) provided the mechanism to make a connection between school improvement goals and professional development—particularly job-embedded professional development—and the role of the principal as facilitator.

Middleton

Middleton (1999) identified job-embedded learning as a factor in altering the opinions of two math teachers regarding the implementation of a math curricula founded on the tenets of Realistic Math Education. Attitudes toward the program were measured prior to implementation and one year following the pilot program. Teachers were asked to introduce a set of curricula that differed from the more traditional texts they were accustomed to teaching, the goal being to make the mathematics they teach more intrinsically motivating. As lessons were taught and the new curricula introduced, researchers came into the classroom to observe *and* to participate. Following the lessons, the researcher and teacher discussed the strategies that were implemented and the impact on student learning and motivation. The two parties consistently collaborated, questioning each other, altering tasks, and making adjustments. Notes were taken after each class, lessons were videotaped, and interviews were conducted so that teachers could reflect on the impact the lesson had on their students, and, more specifically, what made the lesson intrinsically motivating for them as teachers.

Middleton's (1999) results showed that this form of job-embedded learning fostered teachers' development of personal meaning with regard to reforms and innovations. The collaboration and professional dialogue among the teachers in this study created the culture and climate necessary to instigate change. As a result, the job-embedded learning activity helped to shape practice and to motivate both students and teachers.

Clarke

Clarke (2006) believes that both structured and on-the-job learning approaches have individual merit and that an intersection of the two would provide optimal results. Structured learning is defined as "just-in-case learning." In other words, it is a proactive approach. The skills imparted to learners in this method are determined by the organization. It prepares students for the unexpected by providing a broad range of skills, and the learning experiences are longer and less stressful. Often there is a gap between the acquisition of knowledge and the moment of its application.

On-the-job training is timely and provides learners with what they need when they need it. The results are immediate, providing learners with instant feedback. These learning experiences occur within the context of real situations, and as a result, they are often more engaging for learners. Determination of skills is largely the responsibility of the individual and it is through engagement that the individual decides a course of action.

Lankau and Scandura

Lankau and Scandura (2002) explored job-embedded learning in the context of mentorship. This type of relational learning is regarded as personal learning and has two facets: relational job learning and personal skill development. The first is defined as the increased understanding about the interdependence or connectedness of one's job to others. The latter is the acquisition of new skills and abilities that enable better working relationships. According to Lankau and Scandura, both types of learning provide powerful benefits. They assert that the use of a mentor can make learners/mentees more aware of these skills and their importance to workplace efficiency. Through modeling, coaching, and instructing, mentors instill in their understudies the idea of reflective practice. They come to understand their interdependence with others and how their actions and attitudes can affect those critical relationships.

A Case from the Field[1]

When Data Analysis Becomes a Job-Embedded Practice to Support Student Learning

Kelly Nagle Causey, Principal
Latricia D. Reeves, Assistant Principal
Sonny Carter Elementary School
5910 Zebulon Road
Macon, Georgia 31210

Sharon Patterson
Superintendent
Bibb County School District
Bibb County, Georgia

Sonny Carter Elementary School opened its doors in 1994. Sonny Carter Elementary School is a suburban elementary school serving Pre-K through fifth graders in Bibb County, Georgia. During the 2006–2007 academic year, Sonny Carter served approximately 520 students. The population during

---

1 Although the educators described in this case are no longer serving in these leadership positions, for the purposes of this chapter, we are keeping their names and titles to reflect the context of this school at the time this case study was conducted.

that school year was 50% white, 42% African American, and 8% other minorities. Forty percent of the students received free or reduced lunch, 19% received special education services (students with disabilities), and 3% were limited-English proficient. Sixty-seven percent of the 46 certified staff members have advanced graduate degrees.

Involving Teachers in Data Collection and Analysis

Involving teachers in data and test score analysis has been a long-standing practice at Sonny Carter Elementary School. Former principal Karen Yarbrough served as assistant principal at Sonny Carter Elementary School from 1993 to 1997, and became principal in 1997. Kelly Nagle Causey started her teaching career at Sonny Carter in 1993, and taught there for eight years before being appointed to the assistant principalship in 2001. She then assumed the principalship in 2004. Teachers and administrators at Sonny Carter Elementary School have worked together since the school opened to plan instruction based on results of the Iowa Test of Basic Skills (ITBS), the Stanford Achievement Test Ninth Edition (SAT 9), the Georgia Writing Assessment, and most recently, the Georgia Criterion Referenced Competency Test (GA CRCT). Each year teachers compile accountability information on each child in their classroom, which then becomes part of the administrative records. The teachers track how long the students have been at Sonny Carter Elementary School and a variety of achievement information, including test scores. Crafted originally in the 2002–2003 academic year and revised each year, the accountability form (Figure 6.1) helps to develop a baseline profile for each student.

Figure 6.1. Sonny Carter Elementary School Accountability Information

Student's Name _____

Grade_____ Homeroom Teacher_____

Entered Carter School on _____ From _____

Promoted/Retained/Placed _____

Number of schools in which previously enrolled_____

SWD ☐ Gifted ☐ LEP ☐ SST ☐ 504 ☐

CRCT Test Scores			
Subject	2006 Scaled Score	2007 Scaled Score	Gain/Loss
Reading			
English/ Language Arts			

CRCT Test Scores			
Subject	2006 Scaled Score	2007 Scaled Score	Gain/Loss
Math			
Science			
Social Studies			

Norm-referenced Testing Scores (Name of Test _____)						
Subject	2006 NPR	2007 NPR	Gain/ Loss	2006 NCE	2007 NCE	Gain/ Loss
Reading Total						
Reading Advanced						
Language Total						
Math Total						

DRA				Star Assessment Reading Level			
May 2006	September 2006	January 2007	May 2007	May 2006	September 2006	January 2007	May 2007

In School Testing: Name of Test			
Date Administered	Math	Reading	Other

Other Information					
Classroom Performance/Grades					
Reading	English	Spelling	Math	Science	Social Studies

Requesting Help from Within and Beyond the School

Marked improvement on the GA Fifth Grade Writing Assessment from 2000 to 2003 demonstrated the need for the administration to work closely with teachers to make sure they had all of the information they needed about students, testing, and results. After analyzing spring 2000 writing scores, teachers in all grade levels worked with a writing consultant from the Georgia Department of Education in a process called "Power Writing." After spring 2001 scores were analyzed, as the teachers of Sonny Carter Elementary School saw growth in their students' writing, they retrained in "Power Writing" to ensure retention of knowledge of those instructional methods, and used a curriculum specialist from within Bibb County, Dr. Mae Sheftall, to work with teachers on "Writer's Workshop."

Reviewing Efforts and Results of Achieving Goals

There was no teacher turnover in any of the upper grades (fourth, fifth, or sixth) during this time; the same teachers were looking at their students' scores and their teaching practices each year and making adjustments for success. Scores illustrated that this type of analysis was working (Figure 6.2). This prompted the school to expand the process to all areas of instruction.

Figure 6.2. Sonny Carter Elementary School Georgia Fifth Grade Writing Assessment Results

	Spring 2000	Spring 2001	Spring 2002
Emerging Writers	0.0%	0.0%	0.0%
Developing Writers	0.0%	0.0%	0.0%
Focusing Writers	8.5%	0.9%	0.0%
Experimenting Writers	48.5%	28.1%	12.7%
Engaging Writers	40.0%	51.8%	39.7%
Extending Writers	3.1%	19.3%	47.6%

During the 2002–2003 academic year, Mrs. Yarbrough was selected as a first cohort participant in the Georgia Leadership Institute for School Improvement, which is a school improvement initiative for Georgia school leaders funded by the Bill and Melinda Gates Foundation. Participation in this program validated Mrs. Yarbrough's belief that data analysis should be consistent and pervasive throughout the instructional program at Sonny Carter Elementary School. Based on this training, the success of the students, and the empowerment of the teachers from previous data analysis, Karen

Yarbrough and Kelly Nagle Causey then planned a program to assist teachers in understanding and analyzing CRCT and other data. Spring 2002 was the first time all students in grades 1 through 6 were tested on the CRCT, so each grade level had test results with which to work. Teachers were accustomed to analyzing norm-referenced information from the ITBS and/or SAT 9. Because the CRCT is a criterion-referenced test, teachers needed information and focused professional development about how to read criterion-referenced scores and how to use that information to help plan instruction. The leadership team needed to then be able to use the results of data analysis to provide ongoing professional development.

Providing Professional Development to Assist Teachers in Understanding the Results of Data

Mrs. Yarbrough and Mrs. Causey designed a yearlong professional learning program for analyzing student achievement data. This plan provided for 10 hours of release time for teachers in each grade levels 1 through 6, spread out over four days in two- to three-hour increments during the year. Building-level professional learning allotments were used to pay substitute teachers to cover classes while teachers worked in small groups with Mrs. Yarbrough and Mrs. Causey. With only the principal, assistant principal, and four to six teachers at the table at a time, they were able to talk about specific information, specific subdomains on the test, specific children, and to ask questions and present ideas and solutions in a safe, nonthreatening environment. Given the small size of each group, teachers were able to collaborate and to plan what needed to be accomplished to work with students to meet their learning needs.

At the first session with each grade level, teachers received copies of their class roster reports, and they spent time talking about what information the reports actually provided and how to read them. The group discussed scaled scores, percents versus percentiles, and the difference between "meeting" and "exceeding" expectations. As a group, members also devised a color-coded legend for teachers to use in coding their class scores in order to spot trends and patterns, both for individual children and whole-classes. Teachers color-coded the results to reflect children who were brand new to the building, who received free or reduced lunch, and who were "cusp" kids—students who scored within five points either way of the "passing" score. By looking at the performance of individual children and the class performance by subdomain, teachers gained an understanding of their areas of strength and weaknesses, as well as those of their children.

Since the initial work in the 2002–2003 academic year, Mrs. Causey has also been a participant in the Georgia Leadership Institute for School Improvement, and current assistant principal, Latricia Reeves, has participated in the Rising Stars Initiative for aspiring school leaders. In both programs, data analysis is a key component in training. As both the administrators and the teachers have become more sophisticated in their understanding and use of data, much of the professional learning session work has become teacher-directed. Mrs. Causey and Mrs. Reeves have continued the process started by Mrs. Yarbrough, using professional learning allotments to provide release time for teachers to work together throughout the year. Working the same process each year has extended the learning of the staff, and has proved to be essential in helping teachers, parents, and students understand changes in the data as the Georgia state curriculum changed from the Quality Core Curriculum to the Georgia Performance Standards.

In addition, the professional learning process created a stronger collaboration between general education and special education teachers. As more and more students with disabilities moved out of self-contained and into inclusive education settings, it was essential that special education teachers understand the data and work with general education teachers to differentiate instruction around the state standards.

Assessing What Works

In the initial professional learning small group session, teachers received both the scores of the children they taught the previous year to assess their own instructional effectiveness and the scores of the children they were presently teaching to assess their strengths and weaknesses in order to develop a more individualized instructional program. Conversation in that first session centered around what the data were and how to read them. Teachers then completed the CRCT "Class Roster Summary" (Figure 6.3) and determined "Preliminary Strengths" (Figure 6.4, page 137) and "Preliminary Areas for Improvement" (Figure 6.5, page 138) based on these color-coded scores.

Figure 6.3. Sonny Carter Elementary School CRCT Class Roster Summary

Content area: _____

Grade level: _____

Strengths: Subjects/Subdomains where percentage of students Meeting/Exceeding Standards is high—80% or above. This means that 80% or more students are scoring at Performance Levels 2 and 3. Tip: It may be quicker for you to scan the column for Level for any groups that are 20% or less than to add Levels 2 and 3.	
Subject/Subdomain	**Percentage Meeting/Exceeding Standards**

Preliminary Areas for Improvement: Subjects/Subdomains where percentage of students Not Meeting Standards is relatively high—35% or above. This means that 35% or more of the students are scoring at Performance Level 1.	
Subject/Subdomain	**Percentage Not Meeting/Exceeding Standards**

Figure 6.4. Sonny Carter Elementary School CRCT Data Analysis—Preliminary Strengths

Grade level: _____

Preliminary Strengths: Areas where percentage of students Meeting/Exceeding Standards and where year-to-year gains appear relatively high.			
Content Area	**Subgroup**	**Meeting/ Exceeding in Current Year**	**Gain from Previous Year**
Reading			
English/Language Arts			
Mathematics			
Social Studies			
Science			

Figure 6.5. Sonny Carter Elementary School CRCT Data Analysis—Preliminary Areas for Improvement

Grade level: _____

Homeroom teacher: _____

Preliminary Areas for Improvement: Areas where percentage of students Not Meeting Standards appears high and where year-to-year gains appear relatively low.

Content Area	Subgroup	Not Meeting Standards in Current Year	Change from Previous Year
Reading			
English/Language Arts			
Mathematics			
Social Studies			
Science			

Teachers took this information and were given time to "digest" it; they worked together in grade-level meetings for the four to six weeks following the initial session, as well as looking at their scores individually. Going through the process of translating the reports into their own language caused teachers to reflect critically about the data. When the groups came back together for the second and third sessions, teachers brought their coded scores and the results of their analyses. Causey, Reeves, and the teachers talked through the questions that were identified as areas of need, and they created summaries for each teacher and each grade level. Each grade level summarized its individual analyses by completing the "Summary Report of All Student Populations" (Figure 6.6) and made "Data Summary Statements" (Figure 6.7, page 140).

Figure 6.6. Sonny Carter Elementary School CRCT Summary Report of All Student Populations

Content area: _____

Grade level: _____

Strengths: Groups where percentage of students Meeting/Exceeding Standards is high—80% or above. This means that 80% or more students are scoring at Performance Levels 2 and 3. Tip: It may be quicker for you to scan the column for Level for any groups that are 20% or less than to add Levels 2 and 3.	
Subgroup	**Percentage Meeting/Exceeding Standards**
Preliminary Areas for Improvement: Groups where percentage of students Not Meeting Standards is relatively high—35% or above. This means that 35% or more of the students are scoring at Performance Level 1.	
Subgroup	**Percentage Not Meeting/Exceeding Standards**

Figure 6.7. Sonny Carter Elementary School
CRCT Data Summary Statements

Content area: _____

Grade level: _____

Prepare a statement summarizing your results from the analysis of the CRCT data. Complete a summary for each subject area, and include general information about overall performance in the subject area for your grade level. Include relative strengths among the disaggregated student groups and areas that are in greatest need of additional instructional support.

Teachers also used their analysis of individual student results to make accommodations in Student Support Team plans, 504 plans, and Individual Education Plans (IEPs), and to implement strategies in their classrooms to remediate deficiencies. They wrote goals for Annual Improvement based on test subdomains and subpopulations. Teachers conferenced with individual children to discuss strengths and weaknesses and to give the children ownership in the process. Students as well as teachers have become conversant about their "own" data.

The work the teachers did with these scores is kept on file with Mrs. Causey and Mrs. Reeves, and this data serve as a working plan from which to design instruction, create school improvement and professional development plans, and follow the progress of students and teachers (Figure 6.8, page 141).

Figure 6.8. Sonny Carter Elementary School CRCT Student Assessment Annual Improvement Goals

Teacher's name (if applicable): _____

Grade level: _____

Subject/ Subdomain	Population targeted for improvement (Example: Females in Level 1)	2006	Projected 2007	Action steps to be taken

Implications for School Leaders and Staff Developers

School leaders should be cognizant of the benefits of job-embedded learning as they are described by Wood and McQuarrie (1999) when they reveal that job-embedded learning not only promotes practical learning, it also:

- Takes less time away from the job than traditional inservice education;

- Promotes immediate application of what is learned;

- Costs less, in most cases, than paying high-priced consultants to conduct training; and,

- Agrees with what we know about adult learning. (p. 13)

Teachers also are more willing to change practice and take risks if they have the opportunity to decide what problems, mysteries, or new initiatives are focused on in their professional development (Ponticell, 1995). Ponticell also points out that there is an enhancement of professionalism when teachers are involved with job-embedded learning.

Teachers and administrators generally know more about their work than what is actually practiced during the work day (Sparks, 2005). By having meaningful conversations and focusing on the work, teachers and administrators will naturally be inclined to used more of their knowledge and expertise as well as gain knowledge from others. In other words, by experiencing job-embedded learning, teachers not only learn new information in the form of strategies and practices; they also remember those strategies and practices that they have learned, but have left in the back shelves of their minds.

In the best of all worlds, teachers would have extended periods for collaborative planning and learning without having to sacrifice any of their traditional planning time. In the elementary arena, some principals have discovered that by multiplying the school site's workers through innovative use of outside volunteers, this dream can be realized. The varied and complex nature of the curriculum in the secondary arena creates an ideal setting for enlisting the assistance of outside experts. Because district and state attendance mandates, as well as curricular requirements, confine the frequency with which students may be released, schools can multiply their workers through volunteers to provide time for teacher learning. The key is the recruitment of enough volunteers to make release of the teaching faculty for a half-day or full day of learning and planning possible. Volunteers to support this effort could come from parents, patrons of the district, and local business and professional people, especially those who look to the local school district to produce the best possible workforce.

Conclusion

In today's world of high-stakes testing and critical accountability, professional learning must be efficient and swift, and deliver high impact in helping teachers develop as professionals. Recognizing how adults learn and what motivates teachers to learn justifies the shift away from "sit and get" professional development sessions to ongoing job-embedded professional learning. When teachers analyze their own work and share critical feedback in a collegial exchange with peers and supervisors, powerful learning occurs. Regardless of its form, job-embedded learning should be the goal for professional learning. Speck (2002) summarizes that job-embedded learning should be a "part of every school's institutional priorities" (p. 20).

Suggested Readings

Fogarty, R., & Pete, B. (2007). *From staff room to classroom: A guide for planning and coaching professional development*. Thousand Oaks, CA: Corwin Press.

Jalongo, M. R., Rieg, S. A., & Helterbran, V. R. (2007). *Planning for learning: Collaborative approaches to lesson design and review*. New York: Teachers College Press.

Northeastern Nevada Regional Professional Development Program. (2009). *Effective models of professional development*. Retrieved from https://sites.google.com/site/nvnnrpdp/models-of-professional-development

Sparks, D. (2005). *Leading for results: Transforming teaching, learning, and relationships in schools*. Thousand Oaks, CA: Corwin Press.

7

Coaching in the Context of Professional Development

In This Chapter...

- ◆ Coaching
- ◆ Cognitive Coaching
- ◆ Collegial Coaching
- ◆ Instructional Coaching
- ◆ Literacy Coaching
- ◆ Mentor Coaching
- ◆ Peer Coaching
- ◆ Conditions for Successful Peer Coaching
- ◆ Embedding Coaching in Other Forms of Professional Development

The proliferation of coaches and coaching programs targeted in high needs areas (e.g., literacy, math, science) in Pre-K–12 schools has provided numerous learning opportunities for teachers. Albeit there are differences in what coaches do, all coaches support teacher and student learning. Oliver (2007) holds resolute that "the purpose of coaching remains consistent and clear: To improve instructional practices of teachers in order to increase student learning" (p. 2). The scope of this book is on professional development nestled within a learning community structure. This chapter is a critically important one as all models of professional development presented in subsequent chapters support the notion of coaching and the benefits coaches provide.

Regardless of the structure, all models and configurations of professional development can be enhanced with a strong coaching component. Kise

(2006) believes coaching brings together several key elements for effective professional development that if successful,

- uses a common framework for unbiased reflection on education. This forms the platform for the other key elements.

- begins with understanding the strengths and beliefs of the teachers.

- provides information and evidence that can influence those beliefs.

- meets the needs of each teacher in a change process which may involve individual, differentiated coaching. (p. 37)

Coaching is about the development of potential, and Dantonio (2001) positions coaching as an "empowering process that engages teachers in rediscovering themselves, the subject matter they teach, their students and their classroom" (p. 15). Effective coaches know when and how to stretch, when and how to challenge, and when and how to guide those whom they are coaching. The prerequisite coaching skills are collaboration and trust.

Coaching takes into account the needs of the organization as well as the experience, maturity, knowledge, and career path of the individual. To this end, coaching must be developmental and differentiated, relying on adult learning and career stage theories (see Chapter 3), and coaching must be embedded in the work of teachers during the day while they are on the job (see Chapter 6 for a discussion of job-embedded learning). Coaching, regardless of its form, is concerned with

- developing knowledge, thought process, and the creation of supportive environments where coaching is used to develop critical thinking skills (problem posing, problem-solving strategies);

- boosting performance and job satisfaction through the development and codevelopment of ideas and solutions to problems of practice;

- giving feedback on performance to answer the question: "Are we getting closer to meeting the mark?"; and,

- empowering individuals to grow and develop. (Zepeda, 2004a, p. 7)

Coaching can take many forms. Coaches can provide many different types of coaching such as technical coaching, collegial coaching, and challenge coaching (Garmston, 1987). Figure 7.1 summarizes different forms of coaching.

Figure 7.1. **Types of Coaching**

Type of Coaching	Application	Theorist
Executive coaching, transformational coaching and process coaching	Used in business to address working issues	Goldsmith, Lyons, & Freas (2000)
Coactive coaching	Goes beyond working relations and addresses the whole life of a person	Whiteworth, Kimsey-House, & Sandahl (1998)
Cognitive coaching	Used in teaching; is nonjudgmental and aimed at making teachers think about their actions	Costa & Garmston (2002); Dantonio (2001)
Differentiated coaching	Used in teaching and is based on the assumption that there are different types of teachers, so different coaching types should be used to make coaching most effective	Kise (2006)
Literacy coaching	Aimed at professional improvement of the literacy teachers; the coaches usually are literacy professionals, who know a lot of good practices to advice teachers	Casey (2006), Calderon (2007), Dozier (2006)
Instructional coaching	Is performed by full-time professional developers and is aimed at professional development of teachers	Knight (2007)
Technical coaching	Aimed at training sportsmen	Hodges and Franks (2002)
Inner coaching Outer coaching	Aimed at spiritual development Aimed at performance	Hudson (1999)
Mentor coaching	A mentoring assistance proved by a senior teacher to a novice teacher	Nolan (2007)
Culturally proficient coaching	Directed toward embracing different cultures during coaching	Lindsey, Martinez & Lindsey (2007)
Peer coaching	Teachers that coach their colleagues	Gottesman & Jennings (1994), Robbins (1991)
Collegial coaching	Aimed at improving the relations among colleagues and coaching of each other by teachers	Dantonio (2001)

Coaches can come from within the school or coaches can be external to the school. This chapter explores the myriad forms of coaching.

Coaching

Coaching is more successful if the learning environment is friendly, supportive, resource rich, and interactive (Keefe & Jenkins, 1997). Coaches assist with setting goals, encouraging action, acting as a sounding board, and giving feedback (Poe, 2000). Coaching is prompting and questioning, as well as guiding and nurturing. Kise (2006) views coaching as a form of job-embedded learning that supports teachers in

♦ immediate applications;

♦ the impact on individual students;

♦ the details, not the big picture;

♦ a deep understanding of the theories and models;

♦ implementation mechanics;

♦ a say in the plan;

♦ substantive background materials; and,

♦ proof that the changes are better than the present. (p. 27)

Given the complexities of teaching, the increasing needs of students, and the call for higher forms of accountability, all teachers could gain benefit from a coach. Effective coaches know the strengths and concerns of the teachers they are working with, and effective coaches are able to keep in the game of supporting the attainment of individual short- and long-term learning and growth goals.

Coaching often works in tandem with other support structures in schools including mentoring and induction programs, peer coaching programs, and instructional supervision efforts. Figure 7.2 (page 147) illustrates how coaching can be incorporated in a formal supervisory plan that includes the preobservation conference, the extended classroom observation, and the postobservation conference. Later in this chapter, peer coaching is examined.

Given the many forms of coaching, it is important to have a broad understanding of each type of coaching. Although there are several commonalities, there are also specific differences. If your school is just considering implementing a coaching program, it might be helpful to ask a few questions before designing a coaching program (Figure 7.3, page 148). If your school has some form of coaching program in place, you might also want to consider these questions to help assess whether or not more consideration about the coaching program is needed.

Figure 7.2. The Coaching Process Related to Instructional Supervision

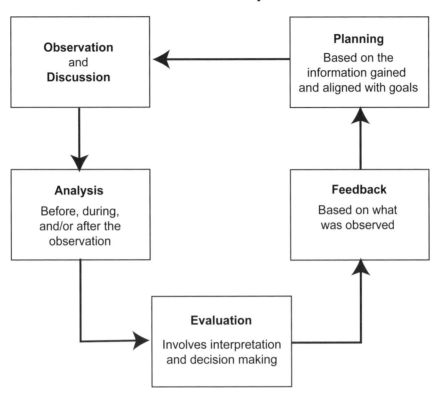

Observation and Discussion

Planning — Based on the information gained and aligned with goals

Analysis — Before, during, and/or after the observation

Feedback — Based on what was observed

Evaluation — Involves interpretation and decision making

Coaching

Figure 7.3. **Guiding Questions—Coaching**

1. What types of professional development are in place?

2. Do any of these types of professional development use coaches? Could these existing professional development programs be enhanced with the use of coaches (e.g., study groups, action research teams, mentor program)?

3. Are there faculty who are willing to serve as coaches? Would there be enough faculty available and interested to diffuse coaching efforts across grade levels, teams, subject areas?

4. What types of resources are available to support the work of coaches (e.g., release time, opportunities for training)?

5. Would the system support paying coaches stipends?

6. Are there other schools within the system that have coaches and/or coaching programs? If so, it might be beneficial to find out as much as possible about what coaching looks and sounds like in these other buildings. Ask questions such as:

   - How did you get started?

   - What lessons have you learned along the way?

   - What have been the benefits to having coaches?

   - How is coaching funded?

   - Is there a job description or a "duty and responsibility" list available?

   - How frequently do coaches meet with the principal, grade-level leaders, department chairs, curriculum specialists?

   - How is the work of coach defined by the site?

7. Is there a way to use Title I funds to support the release of coaches to work in high-stakes subject areas such as literacy, math, and science?

8. How would the work of a coach be configured?

9. Who would configure and define the work of the coach?

Cognitive Coaching

Costa and Garmston (1994) developed the cognitive coaching model. Cognitive coaching is based on the idea that metacognition occurs when there is an awareness of one's own thinking processes and it is this awareness that fosters learning. Cognitive coaching builds flexible, confident problem-solving skills through self-appraisal and self-management of cognition with the assistance of a coach who promotes a focus on learner performance within a given content (Costa & Garmston, 1994). Costa and Garmston (1994) define cognitive coaching across two different levels:

At one level, cognitive coaching is a simple model for conversations about planning, reflecting, or problem resolving. At deeper levels, cognitive coaching serves as the nucleus for professional communities that honor autonomy, encourage interdependence, and produce higher achievement. (pp. 4–5)

Costa and Garmston (1994) assert that the focus is on the cognitive development of the person being coached. The coaching cycle they suggest is cyclical and holds vestiges to the original clinical supervisory cycle of a preobservation conference, a classroom observation, and then a postobservation conference. Techniques that foster cognitive coaching include reflection, dialogue, problem posing (identification), and problem solving. Trust is the cornerstone to building coaching relationships that seek to help people move beyond their current level of performance.

Cognitive coaching is based on the core beliefs that (a) everyone is capable of changing, (b) teaching performance is based on decision-making skills that motivate skill development and refinement, and (c) teachers are capable of enhancing each other's cognitive processes, decisions, and teaching behaviors (Garmston, 1987). The processes inherent in this model of coaching involve many skills in which coaches are actively involved in

♦ applying rapport skills (body matching, intonation, language);

♦ structuring (time, space, purposes);

♦ posing reflective questioning (using positive presuppositions);

♦ using silence (wait-time, listening);

♦ paraphrasing (feeling, content, summary);

♦ accepting (nonverbally, verbally);

♦ clarifying (probing for details, values, meanings); and,

♦ providing (data, resources). (Costa & Garmston, 1987, p. 5)

It is during the conversations before and after classroom observations or while reviewing a lesson plan, the results from action research, or a lesson study discussion in which the coach can assist a teacher to:

explore the thinking behind their practices. Each person seems to maintain a cognitive map, only partially conscious. In cognitive coaching, questions asked by the coach reveal to the teacher areas of that map that may not be complete or consciously developed. When teachers talk out loud about their thinking, their decisions become clearer to them, and their awareness increases. (Garmston, Linder, & Whitaker, 1993, p. 57)

Collegial Coaching

Dantonio (2001) asserts that collegial coaching "facilitates teachers' studies of teaching practices" (p. 19), and its focus is "the reflection and study of teaching practices" (p. 19), not the shortcomings of those practices. Dantonio (2001) summarizes the role of collegial coaching like this:

> Collegial coaching offers teachers occasions to reflect, study, and deliberate on instructional experiences. In doing so, they develop frames of knowing about instruction that contribute to the enhancement of their classroom performance. By collaborating, teachers are afforded opportunities to attain insights into effective practices, building knowledge and confidence in delivering effective instruction for students. And, finally, collegial coaching is a synergetic process that breathes life into a school climate, filling it with dynamic, interactive dialogue about instruction. (p. 22)

Earlier, Garmston (1987) reported that the collegial coaching model, "assumes that teachers acquire and deepen career-long habits of self-initiated reflection about their teaching when they have opportunities to develop and practice these skills. The long-range goal is self-coaching for continuous, self-perpetuating improvements in teaching" (p. 20).

The culture of a school either supports or inhibits teachers from engaging in lifelong learning (Dantonio, 2001). Dantonio suggests collegial coaching as a way to "influence teachers' desires to collaborate, develop a shared vision about instruction, and engage in collective and shared leadership" (p. 31) that can, in many ways, support colleagues engaging in this type of professional learning.

Instructional Coaching

Knight (2007) offers instructional coaching as an alternative to traditional professional development. Instructional coaches are defied by Knight as "individuals who are full-time professional developers, onsite in schools" (p.12). Instructional coaching can be used to promote moral reasoning and technical performance among teachers (Reiman & Peace, 2002). Knight (2007) summarizes the range of work and the roles instructional coaches (ICs) assume:

- ◆ Coaching is about building relationships with teachers as much as it is about instruction. The heart of relationships is emotional connection.

- ◆ To get around barriers to change, coaches often start by working one-to-one with teachers.

- ◆ ICs adopt a partnership philosophy, which at its core means that they have an authentic respect for teachers' professionalism.

- The partnership philosophy is realized in collaborative work between the coach and the collaborative teacher. Together, coach and teacher discover answers to the challenges present in the classroom.

- ICs model in the classroom so that teachers can see what correct implementation of an intervention looks like.

- ICs model in the classroom so that teachers can see what research-based interventions look like when they reflect a teacher's personality.

- To be truly effective, coaches must work in partnership with their principals. (p. 33)

As a support to professional development with targeted teachers (e.g., math or literacy), instructional coaches can support the instructional program, and they can support a broader base of teachers across grade levels while supporting schoolwide improvement efforts.

Literacy Coaching

Dozier (2006) describes that responsive literacy coaching is based on the development of the "respectful, caring, instructional relationship" (p. 9). She points to the importance of engaging both teachers and students and draws a parallel between coaching and teaching. In this model, the coaches work mainly with teachers, but they also work with students, parents, and administrators. Because literacy coaches and other subject-specific coaches work with many teachers in a building, Walpole and McKenna (2004) assert that literacy coaches must be "sensitive to the needs of the teachers in a particular school building" (p. 5).

Symonds (2003) identifies peer accountability, support of beginning teachers, and the ability for teachers to better match instructional objectives and strategies with the needs of students as being among the benefits of literacy coaching. Literacy coaching was studied by Blachowicz, Obrochta, and Fogelberg (2005) who report:

The coach's major role is to provide professional development and support to teachers to improve classroom instruction. This typically involves organizing schoolwide professional development and then structuring in-class training, which includes demonstrations, modeling, support for teacher trials of new instruction, and coach feedback. (p. 55)

Casey (2006) believes literacy coaches should

- support teaching and learning with an eye on improving student achievement;

- effectively make decisions;

- know literacy and pedagogical content knowledge;

- be effective teachers;

- be good communicators; and,

- inspire and lead.

Casey (2006) stresses the importance of good relations with the principal and understanding strengths and weaknesses of the coached teacher. According to Casey, the coach should be fluent about reading and instructional strategies and be able to shift the focus and use of different techniques. The conversations about teaching and learning are critical to the success of a literacy coach.

Walpole and McKenna (2004) present many roles that literacy coaches assume: learner, grant writer, school-level planner, curriculum expert, researcher, and teacher. As one can see, such an approach is much broader than coaching in single classrooms. The literacy coach often assumes many roles and responsibilities for an entire school; hence, the work is not limited to the problems of literacy. In addition, Walpole and McKenna (2004) describe the work of literacy coaches in terms of their efforts across schoolwide reading programs and the support they provide in the development of reading assessments, intervention strategies, and professional support (book clubs, study groups, self-observation, peer observation) in addition to disseminating and interpreting research about reading. Israel, Block, Bauserman, and Kinnucan-Welsch (2005) conclude:

> The role of the literacy coach is evolving to meet the demand for high-quality professional development that is embedded in the daily work of teachers and teaching. Many districts have allocated resources for this role, and despite the challenge of limited resources, it appears that coaching positions will continue to increase in numbers. (p. 386)

The work of coaches continues with the proliferation of coaching programs especially in the areas of literacy and math. The following *A Case From the Field* highlights one districtwide approach to the work of literacy coaches to support the instructional program. A large part of the work of literacy coaches in the Jordan School District (Sandy, Utah) is to support the work of teachers and to provide professional development that is embedded in the workday.

A Case from the Field[1]

Literacy Coaching in Context: One District's Story

Dana L. Bickmore, Ph.D
Executive Director
Curriculum and Staff Development
Jordan School District
9361 South 300 East
Sandy, UT 84070

Kathy Ridd
Elementary Language Arts
and Early Childhood Consultant

The Context: A Balanced Literacy Framework

For more than 100 years, Jordan School District (JSD) has served the students in the south end of the Salt Lake Valley in Utah. Once a rural school district, JSD is now the largest district in the state, serving nearly 80,000 students in a suburban setting. There are 58 elementary schools, 17 middle schools, and nine high schools, as well as five specialty schools serving special education and career technology students. JSD has been recognized nationally for providing a quality education to students, and Shiffman (1999, *Forbes Magazine*) listed JSD as providing one of the best "big city" educations in the country. In the June 12, 2007 special graduation report in *Education Week*, JSD was recognized as having the lowest dropout rate of the 50 largest school districts in the country.

For nearly a decade, the administration of the Jordan School District has placed an emphasis on literacy, particularly literacy skills of elementary age students. In 1999, JSD embraced a Balanced Literacy Framework (BLF) to support the learning of students in kindergarten through sixth grade. The Jordan School District's BLF has the following components:

Shared Reading/Whole-Class Grade-Level Instruction

- Phonological Awareness
- Phonics
- Vocabulary
- Word Work/Spelling
- Comprehension
- Fluency
- Read Alouds
- Before/During/After Strategies

    45–60 Minutes—daily

---

1 Although the educators described in this case are no longer serving in these leadership positions, for the purposes of this chapter, we are keeping their names and titles to reflect the context of this school at the time this case study was conducted.

Guided Reading at Instructional Levels—Before/During/After Strategies

- Phonics
- Vocabulary
- Word Work/Spelling
- Comprehension
- Fluency
- Listen to Students Read
- Ongoing Student Assessments and Records
- Centers/Independent Work/Monitored Independent Reading

  60 Minutes—daily

Writing

- Shared
- Interactive
- Writing Process
- Writer's Workshop
- Independent
- Six Traits Instruction/Evaluation

  45–60 Minutes—daily

In 1999, the district required all elementary teachers and principals to participate in a comprehensive training on the new framework. The superintendent expected that the new BLF was to be implemented in all classrooms. New teachers hired after 1999, while in their first year with the district, continue to participate in district training similar to the original BLF training.

In 2004, through a combination of state and local funds, JSD hired literacy facilitators for each elementary school to support further the district's commitment to literacy and the BLF. The role of the literacy facilitator was three-fold. First, literacy facilitators were to provide direct and indirect support for struggling readers. Direct support might include small group or individual testing or remediation activities. Indirect support might include giving materials and ideas to teachers to support low level readers. Second, literacy facilitators were to model research-based teaching practices that support the BLF to teachers. Third, literacy facilitators were to provide school-based professional development for all teachers related to the BLF and research-based teaching practices that supported the framework. In addition to these school-based expectations, literacy facilitators were to meet together monthly with the district Literacy Administration for their own professional development. The district Literacy Administration includes an Elementary Literacy Consultant, which is a principal-level position, and three district Literacy Specialists who are master-level literacy teachers supporting literacy facilitators and teachers in the field.

Identifying Issues—Looking at Data

In 2006, Kathy Ridd, the district's Elementary Literacy Consultant, and Dana Bickmore, the Executive Director of Curriculum and Staff Development, began to question the implementation level of the Balanced Literacy Framework. Data from 1999 through 2004 showed that students' literacy levels, as measured by state testing, yielded small but steady gains. In 2005 and 2006, however, elementary student reading and language arts skills seemed to plateau. In addition, the district collected quarterly guided reading levels for each student in the district. From this data, it appeared that inconsistencies existed in how teachers reported guided reading levels within schools, as well as between schools. During monthly meetings, literacy facilitators were also expressing concerns about the level of implementation of the components of the Framework, particularly in the upper grades. Acting on these concerns, it was decided that the literacy team needed to develop a systematic approach to determine the level of implementation of the BLF and corresponding teaching practices.

The first step was to examine the research for guidance in developing a district approach to evaluate the implementation of the program. The Concerns-Based Adoption Model (CBAM), developed through the Southwest Educational Development Laboratory (Hord, Rutherford, Huling, & Hall, 2005) provided a method of evaluating the implementation levels of the BLF within and across classrooms throughout the district. The CBAM also offered a means to enhance implementation levels. Although there are three tools that can be used within the CBAM, we were initially interested in the Innovation Configuration tool. The Innovation Configuration, which is a type of rubric, can be used for program evaluation or for teacher self-evaluation. We first developed an Innovation Configuration for the JSD Balanced Literacy Framework and corresponding teacher practices to be used to determine the implementation levels in the district. In our Innovation Configuration, there are 14 Desired Outcomes, or Things that a Jordan School District Elementary Classroom teacher does:

- *Desired Outcome #1:* Teaches ALL literacy components of CBL in a 2.5- to 3-hour daily literacy block.

- *Desired Outcome #2:* Provides students with the opportunity to participate in all of the 20 CBL components.

- *Desired Outcome #3:* Assesses students regularly to diagnose educational needs, monitor progress, plan for reteaching, enrichment, differentiation, and determining student mastery.

- *Desired Outcome #4:* Collaboratively assesses student learning and growth.

- *Desired Outcome #5:* Engages students in Guided Reading.

- *Desired Outcome #6:* Provides quality literacy centers and/or independent work for students to engage in during guided reading.

- *Desired Outcome #7:* Engages students in systematic, explicit word work and language study.

- *Desired Outcome #8:* Provides daily writing instruction through the writing process, including 6 +1 Traits, appropriate for grade level.

- *Desired Outcome #9:* Includes daily monitored independent reading for students as part of independent study.

- *Desired Outcome #10:* Maintains a well-organized, positive classroom environment with a functioning, effective management system in place.

- *Desired Outcome #11:* Provides a literacy-rich classroom environment.

- *Desired Outcome #12:* Provides instruction based on Curriculum Maps created in collaborative grade-level teams.

- *Desired Outcome #13:* Uses multiple sources of formal and informal assessment to improve and verify student learning.

- *Desired Outcome #14:* Provides explicit, whole-class–grade-level instruction for all students

For illustrative purposes, we provide detail about Desired Outcomes #3 and #4 (Figure 7.4) because these two outcomes focus on the uses of assessment of students and the uses of data to develop instructional practices.

Figure 7.4. Innovation Configuration— Things That a Jordan School District Elementary Classroom Teacher Does

Desired Outcome #3: Assesses students regularly to diagnose educational needs, monitor progress, and plan for reteaching, enrichment, differentiation, and determining student mastery.		
1 ☐	2 ☐	3 ☐
♦ Keeps up-to-date running records and guided reading levels for all students	♦ Keeps up-to-date running records and guided reading levels for all students	♦ Designates guided reading level for all students on report cards

Desired Outcome #3: Assesses students regularly to diagnose educational needs, monitor progress, and plan for reteaching, enrichment, differentiation, and determining student mastery.

1 ☐	2 ☐	3 ☐
♦ Submits guided reading levels to principal monthly (or as requested)	♦ Submits guided reading levels to principal four times per year (or as requested)	
♦ Designates guided reading level for all students on report cards	♦ Designates guided reading level for all students on report cards	
♦ Maintains detailed assessment records for all students	♦ Maintains some assessment records for all students	
♦ Maintains a list of below-level students	♦ Maintains a list of below-level students	
♦ Plans for intervention within the regular classroom		

Desired Outcome #4: Collaboratively assesses student learning and growth.

1 ☐	2 ☐	3 ☐	4 ☐
♦ Collaboratively analyzes student assessment data, (i.e., CRT and ITBS screening, progress monitoring, diagnostic assessments, outcome measures, teacher-created common assessments)	♦ Independently analyzes student assessment data, (i.e., CRT and ITBS screening, progress monitoring, diagnostic assessments, outcome measures, teacher-created common assessments)	♦ Reviews student assessment data, (i.e., CRT, and ITBS screening, progress monitoring, diagnostic assessments, outcome measures, teacher-created common assessments)	♦ Has students' data in a file (i.e., CRT scores, ITBS, etc.), but data is not used

Coaching

Desired Outcome #4: Collaboratively assesses student learning and growth.			
1 ☐	2 ☐	3 ☐	4 ☐
♦ Collaboratively uses student data to: • Determine student needs • Identify mastery of concepts • Improve instruction	♦ Uses student data independently to: • Determine student needs • Identify mastery of concept • Improve instruction		
♦ Collaboratively provides students with: • Reteaching • Enrichment • Differentiation	♦ Independently provides students with: • Reteaching • Enrichment • Differentiation		

The work of Joyce and Showers (1981, 2002) related to transfer of learning and ongoing coaching was examined. We realized that for literacy facilitators and the teachers they work with to implement strategies learned during training sessions, they needed ongoing support in the form of coaching. Although literacy facilitators in JSD were providing training to teachers in schoolwide professional development sessions and some were modeling research based practices in classrooms, the district did not expect facilitators to coach. In fact, from the district level there had been no training on coaching given to literacy facilitators.

Moving to Coaching—Getting Into Classrooms to Chronicle Implementation

Using the Balanced Literacy Innovation Configuration developed by the district literacy team, the district consultant and literacy specialists conducted 180-minute observations (see Figure 7.5) in 100 classrooms to determine implementation of the BLF. The results of the observations indicated that implementation levels of the BLF were inconsistent in the district. Although the team identified several model classrooms, in the majority of the classrooms the Framework and corresponding teacher

Figure 7.5. Classroom Observation Checklist

Literacy Block	Guided Reading	Well-Organized Classroom	Literacy-Rich Classroom
○ Read aloud ○ Phonemic awareness (K–2) ○ Concepts of Print (K–2) ○ Shared reading ○ Guided reading ○ Centers/independent work ○ Monitored Independent Reading (MIR) ○ Explicit whole-class instruction ○ Word work ○ Phonics/spelling ○ Comprehension ○ Fluency ○ Oral language ○ Interactive/shared writing ○ Modeled Writing ○ Directed Writing ○ 6+1 Traits of Writing ○ Writer's Workshop ○ Independent writing	○ Small group area evident ○ Uses appropriate narrative texts ○ Uses appropriate informational texts ○ Differentiates instruction to meet all student's needs ○ Uses before, during, after activities ○ Incorporates comprehension ○ Incorporates fluency ○ Teaches vocabulary of text ○ Listens to students read ○ Conducts running records ○ Has up-to-date records ○ Uses appropriate reading strategies (whisper, staggered, choral, paired, etc.) NO ROUND-ROBIN reading!	○ Posts & uses rules, schedules, management system ○ Students routinely follow established rules & procedures ○ Smooth transitions ○ Room organized, labeled ○ Seating arranged for cooperative learning activities and interaction ○ Students accountable for learning ○ Room clutter free, inviting ○ Productive, workable noise level ○ Teacher has positive interaction with students ○ Positive interaction between students	○ Print-rich environment ○ Concept charts ○ Definition chards ○ 6+1 Traits posters ○ Comprehension posters ○ Authentic reading/writing observed ○ Student writing displayed ○ Classroom library evident, with narrative & informational texts in a wide variety of genres, leveled appropriately, for student use ○ Leveled book boxes for MIR ○ Word Wall posted, consisting of general and content words

Literacy Block	Guided Reading	Well-Organized Classroom	Literacy-Rich Classroom
Centers/Independent Work ○ Management system in place ○ Students responsible for learning ○ Engaging activities ○ Authentic reading/writing activities ○ Student accountability system ○ Differentiated work matches student needs ○ Work reinforces previously taught concepts	**Explicit Instruction** ○ Grade-level teacher talk ○ Shared reading: all students ○ Uses Houghton Mifflin for shared reading ○ Other grade-level texts (Big Books, poetry, informational) ○ All students have access to text ○ Book Talk ○ Pre-teaches vocabulary ○ Use comprehension strategies ○ Before, during, after activities ○ Interactive, hands-on activities ○ Integrated content core ○ Incorporates good ESL strategies	**Writing** ○ Writing process ○ Mini lesson ○ 6+1 Traits of Writing ○ Student Accountability/status of class ○ Interactive/shared writing (K–2) ○ Modeled writing ○ Directed writing, independent writing, student-published writing available to other students ○ Writing area & materials evident	**MIR** ○ Minimum 15–20 minutes per day ○ Students self-select books from independent reading level-interest based books provided by teacher ○ Variety of genres provided ○ Monitoring, non-graded (student reflections, cooperative learning discussions, conferences, bookmarks, journals, pictures, etc.) work
Word Work ○ Phonemic awareness (K–2) ○ Phonics ○ Vocabulary ○ Differentiated spelling ○ Grade-level language arts ○ Word Wall posted ○ Word Wall systematically used in instruction	**Assessment** ○ Keeps up-to-date running records with guided reading levels ○ Submits guided reading levels as requested ○ Maintains detailed formal and informal assessment records ○ Maintains list of below level students	**Collaboration** ○ Collaborates with team in analyzing assessment data ○ Collaboratively with team in analyzing assessment data ○ Collaboratively plans for/ provides interventions, re-teaching, enrichment, differentiation	**Curriculum Mapping** ○ Creates curriculum map, based on Utah State Core and student needs ○ Uses curriculum map to guide instruction

practices were applied inconsistently, and at levels that could be stalling student progress. Even more disturbing, the team observed some classrooms where there was little or no implementation of the Framework and teacher practices were at cross-purposes with the Framework. Several teachers were exclusively using whole-class direct instruction for the entire literacy block with no differentiation for literacy levels and no support for struggling readers.

After eight years of district support for balanced literacy and untold hours of teacher training, we concluded from the classroom observation data, the review of research, and the apparent plateau of student achievement that changes in professional development practices needed to occur to improve implementation of the BLF. Although the literacy facilitators were one of the most important assets available to the district and schools, the coaches were not being used in ways to support teachers. We concluded greater implementation of the BLF and associated teacher practices would occur through the development and implementation of a coherent and cohesive district model in which literacy facilitators would act as school based coaches.

Developing the Model—The Art of Coaching

The District Literacy Administration based their coaching model on a combination of the gradual release model of coaching cycle developed by Pearson and Gallagher (as found in Casey [2006]) and a unit of study coaching cycle described by Casey (2006). The gradual release model generally begins with the coach modeling a particular lesson and thinking aloud so the teacher can understand the decision making that occurs. The second phase has the coach modeling a lesson codeveloped by the coach and teacher. The third phase has the coach and teacher teaching side-by-side, with the coach taking the lead on unfamiliar or new aspects of the lesson or strategy. The fourth phase is side-by-side teaching with the teacher taking the lead with the unfamiliar parts of the lesson. The fifth phase has the teacher teaching the bulk of the lesson with support from the coach. In the sixth phase, the teacher practices independently and the coach returns to the classroom for support as the teacher feels the need.

In the unit of study coaching cycle, the coach coconstructs a unit of study, preferably with a group of teachers, usually a grade-level team. The coach teaches several lessons throughout the unit while the teacher team observes. The group, which includes the coach and the observing teachers, debrief the lesson and each observing teacher is expected to "try on" the lesson on their own. The group debriefs after the teachers try each of the lessons.

To support the two coaching models, the District Literacy Team sought to help literacy facilitators develop communication and facilitator skills. Before developing literacy facilitators skills the District Literacy Team felt they needed to improve their own communication and facilitation by involvement in state and district training related to cognitive coaching and facilitation as outlined by Costa and Garmston (1994), Vella (2001), and Garmston and Wellman (1999). The District Literacy Team practiced their new skills on each other, with colleagues, and in various district training sessions.

Facilitating the Facilitators' Coaching Skills—Linkages to Other Forms of Job-Embedded Learning

In the spring of 2007, with their own growing coaching and facilitation skills, the team began in earnest to train the district literacy facilitators. Teams of facilitators were sent to state coaching training. The facilitators participated in a book study of the text, *Literacy Coaching: The Essentials* by Katherine Casey. The Literacy Team facilitated several activities related to the text to model adult learning protocols and to have facilitators learn and practice the gradual release and unit coaching cycles. The facilitators became versed in the district's BLF Innovation Configuration tool. The facilitators learned how the Innovation Configuration would be used as a communication, facilitation, and coaching tool with teachers. The Innovation Configuration would be used by teachers to self-evaluate and the facilitators would coach the teacher based on that self-evaluation. Facilitators had multiple sessions where they role played, one facilitator playing the teacher role, the other facilitator being the coach using the teacher's self-evaluation.

By midyear of the 2007–2008 school year facilitators were encouraged to begin employing their newly developed coaching skills in their schools with teachers. The District Literacy team first required facilitators to use the BLF Innovation Configuration tool with several teachers to start the coaching process. They were then asked to try either a gradual release or unit study coaching cycle.

As the literacy facilitators began to implement coaching, the District Literacy Team debriefed with the facilitators during their monthly facilitators meetings. The District Literacy Team also provided school support by modeling and participating in the coaching cycles with the facilitators. As part of that coaching cycle for the facilitators, an Innovation Configuration self-evaluation tool was developed. The Facilitator Innovation Configuration specifically identified the skills facilitators should demonstrate at various levels of implementation of coaching and other aspects of their job duties. The Innovation Configuration became the springboard for discussion between the facilitators and the district specialists. The facilitators also provided collaborative support to each other through the district Literacy Facilitator listserv, sharing challenges, ideas, and solutions to issues. The District Literacy Team also scheduled time for facilitators to observe each other in their roles as coaches.

There are seven desired outcomes, or things that a Jordan School District Literacy Facilitator does in our *Innovation Configuration for Facilitators*:

- ◆ *Desired Outcome #1:* Meets collaboratively with principal and grade-level teams to determine teacher and student needs for developing educational plans, including interventions.

- *Desired Outcome #2:* Provides training for principal and teachers on assessments (screening, progress monitoring, diagnostics, and ongoing classroom assessments) and helps teachers proficiently use data to guide classroom instruction and Tier I interventions.

- *Desired Outcome #3:* Guides classroom teachers toward proficiency with components of Comprehensive Balanced Literacy (CBL).

- *Desired Outcome #4:* Supports teacher learning and implementation of Comprehensive Balanced Literacy by providing individual, team, and schoolwide professional development based on:

- *Desired Outcome #5:* Helps teachers become proficient with curriculum mapping, integration, assessments and differentiated instruction.

- *Outcome #6:* Supervises and coordinates Tier II student interventions, under the direction of and in collaboration with the principal.

- *Desired Outcome #7:* Serves as an ambassador for Jordan School District's Comprehensive Balanced Literacy Goals.

For illustrative purposes, we provide detail about Desired Outcome #3 (Figure 7.6) because this outcome focuses on coaching teachers with achieving comprehensive balanced literacy (CBL) instruction.

Figure 7.6. Innovation Configuration—Things That a Jordan School District Literary Facilitator Does

Desired Outcome #3: Guides classroom teachers toward proficiency with components of Comprehensive Balanced Litteracy (CBL).			
1 ☐	2 ☐	3 ☐	4 ☐
◆ Builds trust and confidence to enable coaching	◆ Builds trust and confidence to enable coaching	◆ Builds trust and confidence to enable coaching	◆ Builds trust and confidence to enable coaching
◆ Assesses teacher needs and level of implementation of CBL components	◆ Assesses teacher needs and level of implementation of CBL components	◆ Assesses teacher needs and level of implementation of CBL components	

Coaching

Desired Outcome #3: Guides classroom teachers toward proficiency with components of Comprehensive Balanced Litteracy (CBL).			
1 ☐	2 ☐	3 ☐	4 ☐
♦ Models, observes, and provides feedback for teachers	♦ Models, observes, and provides feedback for teachers		
♦ Provides sustained coaching (gradual release of responsibility) for training and support of teachers			

Monitoring Progress

Implementing a coaching model in 58 schools with more than 40,000 students is a daunting task. Bickmore and Ridd believe they are in the second of a five-year implementation process. There are signs that the Jordan School District literacy coaching model is beginning to pay dividends for the facilitators and the teachers they serve. The facilitators are reporting through the facilitator's Innovation Configurations and reflections that they are excited about the coaching model and are improving the quantity and quality of interactions with teachers. Reagan Fay, one of the literacy facilitators, puts it this way:

I went back to school Monday (after our facilitator meeting), looked at my schedule, and made adjustments. I held a meeting with my aides and "coached" them on our Tier 2 interventions program. I like the idea of coaching. I think of myself as a football coach. My players (teachers and aides) know how to play the game. I am just setting them up to be more successful at it. I don't take it over and do it for them. I don't stand back and say "you should have done it this way." We work at it together. I came back to school after the meeting and decided to get my feet wet by coaching this one teacher. She has taught way longer than I have but sees that I can be of help to her. I appreciate her willingness to let me in but know it's because she sees me as a coach and not a spy or whatever. I liked this approach and can't wait for future meetings.

Ridd and Bickmore believe by supporting and monitoring coaching levels of the facilitators and the corresponding improved implementation of the BLF by teachers improved student achievement will occur.

Mentor Coaching

Closely aligned with mentoring, Nolan (2007) defines mentor coaching as a "structured process whereby an experienced person introduces, assists, and supports a less-experienced person (the protégé) in a personal and professional growth process" (p. 3). Nolan believes that mentor coaching can "help staff become more comfortable with one another" and "develop skills and talents that are undeveloped or that have not been previously recognized" (p. 12). Portner (1998) includes coaching as one of the four mentoring functions for new teachers. The other three mentoring functions are relating (trust, paying attention to feelings, body language), assessing (general needs of new teachers, resources), and guiding (different types of guiding for mentees who are at different levels of development). Portner (1998) shares:

> Your goal as a coach is to develop your mentee into a self-reliant teacher. By a "self-reliant teacher," I mean a teacher who is willing and able to (a) generate and choose purposefully from among viable alternatives, (b) act upon those choices, (c) monitor and reflect upon the consequences of applying those choices, and (d) modify and adjust in order to enhance student learning. (p. 41)

Boreen, Johnson, Niday, and Potts (2000) also view coaching as a part of mentoring beginning teachers: "mentors can coach beginning teachers to connect theory with practice" (p. 35). Boreen et al. suggest four techniques to encouraging reflective dialogue with new teachers: "conferring, questioning, mirroring, and reflecting" (p. 39).

These strategies offer ways to coach beginning teachers to "think like a teacher." By using these techniques, mentors help new teachers see beyond the superficial "fun times" of a field trip to the long-range educational benefits that accompany active student engagement. These mentoring strategies allow beginning teachers to get the whole picture. All take time, but benefits to both mentor and new teacher are substantial: many enjoy a collegial relationship not only during the mentoring period but for many years to come. (Boreen et al., 2000, p. 53)

No doubt, new teachers can benefit from coaching as an overall part of an induction program in which mentoring is a part of the plan.

Peer Coaching

Peer coaching provides opportunities for teachers to support and learn from each other and to engage in realistic discussions about teaching and learning—their own and that of their students. Peer coaching derives strength not only from the social nature of the model, but also from its constructivist aspects in which meanings are developed through interacting with others and then from the process of constructing meaning. Learning from each other empowers teachers. Peer coaching can foster ongoing and sustained examination of practices, with those closest to instruction—teachers. Peer coaches provide guidance, encouragement, and motivation to continue learning from the events that unfold in the classroom.

Peer Coaching Extends Learning

As a form of job-embedded learning, peer coaching can extend professional learning opportunities such as action research and lesson study. Joyce and Showers (1981, 1982, 1995, 2002) provided the first documented model of peer coaching as a form of professional development. They developed this model as a means for peers to coach each other while implementing *in the classroom* new strategies learned during in-service (professional development). Joyce and Showers (1982) assert, "Like athletes, teachers will put newly learned skills to use—if they are coached" (p. 5).

Social learning theory as envisioned by Bandura (1986) includes observation and modeling, key aspects of peer coaching. Peer coaching promotes reciprocal learning; the peer who is being observed and the coach who is conducting the observation learn from each other. Modeling is a complex and powerful learning tool that involves three stages: (a) exposure to the responses of others; (b) acquisition of what one sees; and (c) subsequent acceptance of the modeled acts as a guide for one's own behavior (Bandura, 1986).

Peer coaching includes a preobservation conference, an extended classroom observation, and a postobservation conference as depicted in Figure 7.7.

Figure 7.7. Peer Coaching

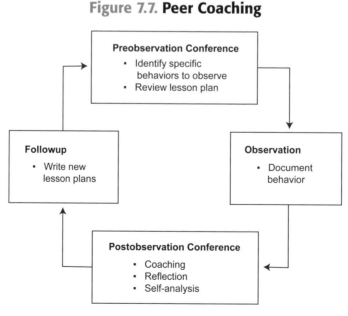

Peer Coaching Fosters Transfer of Knowledge into Practice

Peer coaching helps to ensure the transfer of newly learned skills from an in-service (professional development) learning opportunity into practice. In fact, one of the strengths of peer coaching is the increased likelihood that coaching increases transfer of knowledge to skills applied in the classroom or work environment (Joyce & Showers, 1995). A study by Olivero, Bane, and Kopelman (1997) compared the impact of training alone to a combination of coaching and training. Olivero et al. found

- ♦ Training alone increased productivity by 22.4%; and

- ♦ Training combined with coaching interventions increased productivity by 88%.

The pioneering work of Joyce and Showers (1981, 1982, 1995, 2002) gives a consistent message about the value of peer coaching and transfer of learning to daily practice. Transfer to practice is connected to four interrelated components of coaching related to learning: (a) learning the theory supporting the instructional strategy; (b) watching a skillful demonstration of the instructional strategy; (c) practicing the strategy; and (d) engaging in peer coaching. Joyce and Showers report most recently that if teachers only participate in the first three components, approximately "5% of the teachers transfer and master the strategy in their classrooms" (2002, p. 78). However, if these same teachers would participate in all four components of the peer coaching model by adding engaging in peer coaching, "95%" of the teachers will transfer skills into practice (p. 78).

Defining Peer Coaching

Peer coaching is a multifaceted tool that can be implemented as an instructional strategy, a professional development strategy, and a complement to instructional supervision. Originally conceived as a form of professional development, peer coaching consisted of a cycle that included the presentation of theory as well as a demonstration.

Teachers were then led through practice, given feedback, and coached accordingly as depicted in Figure 7.8. The coaching aspects of the model mirror the clinical supervisory model by including extended "in-class training by a supportive partner who helps a teacher correctly apply skills learned in a workshop" (Joyce & Showers, 1982, p. 5).

The peer coaching model provides a bridge between the topics and skills addressed during large-scale in-service programs (typically delivered by outside experts) and the day-to-day application of newly learned theory. Coaching occurs at two levels: in the classroom with a coach observing a teacher, and in the feedback conference. Because coaching occurs in the classroom, feedback is more realistic, steeped in the context where skills and techniques are applied. Peer coaching is a realistic approach for supporting teachers because, according to Joyce and Showers (1981), coaching involves a collegial

Coaching

Figure 7.8. **Peer Coaching Cycle**

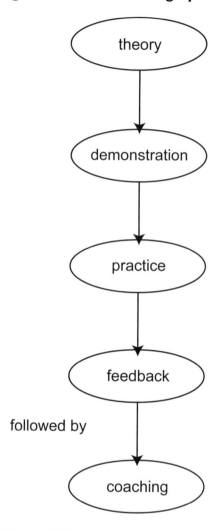

Source: Joyce & Showers, 1995.

approach to the analysis of teaching for the purpose of integrating mastered skills and strategies into

♦ a curriculum;

♦ a set of instructional goals;

♦ a time span; and,

♦ a personal teaching style. (p. 170)

The Job-Embedded Nature of Peer Coaching

Peer coaching is perhaps one of the earliest forms of job-embedded learning—"learning that occurs as teachers and administrators engage in their daily work activities" (Wood & Killian, 1998, p. 52). When learning is job-embedded, transfer of new skills into practice is more likely. In peer coaching, teachers are able to observe one another at work, share strategies, engage in guided practice as followup to professional development, and reinforce learning through feedback, reflection, and ongoing inquiry. In school communities that support and nurture peer coaching, leadership among teachers can be developed and sustained over time.

Coaches Engage Others in Conversations About Teaching

The work of coaches involves engaging in conversations with peers. Zeus and Skiffington (2001) are absolute on the necessity of conversations, and they indicate, "coaching is a conversation, a dialogue, whereby a coach and a coachee interact in a dynamic exchange to achieve goals, enhance performance and move the coachee forward to greater success" (p. xiii). The authors further delineate that

- ◆ coaching is essentially a conversation;

- ◆ coaching is about learning; and,

- ◆ coaching is more about asking the right questions than providing answers. (p. 3)

Given the myriad ways in which coaches can work with teachers (e.g., within study groups, lesson study, peer coaching), it is important to focus on the conversations and the ways that coaches engage in these conversations. The following insights might be helpful in fostering conversations:

- ◆ *Suspend judgment:* Coaches are colleagues who support and nurture the efforts of teachers. Although honesty is always the best policy, effective coaches refrain from making value judgments about the teachers whom they are coaching. Conversations are focused on what was observed or under study.

- ◆ *Listen more, speak less (Oliver, 2007, p. 11):* McGreal (1983) has held that the more teachers talk about teaching, the better they get at it. It is through the talk about teaching that teachers begin to reflect on their practices. Through focused discussion, teachers are able to make better sense of their situations.

- ◆ *Avoid trust blocking responses:* Trust blocking responses as developed by Pascarelli and Ponticell (1994) are conversation stoppers. Figure 7.9 details the range of trust-blocking responses to avoid.

Figure 7.9. Trust-Blocking Responses

♦ Evaluating—Phrases such as the following tend to evoke defensive-ness: "You should…," "Your responsibility here is…," "You are wrong about…"

♦ Advice giving—Advice is best given if requested; responses such as "Why don't you just…," "You would be better off…," or "Your best action is…" can go in one ear and out the other if unsolicited.

♦ Topping—"That's nothing, you should have seen…," "Well, in my class…," "When that happened to me…," "You think you have it bad, well…" are phrases of one-upmanship. They shift attention from the person who wants to be listened to and leaves him/her feeling unimportant.

♦ Diagnosing—Phrases that tell others what they feel ("What you need is…," "The reason you feel that way is…," "You really don't mean that…," "Your problem is…") can be a two-edged sword, leaving the person feeling pressured (if the speaker is wrong) or feeling exposed or caught (if the speaker is right).

♦ Warning—"You had better…," "If you don't…," "You have to…," or "You must…" can produce resentment, resistance, or rebellion if the recipient feels the finger of blame pointed in his/her direction.

♦ Lecturing—"Don't you realize…," "Here is where you are wrong…," "The facts simply prove…," or "Yes, but…," can make the person feel inferior or defensive. Full, descriptive data and problem-solving questioning allow the individual to make logical decisions for him or herself.

♦ Devaluating—"It's not so bad…," "Don't worry…," "You'll get over it…," or "Oh, you really don't feel that way…" take away or deny the feelings of the speaker. Conveying nonacceptance of the speaker's feelings creates a lack of trust, feelings of inferiority or fault, and fear of risk taking.

Source: Pascarelli & Ponticell, 1994.

Barry Zweibel, founder of GottaGettaCoach!, Incorporated (2005) developed the F.R.A.M.E. Coaching Model (Figure 7.10, page 171) as a way to engage in coaching conversations. The F.R.A.M.E. Model has an embedded F.O.C.U.S. that supports coaching conversations that are non-judgmental, seek to extend conversations with open-ended questions, and keep the momentum of the conversation on growth and development.

Figure 7.10. **The F.R.A.M.E. Coaching Model**

F   F.O.C.U.S. each interaction

R   REACT nonjudgmentally

A   ASK thought-provoking questions

M   MONITOR progress and learning

E   ENCOURAGE continued growth

Source: Used with permission of Barry Zweibel, MCC and ICF-Certified Master Coach, GottaGettaCoach!, Incorporated. Retrieved from www.ggci. com

Zweibel (2005) furthers supports coaching conversations through the F.O.C.U.S. for each conversation (Figure 7.11). Zweibel asks, So how *does* a coach help people focus? His answer is to examine conversations from the perspective of the person being coached.

Figure 7.11. **F.O.C.U.S. Interactions**

♦ *F* as in *FACE IT*—Just getting people to talk about where they're stuck, or what they might be avoiding, is often enough to help them stare down their "scary monsters" and get back on track. So coaches have people talk about what's *really* important.

♦ *O* as in be more *OPEN MINDED*—Basketball coaching legend John Wooden said it best, "It's what you learn *after* you know it all that counts." Helping people realize that there may be *other* ways of thinking/feeling about things than how they typically do, is often incredibly liberating and helps them think more creatively and expansively.

♦ *C* as in recognize the *CHOICES*—Once the creative juices start flowing, the next task is to help the client brainstorm a number of concrete alternatives as to how s/he *might* move meaningfully forward. But make sure that you're not the one providing all the answers—that's not coaching, that's consulting. The more you can encourage your client to come up with seemingly absurd ideas, the better.

♦ *U* as in *UNAMBIGUOUSLY* move forward—Once a variety of choices are identified, coaches help people pick one (or more than one), develop specific assignments and plans to get things going, and establish accountabilities to insure proper follow-through.

♦ *S* as in *SOLIDIFY* the learning—Results are nice, but for learning to stick, it's essential to talk about the insights, discoveries, and lessons learned along the way. As Vernon Law said, "Experience is a hard teacher because she gives the test first, the lesson afterward." A good coach makes sure the lessons are clearly understood.

Source: Used with permission of Barry Zweibel, MCC and ICF-Certified Master Coach, GottaGettaCoach!, Incorporated. Retrieved from www.ggci. com

According to Zweibel (2005), there are two basic types of questions: questions that gather information, and questions that deepen the learning of the person being asked. Zweibel elaborates:

> The latter category is far more powerful and thought provoking. Here's the test: if a client is telling you things s/he has already thought about or felt, then you missed the mark. If, on the other hand, new thoughts, feelings, realizations, ideas, insights, and directions start to "pop," then you're in the zone.

Consider the following examples of questions that gather information and questions that deepen learning presented in Figure 7.12 offered by Zweibel (2005).

Figure 7.12. Gather Information Questions and Deepen the Learning Questions

Gather Information Questions	Deepen the Learning Questions
What have you tried so far?	What haven't you tried yet?
Why are you stuck?	What would make that easier for you?
What do you mean?	What aren't you saying?
What are you waiting for?	What are you ready to do?
Why did you do it that way?	What have you learned so far?

Source: Used with permission of Barry Zweibel, MCC and ICF-Certified Master Coach and GottaGettaCoach!, Incorporated. Retrieved from www.ggci.com

Conditions for Successful Peer Coaching

Training

Peer coaches need training and followup support to refine coaching skills in the areas of

- human relations and communication;
- classroom observation processes: preobservation conference, the extended classroom observation, and the postobservation conference; and,
- data collection techniques.

Not all teachers want to be coached and coaches will need support in knowing when and how to gain entrée into teacher's classrooms, how to persevere through difficult conversations, and when and how to seek assistance from others.

Trust

Change means leaving "what we are" and becoming "what we are not" (Barott & Raybould, 1998, p. 31). It can be unnerving to leave behind the comfortable and step into the unknown. Fullan (1982) believes that "all real change involves loss, anxiety, and struggle" (p. 25). Not surprisingly, educators tend to resist change; the reasons may include

- ◆ the perception that change is a personal or professional attack;
- ◆ the loss associated with change;
- ◆ the history of change in the school or district;
- ◆ community or district reaction to change; and,
- ◆ the possibility of added individual responsibility and accountability as a result of change.

Change also means admitting that a practice needs to be modified, extended, or replaced. Teachers must trust coaches, colleagues, and administrators, as well as themselves. Teachers must trust that feedback will be constructive, based on best practice, grounded in research, and not in any way a personal attack. Trust is essential for success in any form of coaching. Costa and Garmston (1994) identify three key areas in which a coach must build trust: (a) in self, (b) between individuals, and (c) in the coaching process.

Trust in Oneself

Trust in oneself is a prerequisite for developing trust in any other area. A person must have a firm sense of her own values and beliefs. Being consistent, open and accessible, nonjudgmental, and freely admitting one's own mistakes are all characteristics of trust in oneself (Costa & Garmston, 1994). Teachers must develop a measure of objectivity when reflecting on their own practices. Artifacts such as journals, videotapes, and portfolios lose their effectiveness when teachers cannot be honest with themselves.

Trust in Each Other

The trust must exist between individuals. This trust is established by knowing what is important to others, how others process information, and what are their current thoughts and concerns. Teachers must be able to trust their coaches. What occurs in a coaching session is sacred and should not be made public information. If supervisors coach teachers, what emerges in the classroom and the conferences must not be used as a basis for a summative evaluation.

Trust in the Process

If peer coaching is to endure, teachers need to trust that peer coaching will be a collaborative effort, not tied to teacher evaluation. Teachers need to feel safe and secure with one another and the process. In part, safety is "having things regular and predictable for oneself" (Gage & Berliner, 1998, p. 337). If teachers are not certain that they can share their ideas without fear of personal criticism or that what is observed in the classroom is confidential (between the teacher and coach), they will be wary of investing themselves in the process or the efforts needed to make changes in practice.

Trust must be forged between teachers and administrators. Blase and Blase (2000) offer that for leaders (both teachers and administrators) to develop trusting relationships, they need to

♦ listen with respect;

♦ be a model of trust;

♦ help others to communicate effectively;

♦ clarify expectations;

♦ celebrate experimentation and support risk; and

♦ exhibit personal integrity. (p. 36)

Teachers will not readily accept administrative support unless trust exists; coaching will not endure without a basis of trust, respect, and good intentions. Trust is the bricks and mortar of coaching.

Administrative Support

Coaching, regardless of its form, needs to be supported before and during the implementation of a peer-coaching program (Gingiss, 1993; Moller & Pankake, 2006; Pankake & Moller, 2007). The research of Pankake and Moller (2007) stresses the need for coaches to learn how to work with adults. Coaches need to be coached in their work with adults. Principals support the work of coaches when they:

♦ encourage networking with coaches at the local, regional, state, or national level.

♦ provide opportunities to attend professional learning experiences that address the skills needed by coaches.

♦ be a coach to the teacher leader by modeling listening and questioning skills.

♦ help teacher leader coaches understand when to support and when to push teachers to move instructional practices forward (Moller & Pankake, 2006, p. 181)

Gingiss (1993, p. 82) believes, "Principals can provide informal encouragement, formal endorsement, personal involvement, and resource designation." Given the complex nature and specific context of each school, the type of administrative support needed to develop, implement, and assess the overall value of a peer coaching program will vary. For coaching to flourish, principals must

- *allocate resources:* Provide substitute teachers to cover classrooms while coaches coach; schedule release time for teachers to coach each other and conduct pre- and postobservation conferences; procure professional development materials on techniques under construction; obtain funds to develop a professional library for teachers (journals, videos).

- *arrange for initial and ongoing training:* Coaches will need training in the processes of peer coaching; followup training might be needed depending on how the program evolves.

- *provide emotional support and encouragement:* Any time teachers try new practices, they need support and affirmative feedback to keep the momentum going.

According to Clutterbuck (2005), in *Creating a Coaching Climate*, there are certain aspects needed to create a coaching climate in which the organization can support coaching. In a climate supporting coaching:

- personal growth, team development, and organizational learning are integrated and the links clearly understood;

- people are able to engage in constructive and positive confrontation;

- people welcome feedback (even at the top) and actively seek it;

- coaching is seen as a joint responsibility;

- coaching is seen primarily as an opportunity rather than as a remedial intervention;

- time for reflection is valued; and,

- there are effective mechanisms for identifying and addressing barriers to learning.

Starting a coaching program means a great deal of upfront work for the principal. Upfront tasks include building momentum for such a program, involving the faculty in its design, garnering support from the central administrative office, and scanning the environment for potential obstacles.

As a peer-coaching program evolves, needs will change and so must the program. In time, the principal might even be able to step back and let teachers run the program. Letting go empowers both the principal and the peer coaches, but it does not obviate the need for ongoing support and some oversight. Some school systems support teacher leadership by appointing a teacher leader to manage the logistics of the program. Effective principals continually seek such opportunities to empower teachers and build collegiality.

Embedding Coaching in Other Forms of Professional Development

Coaching offers the potential to extend learning regardless of its configuration. Coaching can be a standalone strategy as in peer coaching or as a complementary strategy embedded in other forms of professional development such as:

♦ Study Groups, Book Studies, and Whole-Faculty Study Groups (Chapter 8);

♦ Critical Friends (Chapter 9);

♦ Lesson Study (Chapter 10);

♦ Learning Circles (Chapter 11);

♦ Action Research (Chapter 12); and,

♦ Portfolio Development (Chapter 13).

The reader is encouraged to return to this chapter often while reading subsequent chapters in this book. For illustrative purposes, the application of coaching in action research is examined in this chapter.

Through action research, teachers develop a question or a problem of practice to investigate and then gather data from a variety of sources such as instructional artifacts (e.g., lesson plans) and classroom observations. Peer coaches can help teachers make sense of their practice by giving feedback from classroom observations. The original model of peer coaching centered on skill transfer from professional development opportunities. Coaches can examine lesson plans, observe classrooms (with one eye on the teacher and the other on student responses), and give feedback on the application of skills and techniques. Coaching keeps action research alive, as data related to classroom practices and outcomes guide further observations and coaching sessions.

Extending the coaching process to portfolio development can enhance adult learning (Chapter 3). In fact, combining action research with portfolio development and peer coaching yields an even more powerful iteration and supports job-embedded learning (Chapter 6). Teachers can construct, examine, reexamine, and refine their teaching portfolios (along with their practice) based on the observations of peer coaches who give feedback on the artifacts chosen and the reasons for including them in the portfolio.

Conclusion

Coaching situates teachers at the center of their own learning. Coaching in any form breaks the isolation found in most Pre-K–12 schools and promotes collegiality. Coaching supports teachers as they implement new strategies and amplifies the benefits of other forms of professional development.

Administrative support is essential to all coaching efforts. Coaching is a tool for teachers to examine their practices in ways that make sense to them; however, coaching will not flourish until teachers feel valued and supported in their efforts to improve instruction. Effective principals focus their attention here.

Suggested Readings

Arnau, L., Kahrs, J., & Kruskamp, W. (2004). Peer coaching: Veteran high school teachers take the lead on learning. *NASSP The Bulletin, 88*(639), 26–41. doi:10.1177/019263650408863904

Killion, J., & Harrison, C. (2006). *Taking the lead: New roles for teachers and school-based coaches.* Oxford, OH: National Staff Development Council.

Knight, J. (2007). *Instructional coaching: A partnership approach to improving instruction.* Thousand Oaks, CA: Corwin Press.

Steiner, L., & Kowal, J. (2007). *Principal as instructional leader: Designing a coaching program that works.* Issue Brief. The Center for Comprehensive School Reform and Improvement. Washington, DC: Learning Point Associated. Retrieved from www.centerforcsri.org/files/CenterIssueBrief-Sept07 Principal.pdf

Wong, K., & Nicotera, A. (2006). Peer coaching as a strategy to build instructional capacity in low performing schools. In K. Wong & S. Rutledge (Eds.), *System-wide efforts to improve student achievement.* Greenwich, CT: Information Age Publishing.

Zepeda, S. J. (2008). *The instructional leader's guide to informal classroom observations* (2nd ed.). Larchmont, NY: Eye On Education.

Coaching

8

Collaborative Teacher Development: Teacher Study Groups, Whole-Faculty Study Groups, and Book Studies

In This Chapter…

- ◆ Collaborative Teacher Development
- ◆ Teacher Study Groups
- ◆ The Role of the Principal in Teacher Study Groups
- ◆ Whole-Faculty Study Groups
- ◆ The Role of the Principal in Whole-Faculty Study Groups
- ◆ Features That Define Standalone Study Groups and Whole-Faculty Study Groups
- ◆ Book Studies
- ◆ The Role of the Principal in Book Study Groups

Collaborative Teacher Development

Musanti and Pence (2010) noted the complexities of teacher development and the role of collaboration in this process. The authors asserted that "professional development needs to be conceived as a collaborative enterprise, where a space for learning through mutual exchange, dialogue, and constant challenge is created" (p. 87). Levine (2010) examined different theories related to the study and design of collaborative teacher learning:

- Inquiry community;

- Teacher professional community;

- Community of learners;

- Community of practice;

- Activity theory; and,

- Third spaces.

Levine emphasized that all these theories had their strengths and limitations, but for the sake of "understanding and designing experiences with will develop pre- and in-service teachers, we should maintain and refine distinct terms that bring into focus different conditions, resources, and mechanisms which produce teacher learning" (p. 127).

Jacobson (2010) examined the process of structuring teacher collaboration and developing effective professional learning communities and compared two approaches: teacher-led inquiry (inquiry-oriented) and administrator-driven process (results-oriented). Jacobson asserted that although both "approaches are valuable, and many schools have had great success using one or both of these models" (p. 38), neither of them adequately addressed schools' improvement efforts. To combat the limitations of these two approaches, Jacobson suggested the Common Priorities approach that incorporated the characteristics of these approaches and supported "school leaders in balancing twin instructional improvement objectives: developing innovative, effective teacher teams and developing a coherent, schoolwide approach to improving teaching and learning" (p. 44). In summary, Jacobson (2010) emphasized the importance of professional learning communities to teacher and school improvement.

Levine and Marcus (2010) asserted that engaging in collaborative activities may improve teachers and positively impact collaboration, teaching, and schooling overall. Levine and Markus emphasized the importance of meeting structure and focus to the effectiveness of teacher collaborative activities. From the data analysis, the authors reported three types of the meeting structures: protocol guided, strongly-structured and facilitated, and loosely structured meetings. Levine and Marcus identified three intended foci of for collaborative work: instruction-focused, student-focused, and school operation focused. Levine and Marcus concluded that "different types of collaboration can create very different learning opportunities for participants" and therefore, decisions about "the structure and focus of teachers' collaborative activities can both facilitate and constrain what teachers can learn together" (p. 397).

Teacher Study Groups

Teacher study groups, whole-faculty study groups, and book studies are forms of collaborative professional development. By giving ownership to teachers and putting them in charge of their own learning, a deeper level of learning occurs (Cayuso, Fegan, & McAlister, 2004). Although different from whole-faculty study groups, teacher study groups and faculty-led book studies support and nurture teacher learning and can be tied to site-based school improvement initiatives. Teacher study groups and book studies can be formal or informal in nature, and topics can range from learning about specific learning strategies to studying topics such as children of poverty. As a form of professional learning, study groups and book study groups are grounded in promoting professional conversations, collegiality, and learning about issues that affect teaching and learning. Whole-faculty study groups are purposefully focused on "mobilizing" a faculty to examine a schoolwide issue related to a school improvement target (Lick & Murphy, 2007; Murphy & Lick, 1998, 2005).

Interest in study groups as a professional development model for professional educators began in the early 1980s. Joyce and Showers (1982) discovered that qualified trainers were no more effective at providing quality feedback to educators than were teachers themselves. This discovery laid the foundation for a long-term investigation using study groups to implement new practice into classrooms (Murphy, Murphy, Joyce, & Showers, 1988). The rest is history.

Study groups provide a conduit for teachers to become lifelong learners and, to a certain degree, to become action researchers. Because most study groups provide an opportunity for teachers to focus on a topic that they choose for themselves, study groups help establish relevance for the individual. Study groups also serve to promote peer interaction by providing frequent opportunities for the sharing of ideas (Boggs, 1996). More importantly, study groups are comprised of individuals that join together to increase their capacity to meet the needs of students.

Lefever-Davis, Wilson, Moore, Kent, and Hopkins (2003, citing Cramer, Hurst, & Wilson, 1996) share that

> A teacher study group is a collaborative group organized and sustained by teachers to help them strengthen their professional development in areas of common interest. In these groups, teachers remain in charge of their own independent learning but seek to reach personal goals though interaction with others. (p. 782)

Hence, "study groups fill an important need, allowing colleagues to meet and to find wisdom and encouragement" from the collective membership of the group (Cayuso, Fegan, & McAlister, 2004, p. 11).

Study Group Members Learn Together

Study groups, regardless of the configuration, are special interest groups whose mission is to learn in the company of others. Darling-Hammond (1997b) points to the centrality of the teacher as learner linking student learning to teacher learning and development. Teachers need a host of skills "for framing problems; finding, integrating, and synthesizing information; creating new solutions; learning on their own; and working cooperatively" (Darling-Hammond, 1997b, p. 154). Throughout their careers, teachers continually improve their practice through a variety of means including graduate school, reflecting on the lessons learned from teaching, the students they teach, professional development opportunities, and outside of school activities. Study groups and book studies can play a pivotal role in helping teachers learn about instructional strategies, student issues related to discipline, and an infinite number of topics and areas that touch the life of the school and the students who are enrolled. Whole-faculty study groups usually tackle more schoolwide issues that relate to school improvement. This distinction is made here and is elaborated more fully in the section entitled "Whole-Faculty Study Groups."

By giving ownership to teachers and putting them in charge of their own learning, an opportunity for more in-depth learning is created (Cayuso et al., 2004). Through the interactions of the group, teachers can gain a sense of belonging to a community of learners with a focus on a particular aspect of teaching and learning. Teachers can also develop valuable camaraderie amongst group members, and they can overcome the difficult obstacles that often challenge them in the isolation of their classrooms. Belonging to a study group or a book study can increase self-efficacy, or "the belief in one's capabilities to organize and execute the courses of action required to manage prospective situations" (Bandura, 1995, p. 2).

Through a sense of increased self-efficacy, teachers may believe that they are more capable of solving thorny issues of practice. Belonging to a group can also provide a sense of affiliation to the extent that Kruse and Louis (2007) report, "Teachers' sense of affiliation with one another and with the school, their sense of mutual support, and individual responsibility for the effectiveness of instruction are increased by collaborative work with peers" (p. 1). Study groups help members forge "personal and group relationships, creating conditions where members can gain understanding and learn together" (Lick, 2001, p. 43).

What Do Study Groups Do and How Are They Arranged?

The answer to these questions is "it depends"—on the purpose of the study group, why it was formed, and who formed it. Study groups examine issues such as children and poverty, instructional practices (differentiated instruction, pacing, etc.), and dropout prevention. Study groups engage in activities such as reading and discussing books, examining latest research on selected topics, conducting and debriefing on action research, and myriad activities that support the reason why the study group formed.

Figure 8.1 illustrates the work of Cayuso et al. (2004) and Birchak et al. (1998), and describes the ways in which teacher study groups may be arranged according to the work members are undertaking.

Figure 8.1. **Range of Study Group Configurations**

Cayuso et al. (2004)	Birchak et al. (1998)
♦ *Topic Study Group*—members select a book to study and discuss that meets their interest and needs. ♦ *Practice Study Groups*—Metacognitive learning tool where members focus on a strategy. This may involve videotaping, peer observation, etc., with the group discussing what took place in a particular event. ♦ *Online Study Groups*—members join online chats that are about specific areas of interest.	♦ *Issues Discussion Groups*—formed around questions and concerns on a shared issue. ♦ *Job-Alike Study Groups*—educators that have the same type of position in different schools. ♦ *Professional Book Discussion Groups*—initiated by a common interest to read a professional book or set of articles. ♦ *Readers and Writers Groups*—formed to discuss literary works or pieces of writing. ♦ *School-Based Groups*—composed of educators within a particular school. ♦ *Teacher Research Groups*—educators who come together to discuss their systematic, intentional, classroom inquiries. ♦ *Topic-Centered Groups*—educators from different schools who are interested in the same topic or issue.

Organizing Study Groups—Getting Started

As a form of professional development, study groups need to have organizational features such as regularly scheduled meetings and a clearly established focus. In other words, there have to be specific reasons for a study group, and study group members need to have goals to work toward (see Chapter 9 for a discussion about the properties of goals). In a school that embraces the study group as a form of professional development, teacher leadership, and expertise across the faculty, the school could set up a system in which teacher leaders and the principal or the members of the administrative team develop mechanisms for teachers to sign up for membership in study groups. Figure 8.2 (page 183) displays what a signup form could look like.

Figure 8.2. Study Group Signup Form

Please mark the study group topics you are interested in for fall 2012. Let Ms. Cannon know if you would like to see additional study groups added or would be interested in leading a study group.

Name: _____   Date: _____

Study Team Leader	Topic
Ms. Janick	Service Learning
Mr. Foster	Learning Styles
Dr. Benson	Parent Involvement
Mrs. Bonco	Assertive Discipline
Ms. Thomas	Curriculum Alignment
Ms. Cruz	Cooperative Learning
Dr. Tolliver	Content Area Instruction for ESOL Students
Mr. Jenks & Ms. Hanson	Incorporating "Learner Outcomes" in your Daily lesson plans.
Ms. Robine	Portfolio Evaluation and Assessment
Mr. Adams	Enhancing Students' Writing/Reading Skills
Dr. Avern	Increasing Self-Esteem
Ms. Garcia	Higher-Order Thinking Skills

Strategies for Getting Started

If your school has not used the study group as a form of professional development, these strategies might be helpful in getting started.

- *Training:* Identify a few teachers who have content expertise and who are willing to form study groups. Work to find training for these teachers in the development of study groups.

- *Visitation:* If there are schools within the system or nearby that use study groups as a form of professional development, arrange for this small group of teachers to visit with these professionals at their site(s).

- *Outreach:* Contact local universities to see if there are professors who work with study groups and who are willing to help your school or system develop this type of professional development. If the system has a professional development coordinator, consult that person.

- *Professional Development Library:* Invest in books, videos, DVDs, and other materials that deal with study groups. Form a committee of teacher leaders to develop ideas about what a study group should look and sound like given the context of the school.

♦ *Launch:* Ask a teacher leader or a grade-level or subject-level group of teachers to form a study group. After a few months, make the time to ask about the lessons learned through the experience of being in a study group. Use these lessons to develop overall goals and objectives of study groups, purposes for student groups, and a tip sheet.

Organizing Study Group Meetings

Study groups meet regularly, perhaps twice a month; study groups meet for approximately 90 minutes per meeting. Because time is at a premium for teachers, study group time needs to be organized. Birchak et al. (1998) describe four different categories of meetings:

♦ *Brainstorming.* Although a group of teachers might assemble to meet as a study group about the topic, cooperative learning, this is a very broad topic. The first meeting may involve brainstorming through which teachers engage in dialogue that eventually leads to a topic from which the group feels it could benefit in further study. During this first meeting, all ideas are heard and every thought is listed. The first meeting can be lengthy or there may be multiple brainstorming meetings before a topic is developed.

♦ *Narrowing the Topic.* The second type of meeting deals with narrowing the topic and generating the "big" questions that the study group hopes to explore throughout the life of the group.

♦ *Extended Meetings.* The heart of the study group is where the group members engage in extended discussions on the focus the group has determined. During these types of meeting, study group members address questions that are specific to the topic and share ideas, experiences, and findings. Study group members are engaged in animated discussions.

♦ *Reflection on Process and Content.* The fourth type of meeting is when reflection on process and content occurs.

Saavedra (1996) believes: "The most important aspect of the study group is that it provides time for teachers to reflect, analyze, and critique practices together" (p. 273). Saavedra identifies conditions that support transformative learning during study group meetings, the most important include processes that promote

♦ Identity and voice from the experience of being in the study group;

- Ownership and agency where learning is intrinsically motivated as opposed to extrinsic forcers external to the group structure (e.g., required attendance);

- Dissonance and conflict in which study group members often struggle with the materials under study and it is through the struggle that meaning is more likely to occur;

- Mediational events and demonstrations where discussions and activities offer different opinions or thought processes and that lead to an agreement that results in a higher understanding of the problem, strategy, etc.;

- Reflection, action, and collaboration so that group members can act on reflections while generating new knowledge, beliefs, and behaviors;

- Self-assessment and evaluation of the work and efforts of the group done both at the group and individual member levels; and,

- Reflective practice and recreating teaching to improve the learning environment for students whom group members teach.

The specific subjects discussed may originate in a book, an instructional problem in a subject area, examination of student work by subject-area or grade-level teachers; the list goes on and on. Study groups need a quality facilitator, and it is common practice for the facilitator to come from within the membership of the group. The following Discussion Guidelines for Participants (Figure 8.3) are adapted from Kaite Mediatore, Readers' Services Librarian at the Main Branch of Kansas City, Kansas Public Library. These guidelines can help facilitate the discussions.

Figure 8.3. Discussion Guidelines

- Allow everyone the chance to contribute to the discussion—Engage silent readers by posing open-ended questions. Not all people like to share openly in discussion; however, this silence does not mean that the person is not following the discussion. Moreover, not all people will have completed reading the book, chapters, or sections. Sometimes life and work get in the way. Try asking, "Based on the author's message, what applications can you envision in your classroom, David?"

- Keeping the group on the topic of the book—Try not to let readers wander and bring them back if they do. Comments such as, "Let's get back to the end of Chapter 4. What did you think at this point?" "I have a question about the situation on page 125. What's really happening here?"

- Monopolizing conversation—Cut in on a longwinded group member with, "That's an interesting point you just made. Did anyone else get the same impression or a different one?" "You've made some interesting points, Terri. Let's hear from another member. Kimberlee? What did you think?"

- ◆ Listen carefully to what is said by participants—Rephrase comments or questions to be sure you and others understand what was meant. This is an especially necessary technique when dealing with a verbose participant.

- ◆ Interruptions—There will always be someone who breaks in while another person is speaking. Most interrupting during discussion is a result of enthusiasm rather than rudeness. Control the interruptions by saying, "Hold that thought, Sheryl. We'll want to hear it again once Angie has finished."

Remind everyone of the next meeting time and title of next book and send a reminder out a few days before the next meeting.

There is a definite professional focus and a unique culture that is influenced by the different personalities of the members as well as the commonalities of their interest.

The Role of the Principal in Teacher Study Groups

The role of the principal depends on how the study group is configured. According to Birchak et al. (1998), principals can be viewed as positive or negative in a study group. When a principal is a member of the group and is able to function as an equal with teachers in discussing and sharing information related to teaching and learning, a positive value is placed on the principal's role. This provides the study group with a sense of legitimacy and importance within the school's culture. If the principal tries to push too much to promote his or her own agenda, or if teachers are concerned that what is said in a study group in the presence of the principal could influence either directly or indirectly the principal's evaluation of that teacher, a negative value is placed on the principal's role. There must be a "zone of safety" (Lipka & McCarty, 1994) created by the principal so teachers can and will speak freely about teaching issues.

Whole-Faculty Study Groups

Through the pioneering work of Carlene Murphy and the publication of the third edition of *Whole-Faculty Study Groups: Creating Professional Learning Communities that Target Student Learning* (Murphy & Lick, 2005), the value of whole-faculty study groups endures as a professional development model. The whole-faculty study group shows great promise on how professional learning can "mobilize" schools to the action to put student learning as the centerpiece in school improvement efforts. The subsequent book, *The Whole-Faculty Study Groups Fieldbook: Lessons Learned and Best Practices from Classrooms, Districts, and Schools* (Lick & Murphy, 2007), provides concrete applications and results to the whole-faculty study group. Whole-faculty study groups are a structure through which all of the teachers on a faculty meet in small groups for deliberate conversations about a targeted area linked to school improvement centering on student needs and classroom instruction. Murphy and Lick (2005) state:

> The Whole-Faculty Study Group system is a job-embedded, self-directed, student-driven approach to professional development. It is a professional development system designed to build communities of learners in which professionals continuously strive to increase student learning. This is accomplished by practitioners (a) deepening their own knowledge and understanding of what is taught, (b) reflecting on their practices, (c) sharpening their skills, and (d) taking joint responsibility for the students they teach. (p. 2)

Whole-faculty study groups have an organizational focus, focusing on the primary goal of schools, to increase student learning. It is a professional development process that allows individual teachers to design their own learning and to implement what they learn in their classrooms for the benefit of their students. The School Improvement Plan can become the document that drives the whole-faculty study group process, focus, and content.

The guiding principles identified by Murphy and Lick (2005) for whole-faculty study groups can be adopted for any teacher study group. The principles keep a focus on student learning while maintaining and instilling a democratic process that allows for equal opportunity for learning and leading for all teachers. The guiding principles include:

- Students are first;
- Everybody participates;
- Leadership is shared;
- Responsibility is equal; and,
- The work is public.

Implementing whole-faculty study groups involves a commitment to the process. Before implementation of the whole-faculty study group (WFSG) can begin, the principal must be committed to several propositions. Murphy (1999 as cited in Zepeda, 1999) reports that prior to the whole-faculty study process beginning:

- The whole faculty understands the WFSG process;
- The whole faculty participates in some form of decision-making process that acknowledges that a 75-percent majority to support WFSG will obligate all others; and,

♦ The whole faculty participates in reviewing student data that will guide all decisions about how study groups will be organized and what study groups will do. (p. 105)

The Functions of Whole-Faculty Study Groups

Whole-faculty study groups have at least five functions that serve as overall goals:

♦ To support the implementation of curricular and instructional innovations;

♦ To integrate and give coherence to the school's instructional strategies and programs;

♦ To target a schoolwide need;

♦ To study the research and latest developments on teaching and learning; and,

♦ To monitor the impact of innovations on students and on changes in the workplace. (Murphy, 1999 as cited in Zepeda, 1999, p. 106)

From these overall goals, it is apparent that teacher collaboration is one of the centering aspects of the WFSG process. To increase student learning is the primary purpose of WFSG, and teacher collaboration is a means to that end.

Process Guidelines for Whole-Faculty Study Groups

Murphy and Lick (2005) provide guidelines for the structure the WFSG process needs to ensure the intended results of increasing student achievement:

♦ Keep the size of the study groups to no more than six;

♦ Don't worry about the composition of the study groups;

♦ Establish and keep a regular schedule, letting no more than two weeks pass between meetings;

♦ Establish group norms at the first meeting of the study group;

♦ Agree on a written Study Group Action Plan that is shared with the whole faculty by the end of the second meeting;

♦ Complete a Study Group Log after each study group meeting that is shared with the whole faculty;

♦ Encourage members to keep an Individual Reflection Log that is for their own personal and private reflection;

♦ Establish a pattern of rotating group leadership;

♦ Give all study group members equal status;

- Have a curricular or instructional focus;

- Plan ahead for transitions;

- Make a comprehensive list of learning resources, both material and human;

- Include training in the study group's agenda; and,

- Evaluate the effectiveness of the study group, using the intended results stated in the Study Group Action Plan.

The WFSG process requires faculty involvement to the extent that the whole-faculty study group should become the major professional development for the entire school. The intensive nature of the work of whole-faculty study groups necessitates a commitment to the process, the resources needed to support teachers in their work, and the resolve of the principal and the system to guard time and to be a warrior for the work of whole-faculty study groups.

The Role of the Principal in Whole-Faculty Study Groups

In whole-faculty study groups, the role of principal is defined to a greater extent than the role of the principal in standalone study groups, and according to Murphy and Lick (2005), "Today's principal must be a reflective practitioner and must model the value of learning for the faculty, staff, and students" (p. 29). Murphy and Lick (1998, 2005), Lick and Murphy (2007), Lick (2001), and Mahon (2007) detail the practices that principals must perform to be effective as leaders in whole-faculty study groups. Mahon (2007) highlights that principals can be champions of the whole-faculty study group by

- being involved in the WFSG process.

- commenting on action plans and logs.

- keeping study groups focused.

- focusing on research.

- using the decision-making cycle.

- sharing the work.

- using data.

- supporting core practices.

- looking deeper.

- dealing with reluctant teachers.

- celebrating work and success. (pp. 29–33)

Features That Define Standalone Study Groups and Whole-Faculty Study Groups

Several different types of study groups have been identified. Most noticeable, perhaps, is the distinction made by Murphy and Lick (1998, 2005) between whole-faculty study groups and independent or standalone study groups. Independent study groups may or may not be tied to an organizational need, and they are not necessarily composed of teachers from the same school. Standalone study groups are more independent and almost always involve voluntary participants whereas whole-faculty study groups involve the entire school. There is a much more formal structure in the operation of a WFSG than in an independent study group. According to Murphy and Lick (1998, 2005), the most obvious strength of whole-faculty study groups is the support each group receives from other groups. Organizational strength is derived from the collegiality and collaboration fostered by the work of whole-faculty study groups.

A potential weakness of the whole-faculty-study-group system may be the requirement for every faculty member to be involved with a study group, giving up a certain level of independence and individuality while limiting the choices for examining areas of interest for faculty to choose and to participate or not. In contrast, in independent or standalone study groups, the strength is that teachers can voluntarily join these groups in response to a genuine professional interest. A weakness can be found in that independent study groups do not always take the knowledge learned back to the classroom, particularly if the members from the study group are not from the same school (Murphy & Lick, 1998, 2005).

Book Studies

The book study is also a form of individually guided professional development that allows a small group of teachers to meet to have discussions centering on a topic and a book that gives insight about an area of professional interest. Book studies promote conversations among teachers and other school personnel.

Typically, book studies are organized around a topic of interest, an area related to a schoolwide improvement-targeted goal, or an issue of practice at a grade level or with a subject-specific group of teachers. However, it is not uncommon for an entire school to read a common book of interest and for a certain amount of time at general faculty, grade-level, or department meetings to be dedicated to discussing the applicability of the contents of the book at the specific site. This configuration is not a book study, per se, but a common reading.

Effective book studies have the overall goal of supporting the reading of professional materials that will support the development of thinking or refined instructional practice. Ultimately, it is a hope that this increased understanding in an area will lead to applying new ideas in classroom practice and refining existing skills. Book studies can be informal or formal.

There are many advantages of book studies. Book studies support smaller groups of teachers to meet at a regularly scheduled time to engage in discussions, to reflect on what has been read, and then to envision how a new practice might be implemented once back in the classroom. Other book studies focus on issues related to changes a school or teams of teachers are facing such as

♦ changes in demographics—increases in nonmajority students; increase in special needs students; increase of students of poverty;

♦ changes in learning strategies needed to reach students;

♦ changes needed to reach students who are not performing well on standardized tests; and,

♦ changes made in a particular field of study and the subsequent strategies to support implementing new ways of teaching.

The list could continue. Each school resides in a community that enjoys its own context. Because members bring their own characteristics and embrace differing values and beliefs, all book study members should be involved in making decisions.

The Phi Delta Kappa Educational Foundation (2005) suggests a five-step process for how to conduct a book study group. These steps include:

Step 1: Form a Book Study Group

Step 2: Choose a Book and an Objective

Step 3: Decide How to Read the Book

Step 4: Read and Discuss the Book

Step 5: Evaluate the Book and Plan for Future Book Study

Form a Book Study Group

Book studies can be configured around special areas of interest by groups of teachers, or a schoolwide effort, or a combination of the two approaches. Some schools offer the opportunity for teachers to initiate book studies within the overall structure of professional development in the building. Before forming a book study, there is a need to determine the focus of the book study group upfront and seek membership from within the school. Participation should be voluntary and membership should be inclusive—everyone is welcome. There are several ways to form a book study group.

Openly seek membership from grade-level team members, subject-area groups, and departments. Some school systems offer teachers the opportunity to earn professional learning units (PLUs) when they engage in a structured professional learning activity. A structured book study would certainly fulfill a worthwhile self-directed professional learning activity.

Once people sign up to be part of a book study, there are a few decisions that the group needs to make. These decisions include a meeting schedule and the meeting place. Also, the group needs to determine how many times the group will meet, the length of each meeting, and what happens after the book has been read. In other words, will the group read one book and then disband, will the group continue meeting to discuss how the ideas within the book have changed instructional practices, and will the group read more than one book are some questions to consider. A quality facilitator is essential.

High-functioning book study groups have a facilitator to keep the group on task and to assist with running the book study meetings. The facilitator assists with developing and maintaining the group focus and manages each meeting. It is recommended that meetings

- ♦ last no more than one hour;

- ♦ be held at the same time of the day;

- ♦ be held in the same room and building; and,

- ♦ foster the responsibility to try new ideas and practices. (Makibbin & Sprague, 1991)

Choose a Book and an Objective Based on School Improvement Goals and the Needs of Students

A book study group needs a book and objectives for reading the book. Why is the group reading a particular book or series of books? The book or books chosen should relate the overall objective or focus of the book study group. A strategy would be for the members of the group to bring suggestions about books related to the topic and then let the membership of the book study decide which book or books to read. Another strategy is to have up front some overall research on the overall area of study and then to pick a book or series of books that address the need identified by the group.

Decide How to Read the Book

Reading a book for the purposes of a book study is more than merely turning the pages. Depending on the length and complexity of the book, the book could be broken up to be read by chapters or in sections. To qualify to earn a professional learning unit (PLU), a certain number of meetings or hours must be spent to earn this type of credit. It is not recommended that the book study group let time dictate the way in which a book is read. It is suggested that book study groups meet twice a month—this type of frequency will keep the ideas of the book alive in the minds of the teachers who are reading the book and searching for ways to make sense of their practice in light of what is being read.

Read and Discuss the Book

Once the mechanics of how often the book study group will meet and how the book will be read, the real work of the book study group begins. The real work is the discussion and analysis of the book related to classroom practices. Book study members need the opportunity to share insights, to ask tough questions, and to learn from the perspectives of the book study members. This open period of discussion, analysis, and reflection is an important aspect for book study members. Some book study groups encourage members to keep reflective journals as they are reading and to bring these reflections to book study meetings. Journaling can be a powerful learning tool. Conversations are the mainstay of a book study regardless of the configuration. Clark (2001) identifies the qualities of good conversation. Good conversation demands good content; resists the bounds of definition; is voluntary; happens on common ground; requires safety, trust, and care; develops with time; and has a future (meaning that it organizes for future action).

Evaluate the Book and Plan for Future Book Study

Once the book study group has completed reading a book, the work continues as teachers think through the author's message and the rich discussion of the group members. Members need to ask the "so what" and "now what" questions. The so what question is, "so what do we do with the information we have learned from the book?" This type of question will help the members not only make decisions about changes in practices or to explore the meanings they have gained, but also this type of question will help the book study group evaluate the value of the book. Depending on the value of the book, the book study group might be inclined to recommend that other book study groups read the book, that copies of the book be made available to other faculty, or that the school library include a few copies in its collection of books. The "now what" questions prompt members to not only think about what to do with the knowledge learned from the original book, but also this question gets book study members thinking about

- what types of followup are needed to implement changes in practices and the types of support members need: peer coaching, ongoing discussion, action research, lesson study, etc.

- a plan to examine the impact of changes in practices. If members are modifying, extending, or even discontinuing practices based on the knowledge gained in a book study, a followup plan including student data needs to be considered.

- whether there are other materials or books about the original topic that could be examined by book members.

Book study as a job-embedded form of professional learning does not begin and end with the reading of a book. Book study members need time and opportunity to extend conversations over time and with not only members of the book study but also other faculty who might be interested in the topic.

A Case from the Field[1]

Book Studies at Creekland Middle School

Dr. Bill Kruskamp, Principal
170 Russell Road
Lawrenceville, GA 30043

Read a Book—Swap a Book: The Context of Creekland Middle School

Creekland Middle School is a large urban school in Gwinnett County, Georgia. With more than 2,800 students in grades 6 to 8 as the 2007–2008 school year began, Creekland is the largest middle school in Georgia, and certainly one of the largest in the country. Creekland has 201 professionally certified and highly qualified teachers with another 30 certified paraprofessionals. Counting the other staff at Creekland, this middle school employs 290 staff and faculty. The school serves it students through a community concept wherein the students are randomly assigned to one of five communities when they enroll, and every effort is made to maintain that assignment for the duration of that student's enrollment at Creekland. A concentrated effort is made to create communities that are similar in demographics as well as ability levels.

Creekland has a diverse student population with four large subgroups representing nearly 99% of its student population. The percentages for the four largest subgroups are: 48% white, 20% African American, 18% Hispanic, and 12% Asian. The free and reduced student population subgroup is rising quickly at Creekland and is now 30%. The English Language Learner (ELL) population is rising slowly at Creekland but represents less than 10% of the total.

Professional Learning at Creekland Middle School

Professional learning at Creekland Middle School is consistent, pervasive, and delivered on a timely basis. The administration has chosen to spend nearly three times the system allotment on learning activities for the staff at Creekland, including locally prepared professional learning activities

---

1 Although the educators described in this case are no longer serving in these leadership positions, for the purposes of this chapter, we are keeping their names and titles to reflect the context of this school at the time this case study was conducted.

(PLAs), support for attendance at professional conferences and workshops, stipends for local PLAs, and expenditures to bring professional learning professional to Creekland to present to the faculty and staff. Staff that receive local support to attend conferences and workshops are expected to redeliver learning to Creekland staff during Professional Learning Days designated by the system for professional learning and planning.

The Work of the Principal: Observe, Ask Questions, Suspend Judgments, and Focus Efforts

As the new principal at Creekland, I acted as an observer for the first year of my tenure. What I witnessed was a great deal of activity designed to assist teachers in many varied areas such as incorporating technology into their planning, unpacking new state curricula in math, science, and social studies, and use of appropriate teaching strategies. There were some references made to Professional Learning Communities as well as references to Learning Focused School materials. The one thing that soon caught my attention was that there was not any central focus for the varied learning activities. That isn't a criticism as much as it is just an observation. Nevertheless, there wasn't any effort to marshal the efforts being made to support Creekland's Local School Plan of Improvement (LSPI). I determined that the professional learning for the 2007–2008 school year would be concentrated on two specific areas that would also support our LSPI.

The two specific areas of concentration are our Common Classroom Expectations and what we named our cultural awareness initiative, Culturally Proficient Creekland or C3. The Common Classroom Expectations are five specific teaching strategies that were identified as "nonnegotiables"; that is, teaching strategies that all faculty are expected to consciously incorporate into lesson plans on a daily basis. These strategies are as follows:

- ◆ Collaboration
- ◆ Use of essential questions
- ◆ Differentiation
- ◆ Evidence of student learning and engagement
- ◆ Summarization

These five classroom practices serve to drive all teacher observations whether during walkthroughs, peer coaching, instructional supervision (both formal and informal observations), or teacher evaluations. Monthly professional learning activities are designed to support teachers in the appropriate implementation of these practices in their daily lesson plans.

Culturally Competent Creekland

Culturally Competent Creekland is an initiative designed to support teachers as they offer appropriate and differentiated instruction to a growing diversity at Creekland. It isn't enough to provide an "equal opportunity" for students to learn the curriculum and to achieve at high levels. Today's classroom teachers must provide support to children of varied backgrounds, ethnicities and cultures. With more than 50% of the students at Creekland identified as belonging to a minority group it is necessary to equip teachers with an awareness and cultural proficiency so that all students receive the support necessary to achieve at high levels.

How and Why Book Studies Began at Creekland Middle School—It's All About the Kids

Book study groups at Creekland Middle School grew out of an encounter with a seventh-grade four-teacher team who came to me seeking advice concerning students on their team who were difficult to motivate. As a result of our discussion, I agreed to meet with 13 of the students for individual chats. We soon referred to the 13 students as the Baker's Dozen. Not long after this, I began to meet with the students—boys and girls of diverse backgrounds. The one thing that became obvious to me was that these students were not motivated to learn. These were some of the toughest conversations I have ever had.

In February 2007, I attended a large national conference at which I had the privilege and pleasure to listen to Dr. Judy Brough of Gettysburg College speak about the "reluctant student." I immediately thought of the Baker's Dozen. I listened intently to Dr. Brough's account of her research with middle-level learners and decided to purchase her book *Teach Me: I Dare You*. After reading the first couple of chapters, I had the idea that perhaps the teachers of the Baker's Dozen might find this book interesting and supportive of their need to motivate their students. I bought one for each teacher and gave them to the team with the offer of joining them in a book study. It was from this small group that the idea grew that we offer this book to other teachers and create another book study group.

Use Book Studies to Focus the Conversations About What's Important

The need to support our growing diversity was also a source of the book study professional learning activity at Creekland. Dr. Sharon Blackwell-Jones, a faculty member in the Counseling Department at the University of Georgia, has been assisting the staff and faculty at Creekland in their quest to become culturally competent. From this grew our Culturally Competent Creekland initiative as well as the suggestion that we read the book titled *Culturally Proficient Instruction*. In particular, the administrators and counselors at Creekland began to read this book. Members of the administrative team took turns reviewing chapters of this book as part of our regularly scheduled Monday meetings. The counselors began a study group as well.

Success Breeds Success

In planning for the next school year, I proposed that we offer a book study group as part of our formal Professional Learning plan. The list of books grew to five titles, including titles that focused on Culturally Competent Creekland, the Common Classroom Expectations, and reaching reluctant learners. The books for the 2007–2008 year included ones that supported our explorations about diversity, our focus on the "expectations," and our focus on motivating the reluctant reader:

Brough, J. A., Bergmann, S., & Holt, L. C. (2006). *Teach me, I dare you!* Larchmont, NY: Eye On Education.

Gregory, G. H., & Chapman, C. (2007). *Differentiated instructional strategies: One size doesn't fit all* (2nd ed.) Thousand Oaks, CA: Corwin Press.

Robins, K. N., Lindsey, R. B., Lindsey, D. B., & Terrell, D. B. (2006). *Culturally proficient instruction: A guide for people who teach* (2nd ed.). Thousand Oaks, CA: Corwin Press.

Smith, R. (2004). *Conscious classroom management: Unlocking the secrets of great teaching.* Fairfax, CA: Conscious Teaching Publications.

Wormeli, R. (2006). *Fair isn't always equal: Assessing & grading in a differentiated classroom.* Portland, ME: Stenhouse Publishers.

Our book study came alive when Dr. Judy Brough was invited (and accepted) to speak to the entire Creekland staff and faculty at one of our systemwide planned professional learning/planning days.

Book Studies Are Invitational

The idea of the book study groups was floated out to the faculty on several occasions and in several e-mails over the course of the first quarter at Creekland. Teachers have begun to ask for the various books and to start book study groups. Plans have been created to direct teachers on forming study groups of six to ten learners, to choose a facilitator, establish meeting protocols, and requirements to earn a PLU for their efforts. Administrators, counselors and Curriculum Team Leaders—teachers who lead curriculum groups—have been trained to lead various book study groups. Teachers may choose someone other than those mentioned to facilitate if they so choose. Books will be ordered from a signup list and the study groups will be off and running.

Participation in the book study, although encouraged, is not mandatory. The reason for this is that I always resented forced reading as a professional educator. I have read many books or suggested readings along the way in my career. I also have many unopened "book study" titles on my shelves that I failed to read even though I was instructed to do so. For this same reason, teachers have been asked to choose the title from the list of five suggested titles that they want to read—not the one I want them to read. If learners want to choose another book that retains the original focus of the book study, they may do so. After all, the primary reason to offer book studies is to encourage learning for our professional staff. Whether they read one of the five listed books or another matters not in the big picture.

Faculty and staff may participate in more than one study group if they want to commit to that level, and groups may decide to continue reading another title after completing their first title. Group leaders or facilitators will be asked to maintain participation sheets to document attendance for earning the PLU. Groups will be encouraged to share books and to share what they have learned in small and large group settings.

At the beginning of this year, the faculty book studies, entitled *Read a Book–Swap a Book Study Groups*, have flourished. To facilitate the work of our book study professional learning, parameters were developed, as shown in Figure 8.4.

Figure 8.4. Read a Book–Swap a Book

Study Groups at Creekland Middle School

Focus of Book Study Groups

The focus of the book study groups is to promote productive, collegial conversations among staff members with an emphasis on Creekland Middle School'sCommon Classroom Expectations and the Culturally Competent Creekland initiative.

Book Study Groups

1. Participation is voluntary for staff members; administration must participate in a group.

2. Groups should be composed of six to ten learners.

3. Books must be chosen from the list of five titles provided. Other books may be considered if the books relate to a focus on student learning and engagement.

4. Each group must designate one person as the study group leader or facilitator whose duties will include:

   • Schedule meeting times;

   • Assign readings;

   • Maintain attendance log (for PLUs); and,

   • Establish group meeting protocols.

5. To earn a PLU (professional learning unit) a learner must participate in at least eight of ten scheduled meeting hours.

6. Meetings should last one hour and occur at least twice a month.

7. If a group chooses to read and share on more than one book, they will be encouraged to "swap" their books with another group. A group may select an alternate title when choosing a second book as long as the

new title maintains the original focus on Common Classroom Expectations and Culturally Competent Creekland.

8. Study groups will be encouraged to share what they have learned with other groups during faculty meetings or other group settings. Currently, Creekland Middle School is working with a local university to extend our peer-coaching program through the use of video capture. We are presently examining how book study members can use video to capture experimentation with instructional practices and ideas gleaned from the work of book study members.

The Role of the Principal in Book Study Groups

Like in any form of professional development, the principal plays a key role in forwarding the work of the book study. For the book study to work as a viable form of professional development, the principal must be a "warrior" for this type of learning effort. Principals can help support book study by periodically finding time during the day for book study groups to meet. The principal can perhaps be persuaded to use faculty meeting time instead for study groups to meet. Again, the context of the school will dictate whether or not enough substitute teachers can be hired or if others can cover duty periods so that book study groups can meet during the day.

The principal can champion this type of professional learning by promoting book study groups. One way to promote the work of study groups is to ask the members of the group to present their book at a faculty meeting. Members should be encouraged to share the insights they gained about their instructional practices, the changes they made in their instructional practices, and how these changes affected student learning. One principal in the field enlists the support of the parent advisory group by providing this group with a list of books that the faculty have interest in reading. During teacher appreciation week, the advisory group presented to the faculty a substantial gift certificate to a bookstore. Because of the value this principal has for teacher learning, his school media specialist was able to purchase a stable of books for the teacher professional development library. Another principal in the field profiles in faculty newsletters the books that the study groups are reading. This principal reports that this practice encourages other teachers to stay current in the field by reading. This same principal has found the funds to provide soft drinks and light snacks for the book study meetings.

Another principal has invested in remodeling a portion of a reading room in the school media center. He purchased comfortable chairs, a few decorative lamps, had the walls painted, and fashioned the room to resemble a reading den. Students in the advanced art class painted a mural on the wall, and the faculty in this school refers to this room as the "Faculty Reading Den."

Notes from the Field[2]

Judith Harvey, Superintendent
Neal Guyer, Director of Curriculum Services
Maine School Administrative District No. 50[3]
12 Starr Street
Thomaston, ME 04861

The Maine School Administrative District No. 50 (MSAD #50) in Thomaston, Maine, and its superintendent, Judith Harvey, and director of Curriculum Services, Neal Guyer, have used the book study as a form of professional development by connecting this learning to the districtwide improvement plan goals of

♦ using data analysis and assessment to improve instruction;

♦ improving mathematics and science instruction; and,

♦ improving literacy instruction, particularly in reference to student writing.

According to Harvey and Guyer, the format for the book study is intended to be fairly flexible and designed to meet the specific needs of the study group. The following nuts and bolts (Figure 8.5) should guide any study design.

Figure 8.5. MSAD #50 Study Design Guidelines

1. A book study leader needs to be identified. This person is responsible for facilitating the study, organizing concepts/guided questions to be discussed, scheduling meetings (either face-to-face or electronically), establishing timelines for reading, and leading discussion and active reflection for the group. The book study leader will receive an honorarium of $400.

2. Book studies should include a minimum of eight actual meeting hours. Upon conclusion of the study, the book study leader should document actual meeting hours and "contact hour" certificates should be provided to participating members.

3. All book study participants should receive their own copy of the selected book.

4. Book studies should include at least six and no more than ten participants. Members need to make a conscientious commitment to their participation in the book study (application section #5—group norms).

---

2 Although the educators described in this case are no longer serving in these leadership positions, for the purposes of this chapter, we are keeping their names and titles to reflect the context of this school at the time this case study was conducted.

3 The Maine School Administrative District No. 50 merged with a neighboring district and is now a part of the Regional School Unit No. 13. For the purposes of this chapter, we cite the former name of this district where the book study guidelines were developed.

5. All book study applications need to be reviewed and approved by the MSAD #50 Curriculum Team Leaders. One copy of this application should be submitted to Neal Guyer at the Superintendent's Office. A second copy should be submitted to the school principal or principals if more than one school is involved.

6. Approved applications can be amended if group needs/conditions change!

Modified and reprinted with permission of the Maine School Administrative District No. 50 (Thomaston, Maine). www.sad50.k12.me.us/admin/misc/teacherbookstudyinfo.html

To participate in the Maine School Administrative District No. 50 professional development book study, the book study group must complete an application. Figure 8.6 is the application that teachers who wish to participate in a formal and recognized book study must complete.

Figure 8.6. **Teacher Book Study Application Form**

Please complete the following application sections and submit to Neal Guyer at the superintendent's office and to school principal(s) using either e-mail or interoffice mail.

1. *Book Selection:* Please include the title of your selected book and provide a *brief* summary of the concepts & content to be covered.

   Book Ordering Information: Please include full title, author, ISBN, publisher, address, & fax number for ordering. The superintendent's office will complete and process purchase orders.

2. *Learner-Centered Book Study Goal:* Which of the district's staff development themes for the year does this book study address?

   What is the group's goal in pursuing this book study (becoming familiar with research, identifying new instructional strategies, etc.), and hoped for outcomes that will benefit student learning? Please provide *brief* goal statement:

3. *Pre-/Postassessment:* A preassessment activity should be designed to assess the extent of prior knowledge existing within the group, and to establish a "baseline" against which you can measure the extent to which the study group has been successful in achieving the stated goal. A copy of the assessment tool and/or assessment plan should be outlined below or attached to this application.

4. *Group Membership:* Groups should have at least six and no more than ten participants (including the group leader). Please list members below:

   Group Leader:

   Other Group Members:

5. *Group Norms:* The group leader should propose, and the group, through discussion, reach consensus regarding group norms. What do group members agree to in order to keep this collaborative venture

on track (expectations for reading, notifications to others if a members can't attend, **coming** prepared, etc.)? Please list your agreed upon norms below:

6. *Collegial Sharing:* What strategies/activities will be utilized to share the study group's conclusions with colleagues outside of the group?

7. *Study Group Timeframe:* Please indicate when you expect the study group's activities to begin and conclude. Specific meeting dates are not necessary—indicate general timeframe, where/how the group will meet, and the number of hours the group intends to meet:

Thank you for your active interest in this self-directed professional development activity.

Modified and reprinted with permission of the Maine School Administrative District No. 50 (Thomaston, Maine). www.sad50.k12.me.us/admin/misc/TeacherBookStudyApplication10–03.doc

Conclusion

A contributing factor to the success of teacher study groups, whole-faculty study groups, and book studies is the belief that teachers are lifelong learners who have a strong desire to keep learning. For teachers to believe that professional development is more than an event or a series of disconnected workshops, seminars, or in-service hours, principals must support the notion that learning is an ongoing journey, never a completed task. Although the book study is a new component of professional learning, the Creekland Middle School case study illustrates

◆ how professional development is embedded in the workday;

◆ how professional development is engineered to complement the overall focus on student learning; and,

◆ how further tinkering can extend one form of professional learning to other forms such as peer coaching.

With the emphasis on teaming and the absolute need for teachers to work together to improve the instructional program, teacher study groups, whole-faculty study groups, and book studies hold great promise for really getting to the heart of teaching—the students.

Suggested Readings

Birchak, B., Connor, C., Crawford, K. M., Kahn, L., Kaser, S., Turner, S., & Short, K. G. (1998). *Teacher study groups: Building community through dialogue and reflection.* Urbana, IL: National Council of Teachers of English.

Cayuso, E., Fegan, C., & McAlister, D. (2004). *Designing teacher study groups: A guide for success*. Gainesville, FL: Maupin House.

Lick, D. W., & Murphy, C. U. (Eds.). (2007). *The whole-faculty study groups fieldbook: Lessons learned and best practices from classrooms, districts, and schools*. Thousand Oaks, CA: Corwin Press.

Murphy, C. U., & Lick, D. W. (2005). *Whole-faculty study groups: Creating professional learning communities that target student learning* (3rd ed.). Thousand Oaks, CA: Corwin Press.

Study Groups and Book Studies

9

Critical Friends Groups

In This Chapter...

♦ What Is a Critical Friends Group?

♦ The Importance of Goals in the Work of Critical Friends Groups

♦ Build Strong Groups—The Bedrock of Success for Critical Friends Groups

♦ Time and the Job-Embedded Nature of Critical Friends Group

♦ Ongoing Work Needed to Maintain the Work of Critical Friends Groups

♦ Critical Friends Coaches

♦ Critical Friends Protocols

♦ Implications for Leadership

The term *critical friends groups* almost appears to be an oxymoron, combining two seemingly contradictory words—critical and friends. Costa and Kallick (1993) share:

> A critical friend can be defined as a trusted person who asks provocative questions, provides data to be examined through another lens, and offers critiques of a person's work as a friend. A critical friend takes the time to fully understand the context of the work presented and the outcomes that the person or group is working toward. The friend is an advocate for the success of that work. (p. 50)

In the life of schools, the use of critical friends groups (CFGs) as a form of professional development is gaining popularity, and through CFGs, the power of learning in the company of others can be enhanced by the number and the strengths of the members who comprise the group. Implemented properly, CFGs improve teachers' collegial relationships, increase teachers' awareness of research-based practices and reforms, their knowledge of their school, and their capacity to improve their instruction (Curry, 2008). The purpose of CFGs is to promote meaningful professional development and by the design, the group's work is purposefully focused to support job-embedded learning (Dunne, Nave, & Lewis, 2000; Easton, 1999; Richardson, 2001).

What Is a Critical Friends Group?

The Northwest Regional Educational Laboratory (NWREL, 2005) defines broadly that "critical friends groups (or CFGs for short) are cross-curricular groups of teachers that meet once a month, focusing laser-like on student achievement through teaching practice" (p. 2). Critical friends groups were introduced as a professional development model in 1994 through the work of the Annenberg Institute (National School Reform Faculty, 2006). From the early research of Dunne et al. (2000), critical friends groups as a form of professional development was reported as being "satisfying in comparison to other kinds of professional development" because

♦ it is continual.

♦ it is focused on their own teaching and their own students' learning.

♦ it takes place in a small group of supportive and trusted colleagues within their own school (p. 16).

Franzak (2002) describes CFGs as being "practitioner-driven study groups that reflect the growing trend for site-based professional development in which practitioners behave as managers of their own learning" (p. 260). CFGs support teachers taking the lead in their own learning. The rules of the road for how often, when, and where CFGs meet are dependent on the school context and the area under study. At minimum, CFGs meet once a month for an extended block of time lasting approximately three hours (NWREL, 2005).

Usually a CFG is made up of six to ten teachers who meet to address a focused topic (Costa & Kallick, 1993; National School Reform Faculty, 2006). This model is based on a collaborative effort that allows for critical feedback in a nonthreatening environment (Bambino, 2002, Costa & Kallick, 1993), and is "grounded on the belief that teachers of all levels can mentor and support one another" (Franzak, 2002, p. 278). NWREL (2005) reports that the work of CFGs is goal centered with goals that are "specific enough that others can observe them in operation" (p. 5).

The Importance of Goals in the Work of Critical Friends Groups

Goals guide the work of CFGs. Successful CFGs have "goals and values [that] are clear; they are understood and accepted by everyone [because] people are oriented to goals and results" (Dyer, 1995, p. 15). Goals must be clearly established and linked to the group's purpose, and members must understand them. The following goal checklist (Figure 9.1) serves as a primer on the development of goals.

Figure 9.1. Goal Checklist—Attributes of SMART Goals

Lunenburg (1995) suggests that goals should be:

- Specific: Goals are *specific* when they are clearly stated;

- Measurable: *Measurable* goals are precise and can be measured over time;

- Achievable: Goals are *achievable* if they are realistic. The effort needed to reach a goal can inspire greater effort; unrealistic goals are self-defeating;

- Relevant: Goals are *relevant* if they are viewed as important to the individual and to the team. Superficial goals are forgotten because they lack meaning;

- Trackable: Goals need to be *trackable* to check progress. Goals should not be so numerous or complex that they confuse rather than direct teams; and,

- Ongoing: Not all goals will be completed by the end of a specified period. Some goals are achieved over a longer time; others can be reached more quickly.

Throughout the work of a CFG over time, goals will change as group members learn from one another and as short-term goals lead to long-term goal attainment. Refining goals mid-course is a strength of a CFG group, and members should embrace the evolving nature of what is discovered through the work of the group. Shifting work and goals to reflect what is being learned is also a sign of group development.

Build Strong Groups—The Bedrock of Success for Critical Friends Groups

Teacher isolation in schools has been identified as having a negative impact on teacher practice and professional development. When teachers are trained in the use of the CFG model and are engaged in the work of CFGs on a regular basis, the result is less teacher isolation (Nieto, 2000). CFG meetings are not to be used as show-and-tell time, but rather as an opportunity to accomplish the work of the group and to examine and reflect on one or two teacher presentations with an in-depth focus on a specific topic related to pedagogical practice (Costa & Kallick, 1993). Strong teams are crucial because the work of CFGs members is to

- develop shared norms and values.

- focus on student learning.

- make their practice public.

- engage in reflective dialogue and collaborative work.

◆ inquire into, analyze, and reflect upon student work. (The National School Reform Faculty at the Harmony Education Center, n.d., p. 3)

Build Strong Groups

Hudson and Gray (2006) share that in CFGs it is "[t]hrough the use of team and trust building activities [that] teachers in a group develop support for one another" (p. 7). Because CFGs typically include up to 12 members, it is important to establish not only goals related to the problem or issue of practice, but also to have an eye on the structure of the group. The structure of the group composition includes a member who assumes the role of facilitator, manages the overall CFG meeting, and assists in facilitating the work group members do between CFG meetings. Other group members assume roles such as

◆ *Presenter*—prepares and presents the issue; and,

◆ *Discussants*—address the issue and provide feedback to the presenter. (Committee on Institutional Cooperation, 2005)

The National School Reform Faculty (2006) and the framers of CFGs at the Annenberg Institute suggest that the facilitator be trained in group processes associated with the workings of CFGs because the success of the CFGs is the ability of the group to function as a team. Figure 9.2 illustrates the characteristics of effective teams.

Figure 9.2. **Characteristics of Effective Teams**

Clear Goals:

◆ Focus and organize work, tasks, and meetings

◆ Shared vision/mission

Diffused Power:

◆ Power to act and implement decisions

Balanced Membership:

◆ Diversity of membership and inclusion is based on expertise and membership is decided democratically

Positive Behavior of Members:

◆ Team spirit and collaborative

◆ Value for team members

◆ Mutual respect and trust

◆ Open minded, efficient, and flexible

Positive Conflict:

◆ Confident sharing opinions

- Can reach consensus
- Problem solvers
- Conflict-resolution skills

Positive Work Patterns:

- Work is evenly distributed and distributed based on interest and expertise
- Members are motivated to learn together

Positive Support:

- Can find resources and is given authority to make decisions; moreover, decision-making authority is known from the start

Positive Communication:

- Open communication
- Accepts constructive feedback on work and progress
- Positive communication (within the group and with external audiences)

Open Risk Taking:

- Motivated to accomplish goals
- Risk taking is encouraged

> Source: Zepeda, S. J. (2004b). *Instructional leadership for school improvement.* Larchmont, NY: Eye On Education.

Group Development Stages

According to Tuckman (1965), groups go through five common stages:

Stage 1: Forming

Stage 2: Storming

Stage 3: Norming

Stage 4: Performing

Stage 5: Adjourning

The work of CFGs is long-term, and the examination of the five stages of group development can shed light on the parallel work of CFGs—the power of the group structure itself.

- *Stage 1:* Forming: Members scan the group looking for sources of leadership; controversy is avoided; members look for safety and engage in guarded conversations. The forming stage is the orientation to the work, tasks, and goals of the group. Initial concerns emerge. To get to the next stage, storming, members begin to take risks and offer differing points-of-view that lead to storming.

♦ *Stage 2:* Storming: The storming stage is marked by testing the waters and conflict. Without storming, agreeing to disagree with one another, the team members will not move toward interdependence (see the Norming stage). Conflict occurs because members are preoccupied with proving themselves and their role relative to expertise, leadership, and position within the group. Members move from an individual orientation to a group orientation to organize for groupwork. This move involves conflict. Conflict arises over positioning individual members' responsibilities, deadlines, authority to make decisions, and possible power struggles among members of the group. Members learn that they have to make concessions about their own beliefs to achieve the work of the group. Interdependence between team members will not occur until the group has unearthed distrust and conflict. Conflict subsides and the group is ready to transition to the next stage, norming.

♦ *Stage 3:* Norming: Group members adapt a common method of working together. During this phase, members are able to reconcile their own opinions with the greater needs of the group. Cooperation and collaboration replace the conflict and mistrust of the previous phase (The Teal Trust, 2002).

Having gone through the storming and norming stages, groups can begin performing.

♦ *Stage 4:* Performing: The emphasis is now on reaching group goals rather than working on group process. Relationships are settled, and group members are likely to build loyalty toward each other. The group is able to manage more complex tasks and cope with greater change (The Teal Trust, 2002).

♦ *Stage 5:* Adjourning: The work of the team is complete, and the end result has been reached. For some team members, adjourning includes feeling a sense of loss for the work of the team and bonds of interdependence formed through the team development process and through the completion of meaningful work.

As shown in Figure 9.3, Wheelan, Tilin, and Sanford (1996) offer eight tips for improving group effectiveness that can assist CFGs in their work.

Figure 9.3. **Tips for Improving Group Effectiveness**

1. Learn about groups and how they operate.

2. Discuss group functioning each time the group meets.

3. Ask the group for feedback.

4. Take group member's feedback seriously.

5. Keep the focus on the group.

6. Spend time planning how goals and tasks will be accomplished.

7. Allow the group enough time to accomplish its goals and tasks.

8. Do not assume that implementing these suggestions is the responsibility of the group's leader. (p. 15)

Time and the Job-Embedded Nature of Critical Friends Groups

The work of CFGs is dependent on time, not only time to meet once a month for two or three hours, but also time to

♦ examine student work;

♦ work with fellow teachers giving feedback and sharing insights and reflections;

♦ be critically reflective about the feedback from CFG group members; and,

♦ work in between CFG meetings to implement change or suggestions made during CFG meetings.

Time is necessary given the work of CFG members. Adequate time must be allotted so that group members are able to

♦ observe each other's classroom, cueing into instructional practices, student engagement, and student work as it unfolds live in the classroom;

♦ examine artifacts—student work and teacher work samples;

♦ study evidence such as the results of tests, quizzes, and student performances; and,

♦ refine learning objectives, lesson plans, and instructional approaches.

The work of the school system is to find time not only for teachers to meet for CFGs meetings but also time in the day in between the monthly meetings of the CFGs. Creative use of plan time, substitute teacher deployment, and volunteers to cover duty periods are a start to finding the time for teachers to be able to study more in focus the topic under consideration by the members of the CFGs.

Ongoing Work Needed to Maintain the Work of Critical Friends Groups

For CFGs to flourish, they need ongoing team maintenance that includes leadership from the principal "on the sidelines." CFGs need:

♦ *Opportunities to meet:* Time during the day needs to be provided. Given the structure of the CFG and the time needed, two to three hours of uninterrupted time, it is impossible for CFGs to form unless there is time during the regular workday. Additionally, CFG members need time between meetings to learn from their practices by observing other teachers teaching, analyzing teaching and student artifacts, etc.

♦ *Resources:* Resources include, for example, secretarial support to assist with preparing materials (e.g., photocopying). CFG members cannot make good decisions unless they have data (e.g., test scores, discipline records, curriculum and teaching guides), and often accessing data in a school system is an elusive process for teachers.

♦ *Training:* Because of the inherent structures of working in isolation, many teachers who have the desire to work with others may not have the skills needed to work in a group situation as in the case of CFGs.

♦ *Commitment from the top:* CFGs need a firm commitment from the principal that the work of the CFG will be supported from the beginning to the end of the process.

♦ *Leadership from the sidelines:* Principals will need to take on a new role—leading from the side—in other words, getting out of the way so that the group can develop and work through conflict, work, solutions, etc.

♦ *Skill development in critical areas for CFG facilitators:* CFGs are comprised of teachers and other school personnel who may be leaders but who are, for the first time, serving as a CFG facilitator. Critical areas can range from conflict resolution to running an effective meeting.

Critical Friends Coaches

Often there is a coach involved to help facilitate the session (Coalition of Essential Schools Northwest, n.d.; Cushman, 1998; Dunne & Honts, 1998; Franzak, 2002). The Coalition of Essential Schools Northwest (n.d.) offers the following expectations regarding CFG coaches:

1. Be able to plan for and facilitate meetings of colleagues focused on teaching and learning;

2. Use a variety of strategies to promote trust-building, collaboration, reflective practice, and documentation of student learning;

3. Deal effectively with controversy and conflict resulting from

   - the examination of cultural and organizational traditions,

   - differing standards and expectations for students held by individual teachers, and

   - assumptions that underlie practice;

4. Serve as a resource within the school on issues relating to the whole school change and changing teacher practice;

5. Serve as an advocate for the CFG and the professional growth of the staff at the building, district, and community levels;

6. Serve as a collaborator with the school's principal on issues related to the professional growth of the staff and changing the school's culture and practice;

7. Participate in and eventually lead a variety of networking activities (CFG coaches will meet regularly with other school coaches; CFG coaches will have an external CFG coach, as well). (p. 2)

Critical Friends Protocols

To function with purpose as a CFG, there must be a structure based on group norms, a protocol that will help achieve the goal of the session (Franzak, 2002), and a sense of trust in the community of critical friends (Coalition of Essential Schools Northwest, n.d.). Tuning protocols are tools that support and structure the work of critical friends groups. Richardson (2001) offers that tuning protocols "guide conversations…[and they] are designed to break down the barriers that prevent teachers from viewing and commenting on each other's work. They also are designed to build the skills and culture necessary for collaborative work to flourish" (p. 9). Protocols are time managed and can be as long as two hours in length (National School Reform Faculty, 2006). CFG sessions have unique structures that support the particular problem or dilemma that is presented. A session may concentrate on looking at student work, reporting from a series of peer observations, brainstorming on a problem tied to a specific teaching practice, or to provide ongoing feedback. Figure 9.4 (page 213) provides an overview of various types of protocols and the purpose of the protocol. These protocols all have one item in common—the protocols help support ways for teachers to communicate in an organized manner so the focus is on the issue at hand.

Figure 9.4. Critical Friends Groups
Protocols and Their Purpose

Type of Protocol	Purpose of Protocol
Case Story and Sticky Issues	To expand thinking on a professional dilemma, not about giving advice or solving a problem.
Collaborative Assessment	Used to describe work without judgment and without prior information about the work.
Consultancy	To examine work framed around a presenter's question and reflection of the work.
Chalk Talk	To exchange ideas on a particular question or issue.
Descriptive Review	Deepen the understanding of the meanings in the work presented.
Text-Based Seminar and Final Word	Enlargement of understanding of a text; not the achievement of some particular understanding.
Tuning	Formalized way to get feedback on work in progress. To examine work as a means to refine curriculum or practice.

Source: Coalition of Essential Schools Northwest. (n.d.). *Critical friends groups protocols and their purposes*. Retrieved from www.cesnorthwest.org/cfg.php#protocols

A Case from the Field

Using Critical Friends Groups as Induction Support

Dr. Thomas Van Soelen
Assistant Superintendent
Curriculum & Assessment of Instruction & Professional Learning
City Schools of Decatur
758 Scott Boulevard
Decatur, GA 30030
tvansoelen@csdecatur.org

No doubt induction support for novice teachers is one of the most important functions of a school district. The stark statistics of the 1990s moved politicians and state departments of education to mandate teacher induction programs, albeit, most not sure what teacher induction really meant.

Around that same time, a thoughtful group of educators working from the Annenberg Institute for School Reform were redefining what ideal professional learning would look like for teachers. They developed the concepts of CFGs, a voluntary group of eight to 12 educators that come together at least once each month to improve student and teacher learning. CFGs are facilitated by a skilled and trained coach who helps set norms for the group, facilitates protocols, holds the agenda for the group, and keeps the group focused on using reflection to improve their practice. The National School Reform Faculty (NSRF, 2006) is the network of these educators, dedicated to the following:

♦ Everyone is a learner and has expertise;

♦ We improve practice by making it public;

♦ People learn best when working on authentic work;

♦ Only reflective practitioners continue to develop and improve; and,

♦ Protocols offer a reliable and equitable structure for conversations.

I was trained as a CFG Coach in 2002 and soon realized that this reflective stance I was practicing was starting to sink in. As I worked on statewide project focused on teacher induction, I eventually put the concepts together. *Teacher induction through CFGs!*

The premise seemed easy enough: getting novice teachers once each month to discuss their practice, share ideas, and commiserate. I could coach the group. The evaluation also seemed simple: the teachers would remain in teaching.

The naysayers in my peer group offered seemingly valid counterarguments:

♦ What could novice teachers possibly teach each other?

♦ They are novice for a reason, right?

♦ How do they know what they don't know?

♦ Don't we already know what novice teachers need to know?

I chose to practice a tenet believed by many in the NSRF network: assume goodwill. I chose to assume that novice teachers would want to get together, would have something to learn from each other, and would be more energized about teaching and learning.

In my CFG coaches' training, I met a principal from a large middle school in suburban Atlanta. He had new teachers; I had an idea. So, for the second half of the school year, I coached a novice teacher CFG at his school. He was dedicated to retaining new teachers, so he offered professional development funds to get substitutes for them one Wednesday afternoon each month from January through May.

What Was It Like?

I was not working in the school at the time. I relied on e-mail to communicate with my CFG outside of our regularly scheduled meetings. In those e-mails, I checked on their general well-being, as well as asked who would have a dilemma or some adult or student work to bring to the meeting. Although I held the agenda, it was not mine to dictate. Rather, I was facilitating these opportunities for all of us to learn from each other.

In their own works both during and after the experience, CFG members admitted that bringing something the first time was the scariest. Several times an "impromptu" protocol was convened as the members began to realize that the people they were waiting for were, indeed, themselves. Figure 9.5 is a sample agenda from our second meeting.

Figure 9.5. Agenda for the February Meeting

1. Connections

    Connections was a ten-minute experience in which participants could speak about what was currently on their mind or "in the way" of them connecting with what was going to happen during the meeting. Others did not respond to the speaker; it represented a safe place.

2. Norms Review

3. Chinese fortune cookies related to educational practice

    Each fortune was opened and participants related the fortune to their current understandings about teaching and children.

4. Beau's Success Analysis

    Each member engaged in a Success Analysis over the course of three meetings. This 45-minute experience involved a protocol in which the presenter offered a description of the context surrounding the success. Members could ask clarifying questions, which are queries that prompt a quick, short response from the presenter. These questions are for the listeners to get a better picture of the success. The bulk of the analysis occurs as the presenter sits out of the discussion, taking notes on current thoughts and wonderings. The final piece requires the presenter to reengage with the group, presenting current conceptions about the success.

5. Break

6. Susan's Consultancy About Time Management

A consultancy is another protocol used in CFGs. This experiences has similar characteristics to a success analysis: context, clarifying questions, discussion, and reflection by the presenter. A consultancy is a focused conversation about a particular dilemma that a member is experiencing. Thus a vital component of this experience is a section called Probing Questions. After the clarifying questions, probing questions are asked of the presenter that are *for the presenter*, not for the asker. These questions encourage the presenter to perform analysis while tending to the question.

7. Karla's Consultancy About Slave Diaries

8. Zones

Zones is a process of using three concentric circles: comfort as the largest circle, risk as the middle ring, and danger in the middle. During each CFG meeting, participants would record experiences and current wonderings on their zones, which we called our "bulls-eye's."

Figure 9.6 shows the details of the four protocols we used during this four-hour meeting. Each of these protocols is attributed to the person(s) who developed them and can be found on the National School Reform Faculty Web site at www.harmonyschool.org/nsrf/default.html. Figure 9.7 (page 220) shows the zones process.

Figure 9.6. **Protocols Used During February Meeting**

Connections

Developed by Gene Thompson-Grove

What is *Connections*?

Connections is a way for people to build a bridge from where they are or have been (mentally, physically, etc.) to where they will be going and what they will be doing. It is a time for individuals to reflect—within the context of a group—upon a thought, a story, an insight, a question, or a feeling that they are carrying with them into the session, and then connect it to the work they are about to do. Most people engage in *Connections* at the beginning of a meeting, class, or gathering.

There are a few things to emphasize about *Connections* for it to go well...

♦ It is about connecting people's thoughts to the work they are doing or are about to do.

♦ Silence is OK, as is using the time to write, to just sit and think. Assure people that they will spend a specific amount of time in *Connections,* whether or not anyone speaks out loud. Some groups—and people within groups—value the quiet, reflective time above all else.

♦ If an issue the group clearly wants to respond to comes up in *Connections,* the group can decide to make time for a discussion about the issue after *Connections* is over.

The "rules" for *Connections* are quite simple.

◆ Speak if you want to.

◆ Don't speak if you don't want to.

◆ Speak only once until everyone who wants to has had a chance to speak.

◆ Listen and note what people say, but do not respond. *Connections* is not the time to engage in a discussion.

> Facilitating the process is also straightforward. Begin by saying "*Connections* is open," and let people know how long it will last. A few minutes before the time is up, let people know that there are a few minutes remaining, so that anyone who hasn't yet spoken might speak. With a minute or so to go, let the group know that you will be drawing *Connections* to a close, and again ask if anyone who hasn't spoken would like to speak. Before ending, ask if anyone who has spoken would like to speak again. Then end.

> Ten minutes is usually enough time for groups of ten people or fewer, 15 minutes for groups of 11 to 20 people and 20 minutes for any groups larger than 20 people. *Connections* generally shouldn't last more than 20 minutes. People can't sustain it. The one exception is when there is a group that has been together for a period of time doing intensive work, and it is the last or next to the last day of their gathering. Some people will say that *Connections* is misnamed, since people don't connect to (or build on) what other people have said. However, the *process* is a connecting one; and powerful connections can still occur, even though they are not necessarily the result of back and forth conversation.

The Connections Protocol was developed by Gene Thompson-Grove and can be found at the National School Reform Faculty site at www.nsrfhar-mony.org/protocol/doc/connections.pdf. Used with permission.

The Consultancy Protocol

The Consultancy Protocol was developed by Gene Thompson-Grove as part of the Coalition of Essential Schools' National Re:Learning Faculty Program, and further adapted and revised as part of work of NSRF.

A consultancy is a structured process for helping an individual or a team to think more expansively about a particular, concrete dilemma. Outside perspective is critical to this protocol working effectively; therefore, some of the participants in the group must be people who do not share the presenter's specific dilemma at that time. When putting together a Consultancy group, be sure to include people with differing perspectives.

Framing Consultancy Dilemmas and Consultancy Questions

A dilemma is a puzzle, an issue that raises questions, an idea that seems to have conceptual gaps, something about process or product that you just can't figure out. Sometimes it will include samples of student or adult work that illustrate the dilemma, but often it is a dilemma that crosses over many parts of the educational process.

1. Think about your dilemma. Dilemmas deal with issues with which you are struggling or that you are unsure about. Some criteria for a dilemma might include:

   - Is it something that is bothering you enough that your thoughts regularly return to the dilemma?

   - Is it an issue/dilemma that is not already on its way to being resolved?

   - Is it an issue/dilemma that does not depend on getting other people to change (in other words, can you affect the dilemma by changing your practice)?

   - Is it something that is important to you, and is it something you are actually willing to work on?

2. Do some reflective writing about your dilemma. Some questions that might help are:

   - Why is this a dilemma for you? Why is this dilemma important to you?

   - If you could take a snapshot of this dilemma, what would you/we see?

   - What have you done already to try to remedy or manage the dilemma?

   - What have been the results of those attempts?

   - Who do you hope changes? Who do you hope will take action to resolve this dilemma? If your answer is not you, you need to change your focus. You will want to present a dilemma that is about your practice, actions, behaviors, beliefs, and assumptions, and not someone else's.

   - What do you assume to be true about this dilemma, and how have these assumptions influenced your thinking about the dilemma?

   - What is your focus question? A focus question summarizes your dilemma and helps focus the feedback (see the next step).

3. Frame a focus question for your consultancy group: Put your dilemma into question format.

   - Try to pose a question around the dilemma that seems to you to get to the heart of the matter.

- Remember that the question you pose will guide the consultancy group in their discussion of the dilemma.

4. Critique your focus question.

  - Is this question important to my practice?

  - Is this question important to student learning?

  - Is this question important to others in my profession?

The Consultancy Protocol was developed by Gene Thompson-Grove as part of the Coalition of Essential Schools' National Re:Learning Faculty Program, and further adapted and revised as part of work of NSRF. The Consultancy Protocol can be found at the National School Reform Faculty homepage at www.nsrfharmony.org/protocol/doc/consultancy.pdf. Used with permission of the National School Reform Faculty.

Success Analysis Protocol

Developed by Daniel Baron, NSRF

Roles

- A timekeeper/a facilitator

Steps

1. Reflect on and write a short description of the "Best Practice" of your CFG. Note what it is about the practice that makes it so successful. (5 minutes)

2. In groups of four, the first person shares their CFG's "Best Practice" and why it is so successful. (3 to 5 minutes)

3. The group of four discusses how this practice is different than other CFG practices. (3 to 5 minutes)

4. Each of the other three members of the group shares their CFG's "Best Practice" and why it is so successful, followed by a group discussion analyzing how this practice differs from other CFG practices. (Each round should take 6 to 10 minutes)

5. The small group discusses what was learned by the analysis and what are the implications for other CFG work. (10 minutes)

6. Debrief the protocol and write four "CFG Best Practice" headlines on one piece of chart paper. (5 minutes)

The Success Analysis Protocol was developed by Daniel Baron. The Success Analysis Protocol can be found at the National School Reform Faculty homepage at www.nsrfharmony.org/protocol/doc/success_analysis_cfg.pdf. Used with permission of the National School Reform Faculty.

Figure 9.7. Zones of Comfort, Risk and Danger: Constructing Your Zone Map

The Zones Exercise comes from an unknown source (to me) within the NSRF organization. I first experienced it at the Fall 2000 Critical Friends Group Symposium in Boca Raton, Florida. I have found the exercise useful and have tried to make notes for others. I hope the originator will claim the invention, and that others will add to this useful exercise as they discover new applications. Marylyn Wentworth, January, 2001.

1. Draw a diagram of concentric circles in the following manner:

    a. The middle circle is Comfort, the second is Risk, the third is Danger.

    b. Consider the various aspects of your work (as a CFG Coach, for example). Think about the aspects that feel really comfortable to you, those that feel like there is some risk involved, but generally positive, and those aspects that you know get your hackles up, make you feel defensive, cloud your judgment, make you want to retreat.

    c. Decide on the size of each Zone based on your consideration. Do you work a lot in your Comfort Zone, your Risk Zone? Do you work only a little in your Danger Zone? Make the size of the Zones reflect the quantity of time you work there.

2. Think about the different activities you do and/or affective domains in which you work (i.e., facilitating groups, leading protocols, designing meetings, guiding peer observation, responding to conflicts between group members...). Make a list if it helps.

3. Put each activity or affective domain into the Zone that best represents your sense of relative Comfort, Risk or Danger.

Source: Unknown author. Zone of Comfort, Risk and Danger: Constructing Your Zone Map can be found at the National School Reform Faculty homepage at www.nsrfharmony.org/protocol/doc/zones_of_comfort.pdf. Used with permission of the National School Reform Faculty.

The work with this novice teacher CFG was unique in that we had intense time once/month for our work. As I structure meetings now, 1.5 to 2 hours are the maximum amount of time teachers can offer for collaborative work. For those situations, I would use the following sample agenda.

1. Connections

2. Protocol work (e.g., Consultancy, looking at student work)

3. Peer Observation Learnings

4. Planning for the next CFG meeting

What Did the CFG Group of Novice Teachers Learn?

This group of novice teachers did not examine issues of classroom management. They did not talk about how to negotiate parent communications or complaints. In fact, their agendas ran counter to most "canned" teacher induction programs, which offer modules on report cards, parent/teacher conferences, classroom management, and the like. This novice teacher CFG examined issues of assessment, grading and reporting, and relationships with teammates. These issues, which they said they needed to address, may have never arisen without a structure that honored their current needs.

They also learned the power of peer observations and learning. Peer observations are an important part of a CFG's life. The observations foster accountability while pushing participants to make their practice public. Observations are structured through protocols, so teachers are clear about intent.

One member of the group quit after the first meeting. She purported to be "too busy" to collaborate. As I looked at what she said during the first meeting as being her needs, this novice CFG organically examined each of those issues. Interestingly enough, the only person who left teaching after that year was the teacher who quit the group.

So What?

There are two counties in Georgia that use CFGs as their primary source of teacher induction and support. Barrow County Schools (enrollment = 11,000 students) and Fulton County Schools (enrollment = 82,000 students) train excellent teachers to function as CFG coaches. These coaches support novice teachers by leading a CFG that honors the voices of what the novices in identifying what they need.

Why did these counties choose CFGs? Perhaps Gene Thompson-Grove's keynote speech from the Ninth Annual National School Reform Faculty Winter Meeting in January 2005 will help explain:

> So, a group of people reading together can be useful work, but that's a book group, not a CFG. People coming together to research best literacy practices is important work, but that's a study group, not a CFG. People learning to look at student work on a professional development day can produce new insights and new learning, but that's

a workshop, not a CFG. Faculty participating in team building and conflict resolution activities might be vital to the health of a school, but that's not a CFG. People being told by the district to bring curriculum units to a districtwide meeting to be tuned might produce better alignment of the curriculum to the standards, but it is not a CFG.

A CFG supports teachers learning from each other through job-embedded structures to support collaboration.

Not Just New Teachers

CFGs are a meaningful and effective professional learning community for varied levels of experience as well. Some CFGs include university professors, veteran teachers, novice teachers, and university teacher candidates. Some CFGs involve only superintendents or principals. In the City Schools of Decatur, Georgia, each monthly superintendent's meeting includes a segment of professional learning. In 2007, the superintendent agreed that 90 minutes would be used in three smaller groups (CFGs). The CFG coaches are three individuals in the district (assistant superintendent, principal, and elementary instructional coach) that were trained in a CFG Coaches' Institute. Each group uses its own agenda to improve the work of the individuals in the group. For more information about the NSRF and CFGs, visit the National School Reform Faculty Harmony Education Center Homepage at www.nsrfharmony.org.

Implications for Leadership

Dunne and Honts (1998) identify four factors that can enable or disable the CFG model's success. School principals, professional development coordinators, subject area supervisors, and CFG coaches should be aware that (a) internal group dynamics, (b) administrative structure, (c) school culture, and (d) access to resources are factors that influence job-embedded professional learning.

Internal group dynamics vary between schools as well as between subgroups within a single school. Groups with a high level of trust between members will find a smoother journey to becoming a CFG. Trust must be collegial in nature, not to be mistaken for congenial trust (Dunne & Honts, 1998). Schools that have a high level of teacher isolation and autonomy will find a tougher road to establishing a CFG, and time will be required to develop the appropriate internal group dynamics. Leadership is of substantial importance in such cases.

Administrators must show support in the manner in which they participate in the CFG process. Some school leaders may choose to be coaches or participants. In either case, there must be a relationship that enables participants to be critical in a productive and nonthreatening way. CFGs require administrators to be open to high levels of collaboration among staff, and to have the trust in teachers to be effective participants in the process. When administrators require every staff member to become a part of a CFG, what usually results is what Hargreaves (1994) terms "contrived collegiality" (p. 195), the development of a CFG is slow and troubled. The same applies when leaders are passive to the process (Dunne & Honts, 1998). Leaders who are supportive of teacher development in collaborative settings most often are associated with strong school cultures.

School cultures that consistently reflect collegial work are likely to find CFGs are an extension or modification of what they have experienced in the past. In schools that support and embrace teacher individualism, autonomy, and isolation, there is likely to be greater incidence of conflict or rejection of the CFG model (Dunne & Honts, 1998).

Teachers need access to information that is beyond the scope of what they already know or have experienced. This type of resource is identified by Dunne and Honts (1998) as being important to the quality of work that the CFG does. Information regarding change, learning, and culture are examples of a needed resource. Supervisors and coaches should recognize that note every teacher comes to the table with the same level of professional background and knowledge. When problems are being addressed that really need additional information, those resources should be sought out and provided.

Conclusion

The underlying assumption about the value of the CFG model is that "students whose teachers have participated in CFG work over time will exhibit improved performance..." (Coalition of Essential Schools Northwest, n.d., p. 5). As a professional development model, the CFG can act as a framework for high levels of collaboration. Critical friends can be a source of data for action research projects and can provide the energy to seek out additional knowledge about the practice of teaching. It could be argued that a CFG actually broadens the field of supervisors for any one teacher.

Suggested Readings

Curry, M. W. (2008). Critical friends groups: The possibilities and limitations embedded in teacher professional communities aimed at instructional improvement and school reform. *Teachers College Record, 110*(4), 733–774.

Gregory, G. H., & Kuzmich, L. (2007). *Teacher teams that get results: 61 strategies for sustaining and renewing professional learning communities.* Thousand Oaks, CA: Corwin Press.

Handal, G. (1999). Consultation using critical friends. *New Directions for Teaching and Learning, 1999*(79), 59–70. doi:10.1002/tl.7907

Silva, P. (2005). A day in the life of schoolwide CFGs. *Educational Horizons, 84*(1), 29.

Southern Regional Education Board. (2005). *Teachers teaching teachers: Creating a community of learners to improve instruction and student achievement. Best practices for implementing HSTW and MMGW.* Atlanta, GA: Author. (ERIC Document Reproduction Service No. ED486512)

Wheelan, S.A. (2004). *Faculty groups: From frustration to collaboration.* Thousand Oaks, CA: Corwin Press.

10

Lesson Study

In This Chapter...

♦ The Lesson Study Process

♦ Implications for Professional Development

♦ Challenges for Lesson Study Implementation

♦ Focusing on Student Work as Professional Development

The phrase *lesson study* is derived from the Japanese terms *jugyo* (lesson) and *kenkyu* (study). When reversed in translation, the term, *jugyokenkyu*, carries the meaning of "research lesson" (Wiburg & Brown, 2006). Lesson study can be approached as research that combines collaboration, reflection, and professional development into one structured experience for teachers that engages them in constructing new meanings about instructional practices (Fernandez & Chokshi, 2002; Lewis, Perry, Hurd, & O'Connell, 2006). By design, lesson study is a form of job-embedded learning that is grounded in data. According to the National Education Association Foundation for the Improvement of Education (NFIE), data are collected by teachers observing teachers. Through these purposeful interactions, "teachers have the opportunity to discuss the lessons and their analysis, while refining their practices according to what the evidence suggests works well with their students" (2003, p. 3).

According to the Lesson Study Research Group (LSRG, n.d.) housed at Columbia University:

Lesson study is a professional development process that Japanese teachers engage in to systematically examine their practice, with the goal of becoming more effective. This examination centers on teachers working collaboratively on a small number of "study lessons." Working on these study lessons involves planning, teaching, observing, and critiquing the lessons. To provide focus and direction to this work, the teachers select an overarching goal and related research question that they want to explore. This research question then serves to guide their work on all the study lessons. (p. 1)

Lesson study originally was applied in the area of mathematics, but the process has spread in application to other subject areas.

The Lesson Study Process

The process of lesson study is an iterative cycle involving teachers in activities across four basic steps (Lewis, Perry, & Murata, 2006):

- ♦ Study curriculum and formulate goals;

- ♦ Plan;

- ♦ Conduct research; and,

- ♦ Reflect.

The lesson study cycle is highly interactive. Teachers are continually engaged in the work of improving instruction, and they are supported by peers as they analyze teaching strategies, evaluate methods, give and receive feedback to lessons, and study the results of their efforts. Figure 10.1 illustrates the iterative and cyclical nature of lesson study.

Figure 10.1. The Iterative Nature of Lesson Study

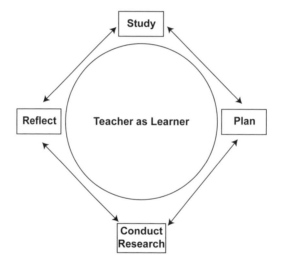

Study Curriculum and Formulate Goals

In studying the curriculum, teachers identify a topic that encompasses a learning problem they would like to pursue. The learning problem is related to the learning goals of the school, and it is initially found by studying the curriculum as it relates to the overarching goals of the school. Wiburg and Brown (2006) suggest that the study of the curriculum needs to be two-pronged. The written curriculum needs to be studied, but so does the learned curriculum. One lens looks at what the teacher is doing in relation to the written curriculum, the other lens is looking at what learning problems the students may be experiencing.

Plan

In the planning stage, teachers identify a specific learning problem and how this problem affects the learning goals of the students. Questions dealing with the level or depth of understanding desired, the assessments that will be used to determine the degree of understanding, and the strategies that will be most suitable need to be asked and debated during this initial step (Wiburg & Brown, 2006). The formulation of planning goals can result in answering questions about

♦ the depth or level of understanding, for example: "What are the enduring understanding we want our student to have?"

♦ assessment methods, for example: "How will we assess students to determine if they have these understandings?"

♦ learning opportunities, such as: "What learning opportunities can be designed to support students' gaining this understanding?" (Wiburg & Brown, p. 25)

Conduct Research

Once the learning problem is identified, a research question is developed to address that problem. The development of this research question needs to relate to the overarching learning goal(s) involved and must have a certain degree of anticipation regarding student thinking and learning. For example, if the problem is that students cannot see relationships between numbers to solve problems involving multiplication, then the question might be: Does instruction using the *say why* method of problem solving help students understand how to apply relationships between numbers to multiplication problems? Included in the plan is a rationale for the approach that has been chosen, an explanation of how data will be collected, and a learning trajectory.

Conducting the research involves the actual teaching of planned research lessons. These lessons involve a team of teachers observing and collecting data as one teacher teaches the lesson. This lesson may be repeated over time to allow the teacher to make adjustments and revisions (Wiburg & Brown, 2006).

Reflection

The fourth stage of the lesson study cycle is reflection. The team collectively reflects on the process. The team reconvenes, the lesson is discussed, and data are shared. During this reflection time, data should be used to explore and uncover concerns, new information, or celebrations. Areas that should be recognized in the survey of data are: (a) student learning, (b) disciplinary content, (c) lesson and unit design, and (d) broader issues in teaching and learning (Lewis, Perry, & Murata, 2006). This stage can culminate in a written report of the findings and recommendations of the team.

Information from the reflection of the lesson study leads the team back to the first stage of the cycle: the study of the curriculum and the formulation of goals. The lesson may be modified as necessary, and the same or another teacher will teach the modified lesson with the team observing once again. The team may decide that as part of their research, they will conduct the same research lesson with a different group of students and compare results (Lewis, Perry, & Hurd, 2004). The team could find that they have solved the learning problem and then would identify a whole new problem, related problem, or research whether the strategies used would work on another problem.

It is important that the two-pronged view of the curriculum (written/taught vs. learned) is keenly adhered to as the discussion of the team needs to involve whether the learning problem actually originates with the learner or with the written/taught curriculum (teacher).

Implications for Professional Development

As a form of professional development, what does lesson study do? How does it improve teaching? Those are important questions to explore. Lewis et al. (2004) offer seven "key pathways to instructional improvement" provided through the practice of lesson study (p. 19). Figure 10.2 presents these pathways and the related challenges.

Figure 10.2. The Seven Pathways to Instructional Improvement and the Related Challenges

Seven Pathways to Instructional Improvement	Related Challenges
♦ Increased knowledge of subject matter	♦ Textbook-bound thinking, isolation, lack of accountability, failure to relate to being a researcher
♦ Increased knowledge of instruction	♦ "This is the way I have always done it," lack of accountability, failure to relate to being a researcher
♦ Increased ability to observe students	♦ Lack of time and trust, failure to relate to being a researcher, fear of failure (risk)

Seven Pathways to Instructional Improvement	Related Challenges
◆ Stronger collegial networks	◆ Lack of time, trust, and shared purpose
◆ Stronger connections of daily practice to long term goals	◆ Lack of goals, not understanding the connectivity required between goals and practice
◆ Stronger motivation and sense of efficacy	◆ Negative environment, lack of administrative support, low standardized test scores
◆ Improved quality of available lesson plans	◆ Lack of trust, autonomy, competition

Increased Knowledge of Subject Matter

Subject-matter knowledge must be discussed and investigated during the planning stage of lesson study. This collaborative examination of the content matter offers the opportunity for new questions and insights about the content to be discovered. As these new questions and insights are uncovered, the group may answer or refine them through their discussion, or they may go outside of the group for enlightenment. Students may also produce unique insights or inquisitions about content that can be discussed by the team resulting in an increase in content knowledge.

Increased Knowledge of Instruction

Teachers have reported an increase in their knowledge of instruction when they are involved with lesson study (Lewis et al., 2004). Lesson study does not create completely new lessons, but the process helps teachers perfect a lesson that is already in existence (Chokshi & Fernandez, 2004; Lewis, 2002). The result of a lesson study may be much different from the original lesson that was first researched.

Chokshi and Fernandez (2004) offer:

The lesson study should investigate issues of pedagogy and content that teachers typically struggle with, it should be grounded in the realities of the school, and should not be isolated from the curriculum or everyday experiences of the students. In other words, the driving force for the lesson should not be originality alone, but the fact that it provides a rich vantage point from which teachers can think about their teaching. (p. 522)

Studies reveal that teachers believe lesson study helps them learn new strategies that can be used throughout the curriculum (Lewis, 2002). The key characteristics of lesson study as a professional development model are that it is teacher driven and classroom based (Stepanek, Appel, Leong, Mangan, & Mitchell, 2007), and data about teacher practices and how students respond to these practices can be captured. These characteristics allow lesson study to be an instrument of job embedded professional development.

Stronger Collegial Networks

Observation by teams of teachers as a practice can be a dynamic springboard towards building stronger collegial relationships, particularly when they are structured, planned, and focused. Lesson study provides such structure to group observations. Lesson observations are more than simply seeing what a teacher is doing or not doing in the classroom. It is designed to produce data that should be meaningful to all involved and offer a professional focus to guide the discussions that follow. Lewis (2002) writes: "As another Japanese teacher said: 'What's a successful research lesson? It's not so much what happens in the research lesson itself that makes it successful or unsuccessful. It is what you learned working with your colleagues on your way there'" (p. 4). This realization has strong implications for professional development as lesson study is a form of collaboration with a very specific focus that allows for teachers to share their expertise, observations, and questions in order to generate a higher level of teaching and learning. If there is consistency in the makeup of the lesson study team, the collaboration and relationships built will also have a positive effect on the culture of the school (Lewis et al., 2004).

Stronger Connections of Daily Practice to Long-Term Goals

The goals that are established in the initial stage of the cycle are connected to the overarching goals of the school (Lewis et al., 2004). These can be the "enduring understandings" that a school wants their students to have, or it could be abilities related to problem-solving, communication, and civility (Wiburg & Brown, 2006, p. 5). When the lesson study team observes, they are looking through the lens of these broad goals, even though there are specific learning and teaching strategies with which they may be concerned.

Stronger Motivation and Sense of Efficacy

Collaboration practiced through lesson study has a profound effect on teacher efficacy (Puchner & Taylor, 2006). Along with this sense of efficacy is a sense of shared responsibility (Lewis, Perry, Hurd, & O'Connell, 2006). Studies show that teachers generally develop a level of self-efficacy before a group or collective efficacy develops. This can be attributed to the isolation and independence traditionally found in schools (Hipp, 1996). Furthermore, it has been found that "People who have a sense of collective efficacy will mobilize their efforts and resources to cope with external obstacles to the changes they seek. But those convinced of their inefficacy will cease trying even though changes are attainable though concerted effort" (Bandura, 1982, p. 144). This increase in teacher efficacy, whether group or individual, can lead to higher teacher retention as well as a willingness to broaden the teaching practices presented in the classroom (Cowley & Meehan, 2001). Lesson study provides the opportunity for teachers to increase their efficacy while sharing responsibility for student learning and professional growth.

The collaborative practice found in lesson study groups has five characteristics that help define a genuine sense of collaboration as opposed to teachers simply meeting to discuss or communicate: (a) collective responsibility, (b) philosophical conversations, (c) addressing problems together, (d) valuing dissent, and (e) community as an end (Stepanek et al., 2007).

Improved Quality of Available Lesson Plans

The sharing of findings from the research lessons along with the revised plans allows for a school or department to collect and distribute strong lesson plans with strategies that have been developed through the research of the team. This is not to imply that all revised plans will work across all classrooms and for all teachers, but instead, that these "tested" lessons will provide a starting point for further lesson study groups. For example, if a lesson study team discovered a particular worksheet had been used for multiple years in a math class but was not very effective in accomplishing the learning goals of the curriculum and the use of manipulative tools, then math teachers would be able to make informed decisions about what teaching strategy to use.

School leaders looking to increase student learning and instructional effectiveness are most likely aware of some if not all of these pathways to instructional improvement. However, the potential benefits of these pathways applied to the work of lesson study must be examined within the context of the school in which lesson study is being considered. Lesson study requires a shift in thinking, behavior, and how teachers go about their work. School leaders need to be aware of the obstacles and challenges that exist.

Challenges for Lesson Study Implementation

Schools that have developed a collaborative culture with high levels of trust and a pervasive shared vision, values, and goals are well-equipped to incorporate lesson study as a professional development practice. However, many schools need to acknowledge various challenges that exist in implementing lesson study. Figure 10.2 (page 228) identifies, based on the work of Lewis et al. (2004), the challenges that exist for the seven pathways to instructional improvement.

The most obvious challenge for schools is finding the time for teachers to develop a research lesson through the lesson study process. Some teachers in Japan are paid to stay at school in the afternoon for two hours to plan together and to share experiences (Kelly, 2002). Lewis (2002) states: "It is *not* the case (despite accounts to the contrary) that Japanese elementary teachers have more time for collaboration during the school day than their U.S. counterparts; daily time with students is comparable or longer in Japan" (p. 14, emphasis in the original). The concern for time to collaborate has been voiced from elementary school principals and teachers more than from secondary level educators in the United States. This is reflected in discussions throughout the nation about developing professional learning communities in schools. Lesson study is a prime example of how a professional learning community can operate if time is available for meaningful collaboration to occur.

For lesson study to be powerful and meaningful, research teams should work together through the entire cycle. Schools that simply put together a team of teachers that may be available at a certain time and send them in to take notes on "what they see" are not going to improve instruction. If the team members have had input into the goal creation and planning, then they will have a much better opportunity to research a learning problem effectively and provide meaningful feedback in their discussions about teaching and learning. A team that goes through the lesson study together develops a sense of purpose, efficacy, and trust. School leaders need to be innovative in how they work with teachers on utilization of time as a resource.

The willingness and ability to take on the role of the researcher has proven to be a challenge for teachers (Fernandez, Cannon, & Chokshi, 2003). Teachers have generally relied on information from the world of educational researchers to reach them through professional development sessions, books, and tapes. In lesson study, they must develop the skills and abilities needed to ask the right questions to conduct the research lessons. According to Fernandez et al., "…Japanese teachers emphasized four critical aspects of good research: the development of meaningful and testable hypotheses, the use of appropriate means for exploring these hypotheses, the reliance on evidence to judge the success of research endeavors, and the interest in generalizing research findings to other applicable contexts" (p. 173). School leaders need to recognize that teachers need the opportunity to become comfortable with their roles as researchers.

Teacher isolation or autonomy can make lesson study difficult (Puchner & Taylor, 2006). The common belief today is that a collegial and collaborative culture must exist for successful professional development to take place. Lesson study requires teachers to be open and trusting of other teachers about teaching and learning. Collaborative inquiry has been found to have a substantial positive effect on teacher efficacy, content area knowledge, classroom teaching, and student learning (Huffman & Kalnin, 2003).

The initial goal setting in lesson study is overarching in nature. Thought goes into what the team envisions their students being able to do (Fernandez et al., 2003; Fernandez & Chokshi, 2002; Wiburg & Brown, 2007). The overarching goal of the lesson study, although broad in nature, has a determined focus on what students will be able to do and learn.

Lesson study teachers are open to learning new information about the subjects they teach and how they teach them. This involves a level of trust and willingness to expose one's practice as a teacher (Stewart & Brendefur, 2005). The research that occurs generates questions and demands answers to those questions. Teachers generally tend to be timid about opening their classroom door and having a team come in to observe critically. This is why it is important that the questions asked by the team need to be focused on what the students are doing or not doing as learners.

Increased Ability to Observe Students— Focus on Student Data

Student observation occurs at a much higher level of intensity with some members of the lesson study team concentrating on the learning activity of small groups or individual students. Collecting narrative data from select students is a strategy found in lesson study, and this collection is often concentrated on particular students who either have difficulty with achieving the learning goal or on students who excel with the goal (Lewis et al., 2004). A comparison of the thinking of both levels of students can lead to valuable insights of individual learners and help teachers understand which teaching strategies work with which students. Simply put, the more sets of eyes that are observing, the more data can be collected.

Focusing on Student Work as Professional Development

Effective professional development is job-embedded where the work of teaching and learning how to teach, to improve, and to meet the needs of students coalesce into opportunities to see live the impact of efforts on student learning. Examining student work leads teachers to learn more about the efforts of their teaching based on the student work.

When teachers examine student work alone or in the company of others, they can reflect on how and why students are or not learning. The National Education Association (2003) believes, "when teachers analyze and discuss instructional practice and the resulting samples of student work, they experience some of the highest caliber professional development available" (p. 2).

Teachers can identify the gaps in their own teaching and student understanding. Teachers can identify cues on what instructional practices or curricular materials need to be modified. When teachers examine student work together, they can share ideas, approaches, and instructional materials; they can codevelop curricular materials and they can make comparisons about which materials or approaches appeared to work. Examining student work can help teachers make better decisions relating to the curriculum and its development, instructional strategies, and assessments.

In their large-scale study of professional development, Garet, Porter, Desiome, Birman, and Yoon (2001) found that active learning occurs when teachers can learn from their own work, and this type of learning had greater levels of impact on academic gains of students. One of the strategies that constituted active learning was reviewing student work. Garet et al., report, "examining and discussing examples of student work may help teachers develop skills in diagnosing student problems and designing lessons at an appropriate level of difficulty" (p. 926). Similarly, Kazemi and Franke (2003) report:

> Close analysis of student work can provide opportunities for teachers to pause and see ideas in their students' thinking that the day-to-day rush of instruction may not necessarily foster. Discussions of student work allow teachers to raise their own questions about practice and to deliberate about what it is that they want and need students to learn. Such professional inquiry can allow teachers to form generalizations and conclusions from the particular instances of students' reasoning that would guide future interactions in their classrooms. In this way, the study of student work can also stimulate discussions about how and what to teach. By collectively engaging in the study of student work, teachers can make public their own assumptions about teaching and learning and deliberate differences they see in the ways their practices affect students' thinking. (p. 6)

Studying Student Work Is Professional Development

Studying and examining student work promotes key constructs that are at the heart of professional development—inquiry, site-based research, and collaboration—situating the teacher as an active learner. The National Education Association (NEA, 2003) reports that data can be used in two equally important ways to improve professional development:

1. As the actual substance of professional development, as educators convene with each other to study student work and analyze the instructional practice that produced such results; and,

2. As a basis for making decisions about educators' on-the-job learning, including decisions pertaining to professional development resource allocation, content, and delivery (p. 2).

Getting Started with Examining Student Work

Getting started examining student work can be awkward. A teacher shared with me that the first time she and her colleagues examined student work together—it was "awkward, awkward, awkward." She elaborated that the team members had never worked together in ways that their "vulnerabilities" were in full view of one another. However, she shared that after a few meetings, the defensiveness associated with sharing student work was replaced with learning about how to teach better, how better to develop curricular approaches, and how to modify instructional and curricular approaches based on what members were learning from each other while examining student work.

The NEA (2003) underscores that "data are more than test scores" (p. 1). Teachers, who are at the beginning stages of examining student work, can be assisted with agreeing on a single standard (curricular/learning) and then by examining student work samples that reflect that standard. Work samples could include

- essays;

- quiz or test sample responses;

- video clips of students completing tasks; or,

- drawings.

Any item that is a sample of student work can be studied. The objective is to study not only the artifact but also the learning objective, the standard, and the instructional approach to see how students perform, what have they mastered, and what shifts in instructional practices need to be made. A primary objective behind studying student work is to "invite conversations about the work and the teaching associated with it" (McDonald, 2001, p. 121). However, McDonald offers that the conversations are "highly structured," employ some type of "protocol" and that "the activity of talking productively with peers about the intentions behind and the actual effects of one's work demands assertiveness and frankness but also requires delicacy and some buffer against quick judgments and harsh words" (p. 121).

McDonald (2001) believes "the discipline and structure make the process safe" (p. 122). The intent of predetermined protocols is to allow members of the group to "suspend judgment" so "that the teacher finds her capacity to make judgments enriched by other perspectives" (p. 122). ATLAS Learning Communities, Inc. (2007a, 2007b) offers sound strategies (Figure 10.3) to get teachers reflecting, listening, and collaborating while studying student work

Figure 10.3. Thinking, Listening, and Reflecting with Colleagues About Student Work

Reflecting on the Process

Looking for evidence of student thinking…

- What did you see in this student's work that was interesting or surprising?

- What did you learn about how this student thinks and learns?

- What about the process helped you to see and learn these things?

Listening to colleagues thinking…

♦ What did you learn from listening to your colleagues that was interesting or surprising?

♦ What new perspectives did your colleagues provide?

♦ How can you make use of your colleagues' perspectives?

Reflecting on one's own thinking…

♦ What questions about teaching and assessment did looking at the students' work raise for you?

♦ How can you pursue these questions further?

♦ Are there things you would like to try in your classroom as a result of looking at this student's work?

Copyright 2007 ATLAS Learning Communities. Used with permission.

A suggested process offered by ATLAS (2007a) supports teachers learning from student work (Figure 10.4).

Figure 10.4. ATLAS—Learning from Student Work

1. Getting Started

  • The facilitator reminds the group of the norms: no fault, collaboration, and consensus, and, with the group, establishes time limits for each part of the process.

  Note: Each of the next four steps should be about 10 minutes in length. The presenter is silent until the "Reflecting on the Atlas," step 5. The group should avoid talking to the presenter during steps 2–4. It is sometimes helpful for the presenter to pull away from the table and take notes.

  • The educator providing the student work gives a very brief statement of the assignment. The educator should describe only what the student was asked to do and avoid explaining what he or she hoped or expected to see.

  • The educator providing the work should not give any background information about the student or the student's work. In particular, the educator should avoid any statements about whether this is a strong or weak student or whether this is a particularly good or poor piece of work from this student.

  Note: After the group becomes more familiar with this process for looking at student work, you may find it useful to hear the educator's expectations. However, this information will focus more of the group's attention on the design of the assignment, the instruction, and the assessment, rather than on seeing what is actually present in the student's work.

2. Describing the Student Work

- The facilitator asks: "What do you see?"

- During this period the group gathers as much information as possible from the student work.

- Group members describe what they see in the student's work, avoiding judgments about quality or interpretations about what the student was doing.

- If judgments or interpretations do arise, the facilitator should ask the person to describe the evidence on which they are based.

- It may be useful to list the group's observations on chart paper. If interpretations come up, they can be listed in another column for later discussion during step 3.

3. Interpreting the Student Work

- The facilitator asks: "From the student's perspective, what is the student working on?"

- During this period, the group tries to make sense of what the student was doing and why. The group should try to find as many different interpretations as possible and evaluate them against the kind and quality of evidence.

- From the evidence gathered in the preceding section, try to infer: what the student was thinking and why; what the student does and does not understand; what the student was most interested in; how the student interpreted the assignment.

- Think broadly and creatively. Assume that the work, no matter how confusing, makes sense to the student; your job is to see what the student sees.

- As you listen to each other's interpretations, ask questions that help you better understand each other's perspectives.

4. Implications for Classroom Practice

- The facilitator asks: "What are the implications of this work for teaching and assessment?"

- Based on the group's observations and interpretations, discuss any implications this work might have for teaching and assessment in the classroom. In particular, consider the following questions:

  - What steps could the teacher take next with this student?

  - What teaching strategies might be most effective?

  - What else would you like to see in the student work? What kinds of assignments or assessments could provide this information?

  - What does this conversation make you think about in terms of your own practice? About teaching and learning in general?

5. Reflecting on the ATLAS

- The presenter shares back what they learned about the student, the work, and what they're now thinking. The discussion then opens to the larger group to discuss what was learned about the student, about colleagues, and self.

6. Debriefing the Process

- How well did the process work—what went well and what could be improved? If the group has designated someone to observe the conversation, this person should report his or her observations.

Source: Copyright 2007 ATLAS Learning Communities. Used with Permission.

Conclusion

Both lesson study and analyzing student work are valuable forms of professional development for teachers and leaders. The data gleaned from these analyses enrich the knowledge base of an educator and situate them as action learners. Student observation, collecting narrative data, and a comparison of student thinking lead to quality professional development and training for teachers.

Lesson study is a strong model of professional development; however, school leaders need to recognize that "…lesson study is easy to learn but difficult to master" (Chokshi & Fernandez, 2004, p. 524). There has been significant progress in the use of lesson study as a professional development model. As the trend in the professional development continues to emphasize the use of job-embedded professional learning opportunities, lesson study offers a promising approach to advancing the learning and development of teachers.

School leaders must be knowledgeable of lesson study and act as participants and evaluators of the process, not the personnel who engage in this type of professional development (Liptak, 2002; Stepanek et al., 2007). The development and continued focus of the research lesson goals should be constantly monitored by administrators to assure that lesson study teams remain disciplined in their research. There may be opportunities for teachers to form research teams with teachers from other schools, or include subject area specialists from the district office or regional support office. Administrators should be open to developing and supporting such interactions and to providing the necessary resources to do so.

Suggested Readings

Chokshi, S., & Fernandez, C. (2004). Challenges to importing lesson study: Concerns, misconceptions, and nuances. *Phi Delta Kappan, 85*(7), 520–525.

Lewis, C., Perry, R., & Hurd, J. (2004). A deeper look at lesson study. *Educational Leadership, 61*(5), 18–22.

Stepanek, J., Appel, G., Leong, M., Mangan, M. T., & Mitchell, M. (2007). *Leading lesson study: A practical guide for teachers and facilitators.* Thousand Oaks, CA: Corwin Press.

Wiburg, K., & Brown, S. (2006). *Lesson study communities: Increasing achievement with diverse students.* Thousand Oaks, CA: Corwin Press.

Lesson Study

11

Learning Circles

In This Chapter...

- ◆ What's in the Learning Circle?
- ◆ Quality Learning Circles
- ◆ Online Learning Circles
- ◆ Getting Started with Learning Circles
- ◆ Challenges and Concerns for School Leaders

Learning circles have been in existence since humans learned to communicate and recognized the need to solve problems collaboratively. In early native cultures, these meetings were called "wisdom circles" (Riel, 1997). Learning circles can also be described as Study Circles. Bjerkaker (2003) states: "As a Nordic traditional method for liberal adult education, the *Study Circle* has been active for more than 100 years. From the beginning the Study Circle has been seen as a democratic and emancipatory method and arena for learning, particularly among adults" (p. 1). From the business world, Siegel, Kappaz, and Dowell (2006) offer: "A Learning Circle is a focused discussion group that harnesses the wisdom and experience of professional peers" (p. 2). In the education profession, learning circles can be described as "...small communities of learners among teachers and others who come together intentionally for the purpose of supporting each other in the process of learning" (Collay, Dunlap, Enloe, & Gagnon, 1998, p. 2).

Learning circles can consist of any group of teachers that meet on a continual basis over a long or short period of time. A learning circle is not simply a group that gets together to discuss a single issue in a single session, but rather a professional development model that can entail components of action research, critical friends, or any other collaborative professional development model. Teachers who regularly meet as a team and discuss instructional issues with the goals of improving student learning teacher performance may already be participating in a learning circle model (Collay et al., 1998; Funk, 2002).

According to Riel (1997):

Learning circles, generically described, are small diverse, democratic groups of people (generally 6–12) who meet regularly over a specified period of time to focus their different perspectives into a common understanding of an issue or problem. The discussion [*sic*] take place in an atmosphere of mutual trust and understanding. The goal is deeper understanding by the participants and their efforts are often directed towards the construction of a final product or recommendation for a course of action. Online Learning Circles are groups of 6–12 classrooms that work together as a team using their diversity as a resource to understand a topic or problem they share. (p. 1)

What's in the Learning Circle?

Learning circles as a professional development model create smaller groups, enabling a more efficient and effective means of establishing learning communities (Collay et al., 1998; Funk, 2002). Learning circles might exist as subject area departments in high schools, interdisciplinary teams in middle schools, or grade-level groupings in elementary schools. That any of these groups exist as a result of the structuring of most schools, however, does not necessarily mean that they can be identified as learning circles. Learning circles have a purpose, a shared commitment to and interest in a specific topic, and a climate of democracy and trust. Any group of educators who share a common professional problem, concern, or interest can form a learning circle.

Learning circles require six conditions to be met (Collay et al., 1998):

- Building community
- Constructing knowledge
- Supporting learners
- Documenting reflection
- Assessing expectations
- Changing cultures (p. 8)

Schools seeking to develop a culture of professional learning communities find that these six conditions are more obtainable when created through smaller groups of individuals. The ability to focus on problems and issues of personal interest allows smaller groups to create and sustain collegial relationships more efficiently and powerfully than a large faculty attempting to become a learning community all at once as a single unit.

Quality Learning Circles

Adapted from the Total Quality Management professional development practice of Learning Circles in the business world, the Quality Learning Circle has been implemented as a model of professional development in education, particularly in New Zealand (Lovett & Gilmore, 2003). Quality Learning Circles are often designed for teachers sharing a common interest or concern who are willing to meet outside of their own school building with teachers from other buildings. Lovett and Gilmore studied the implementation of Quality Learning Circles and documented the positive effects of such circles on the teachers involved.

Stewart and Prebble (as cited in Lovett & Gilmore, 2003) identified the following features of Quality Learning Circles:

♦ Selection of a theme for exploration.

♦ Discussion and storytelling within the group about experiences related to the theme.

♦ Observation in classrooms to provide an authentic context for sharing perspectives on the learning and where the observer in the classroom is the learner.

♦ Discussion of these observations in pairs and then with the whole group.

♦ The sharing of examples of practice with the group. (p. 195)

Lovett and Gilmore identify four themes that are characteristic of Quality Learning Circles. These are described as structuring meetings; sharing experiences; visiting one another's schools and classrooms; and dissemination of knowledge gained.

Online Learning Circles

The emergence of technology as a support for professional development is at the forefront of schools and according to Dede, et al. (2006):

The need for professional development that can be customized to fit teachers' busy schedules, that draws on powerful resources often not available locally, and that can provide real-time, ongoing, work-embedded support has prompted the creation of online teacher professional development.... (p. 13)

A type of learning circle has evolved with the use of the Internet for online exchanges and discussions. The online learning circle has been found to be effective in the learning experiences of both teachers and students (Riel et al., 2002; Riel, 1997). Riel et al. identify six phases that constitute the structure of the online learning circle (Figure 11.1):

♦ *Phase I:* Getting Ready involves finding the partners, selecting and setting up the electronic structure, and setting the stage for interaction.

- *Phase II:* Opening the Circle focuses on group formation and cohesion.

- *Phase III:* Planning the Project requires each participant to describe the project or task they sponsor for the group.

- *Phase IV:* Exchanging Work on projects constitutes the major part of the process.

- *Phase V:* Organizing the Publication is time for organizing results of work on projects.

- *Phase VI:* Closing the Circle provides time for final reflections on the process. (Project Summary section, p. 3)

Figure 11.1. The Six Phases of the Online Learning Circle Identified by Riel et al. (2002)

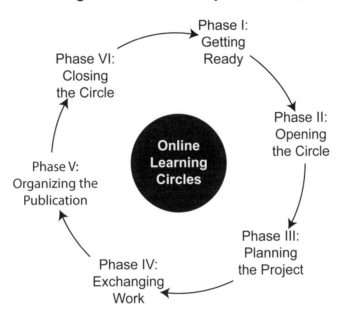

Getting Started with Learning Circles

When establishing learning circles, the first task involves identifying participants and setting up clearly defined roles with which teachers can become comfortable and familiar. These roles should help participants develop an understanding of how they should interact with each other, share their experiences, and contribute to overall learning experience. Through the creation of clear guidelines and expectations, participants will have the opportunity to work more cohesively and efficiently toward a common goal or purpose. The objective is for each member of the circle to discuss areas of concern as well as individual strengths and weaknesses so as to develop a direction in which all participants can move together and from which each member can derive benefit.

After participants are selected and initial goals are established, members of the learning circle will begin sharing and exchanging knowledge, advice, support, and suggestions as to how other members' might improve their practice and pedagogy. With classroom observations serving as the foundation for discussion, circle participants will examine practical and contextual examples of teaching and learning. Additionally, these observations and discussions will aid in the creation and sustainability of healthy collegial relationships that promote professional growth. As relationships strengthen, members of the learning circle progress toward the realization of its previously established goal.

Challenges and Concerns for School Leaders

Learning circles can be powerful and democratic ways to develop job-embedded professional development; however, they require school leaders to be aware of the differences between true communities of learners and simply groups of teachers getting together to talk about the issue of the day. Learning circles require teachers to think independently and to identify professional problems or topics that are of interest to them. School leaders need to be present to help ensure that learning circles are dealing with issues that are meaningfully related to the enhancement of teaching and learning. Teachers traditionally have not been required to generate topics for professional development. In describing the initial structuring of a Quality Learning Circle, Lovett and Gilmore (2003) report: "The group initially struggled with its chosen focus because its members were accustomed to linear change models in which professional development included a definite sequence and content to be followed" (p. 198).

Research dealing with online learning circles has determined that participants tended to withdraw from the circle as the final three stages occurred (Riel et al., 2002). Riel et al. also found that defining the project proved to be difficult because there can be disagreement about common interests. For obvious reasons, online circles can make establishing and nurturing collegial relationships more difficult.

Conclusion

The learning circle is a model of professional development that requires a group of teachers to work together as they identify a common area of concern and establish a strategy with which to address the concern. The collaborative nature of learning circles encourages the development of strong collegial relationships, and promotes reflection amongst teachers as they make strides toward the achievement of a common goal. Because learning circles rely heavily on discussion and reflection amongst peers, the establishment of trusting professional relationships is of the utmost importance. Research suggests that such relationships are more easily established when learning circles are smaller rather than larger.

Additionally, supervisors can help ensure the success of learning circles by encouraging teachers to select adequate and relevant issues that will provide a valuable springboard for ideas, discussion, and reflection. Supervisors should also emphasize the monitoring of learning circles so as to make sure the identified goals are being pursued with appropriate rigor and dedication.

Suggested Readings

Bishop, M., & Gibson, G. (1999). *Learning circles: Do-it-yourself. A guide to preparing your own learning circle material*. (ERIC Document Reproduction Service No. ED480824).

Collay, M., Dunlap, D., Enloe, W., & Gagnon, G. W. (1998). *Learning circles: Creating conditions for professional development*. Thousand Oaks, CA: Corwin Press.

Dede, C. (Ed.). (2006). *Online professional development for teachers: Emerging models and methods*. Cambridge, MA: Harvard Education Press.

Hannan, M., & Kicenko, J. (2002, January 1). *Facilitator's guide to run a learning circle*. Yarracille, AU: Panther Publishing and Printing. (ERIC Document Reproduction Service No. ED475005).

Polirstok, S., Delisle, R., Deveaux, F., Gottlieb, B., Qian, G., Thompson, P., & Zuss, M. (2002, February 1). *The learning circle model: A vehicle for exploring critical perspectives in teacher education*. Paper presented at the annual meeting of the American Association of Colleges for Teacher Education. (ERIC Document Reproduction Service No. ED463255).

Learning Circles

12

Action Research

In This Chapter...

♦ Why Engage in Action Research?

♦ The Action Research Model

♦ Getting Started with Action Research as a Form of Professional Development

♦ The Importance of Reflection in the Action Research Process

♦ Connecting Action Research to Teaching: The Job-Embedded Nature of Action Research

♦ Leadership Needed to Support Action Research

Action research shows promise as a professional development model in that teachers and other members of the learning community are the researchers. As action researchers, teachers can study their practices with data guiding informed discussions as well as future decisions they make regarding their practices. Action research promotes dialogue, reflection, and inquiry. McNiff and Whitehead (2005) suggest that "improving practice and generating new theory" about teaching and learning should be the two broad reasons why teachers engage in action research (p. 2). According to the North Central Regional Educational Laboratory (n.d.),

> Action research is inquiry or research in the context of focused efforts to improve the quality of an organization and its performance. It typically is designed and conducted by practitioners who analyze the data to improve their own practice. Action research can be done by individuals or by teams of colleagues. The team approach is called *collaborative inquiry*. (p. 1, emphasis in the original)

Action research can transform the ways teachers work and learn with and from one another while improving their classroom practices. The results of action research can inform school systems and can aid in formulating and reformulating goals related to school improvement.

Action research as a form of job-embedded learning (Chapter 6), can be a strategy used by lesson study groups (Chapter 10), and its results can inform the ongoing work of critical friends (Chapter 9), teacher study groups, whole-faculty study groups, and book study groups (Chapter 8).

Why Engage in Action Research?

Action research can be a powerful way to engage in learning more about teaching and because "learning is a messy, mumbled, nonlinear, recursive, and sometimes unpredictable process; action research (undertaken by teachers) is research that occurs in conjunction with, and often concurrently with, day-to-day classroom or school activities" (Avery, 1990, p. 43). Dewey's (1929) beliefs about the importance of self-reflection and analysis about teaching and the pivotal role of the teacher provide the rationale for action research, "each day of teaching ought to enable a teacher to revise and better in some respects the objectives aimed at in previous work" (p. 75).

Teachers make quick decisions every day, both in and out of the classroom environment—teaching a lesson, interacting with students, and handling situations that pop up. Such split-second decisions allow little time to stop, analyze, and reflect on the data underlying them. Good decisions are based on data. Better decisions are made after collecting and examining data, reflecting on alternatives, and getting feedback from another person. Fairbanks and LaGrone (2006) state:

> Perhaps more importantly, though, action research engages teachers in reading and writing about their practice, enlarging their professional knowledge through text-based study, and it generally engages them in collaboration with their colleagues, garnering feedback and support for their work as well as access to additional perspectives about observations or interpretations. (p. 8)

Action research engages teachers in their own intentional actions of collecting, analyzing, reflecting, and then modifying practice. Action research is about change. The process of conducting action research propels change, and the results of action research can support teachers in making informed decisions about changes in practices. In fact, Schmuck (2006) asserts, "Change is where action research leads" (p. 27). Action research is about improvement (Heydenrych, 2001; Howden, 1998). According to Howden (1998), who reports the work of Grundy and Kemmis (1981), action research can focus teachers toward (a) the improvement of a practice, (b) the improvement (or professional development) of the understanding of the practice by its practitioners, and (c) the improvement of the situation in which the practice takes place (p. 7).

What Is Action Research?

McNiff and Whitehead (2005) define action research as a "common sense approach to professional development" (p. 1) so that teachers can ask specific questions to extend their thinking about teaching and learning. Macintyre

(2000) focuses her discussion of action research on the immersion of teachers and others in the processes and purposes of action research. Macintyre states:

> Action research…is a recognized and approved way of carrying out self-appraisal through evaluating any or all of the activities which make up classroom practice. It is a disciplined method of investigation which gives credibility to the claims that are made. It is a research method that "fits" the parameters and ethos of the classroom for it allows teachers and pupils to be active change agents, not simply participant observers. (p. xii)

Sullivan and Glanz (2005) add "[a]ction research is not a narrow, limited practice but can use a range of methodologies, simple and complex, to better understand one's work and even solve specific problems" (p. 155). Action research is based on many assumptions and premises that are highlighted in Figure 12.1. These assumptions and premises give value to action research and promote professional learning that is tailored to individuals.

Figure 12.1. Assumptions and Premises: The Value of Action Research as a Model of Professional Development

Koshy (2005, p. 10)	Madison Metropolitan School District, n.d., p. 1
◆ involves researching your own practice—it is not about people out there; ◆ is emergent; ◆ is participatory; ◆ constructs theory from practice; ◆ is situation-based; ◆ can be useful in real problem solving; ◆ deals with individuals or groups with a common purpose of improving practice; ◆ is about improvement; ◆ involves analysis, reflection, and evaluation; ◆ facilitates change through enquiry.	◆ teachers and principals work best on problems they have identified for themselves; ◆ teachers and principals become more effective when encouraged to examine and assess their own work and then consider ways of working differently; ◆ teachers and principals help each other by working collaboratively; ◆ working with colleagues helps teachers and principals in their professional development.

What Do Teachers as Action Researchers Do?

Essentially, learning, acting, and doing are all part of the action research process. The Fairfax County Schools System (2007) outlines that educators who engage in action research:

- Ask questions and examine their underlying assumptions about teaching and learning.

- Develop research questions based on their own curiosity about teaching and learning in their classrooms.

- Learn to observe, reflect, and analyze their teaching and student learning.

- Discuss with colleagues relationships among theory, practice, and research.

- Systematically collect data and research methodology with fellow teacher researchers.

- Analyze and interpret their data and research methodology with the support of colleagues and fellow teacher researchers.

- Share their findings with students, colleagues, and members of the educational community.

- Write about their research.

Action research is a powerful approach to professional learning. Action research derives its power because action research is job-embedded learning.

What Action Research Is Not

Kemmis and McTaggart (1988) offer that action research is not

1. the usual things teachers do when they think about their teaching.

2. just problem solving [but rather] involves problem posing.

3. research on other people. Action Research is research by particular people on their own work to help them improve what they do, including how they work with and for others. Action Research does not treat people as objects. It treats people as autonomous, responsible agents who participate actively in making their own histories by knowing what they are doing.

4. the scientific method applied to teaching. Action Research is not just about hypothesis testing or about using data to come to conclusions. It is concerned with changing situations, not just interpreting them. It takes the researcher into view. (p. 21)

The Action Research Model

Basic Processes and Steps of Action Research

Although some variations exist, there are common processes, components, and models of action research. No one aspect of these processes or components are championed in that what makes sense is dependent on the contextual factors of the school and the personnel who engage in the action research. The maxim should be for teachers to examine these basic premises and to begin the work of action research. Figure 12.2 illustrates the processes that all models of action research have in common.

Figure 12.2. The Processes of Action Research

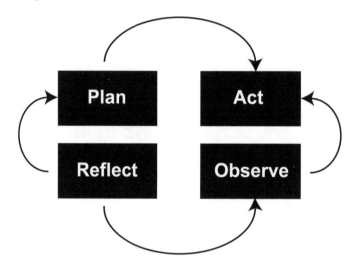

Source: Dick, 1999.

Steps of Action Research

There are many steps involved in action research (Glanz, 1999, 2003, 2005; Sagor, 2000). The work and activity involved in each one of these steps situates the teacher as actor in numerous activities highlighted in Figure 12.3.

Figure 12.3. **Overall Steps to Action Research**

Steps	Framing Questions	Questions to Extend Thinking Throughout the Action Research Process
Based on: Glanz, 1999, 2003, 2005; Sullivan & Glanz, 2005	Based on: Sagor, 2000	Based on: McNiff & Whitehead, 2005, p. 31; adapted from the St. Louis Action Research Evaluation Committee, Metropolitan School District, n.d., as cited by the Madison Metropolitan School District
♦ Defining the focus	♦ What do I want to accomplish?	♦ What is my concern (about what I know?) ♦ What do I need to learn? ♦ What kind of evidence do I produce to show my concern (about what I know and what I need to learn)? ♦ What can I do about it (about what I know)? ♦ How do I critique what I know? ♦ How am I going to learn more? ♦ What will I do about it?
♦ Developing research instruments	♦ What do I believe is the approach with the greatest potential for achieving my goal(s)?)	♦ What kind of evidence do I produce to show the potential influence of my learning?

Steps	Framing Questions	Questions to Extend Thinking Throughout the Action Research Process
◆ Collecting the data	◆ What data will I need to collect to understand the efficacy and workings of my theory of action?	◆ What types of data should you try to collect to answer your question? ◆ How will you ensure that you have multiple perspectives? ◆ What resources exist and what information from others might be useful in helping you to frame your question, decide on types of data to collect, or to help you in interpreting your findings?
◆ Organizing and analyzing the data	◆ What do I do with the data once I have collected the data? ◆ Who should be involved in analyzing the data?	◆ What can you learn from the data? What patterns, insights, and new understandings can you find? ◆ What meaning do these patterns, insights, and new understandings have for your practice? for your students?
◆ Creating action plans	◆ Based on this data, how should I adjust my future actions?	◆ What will you do differently in your classroom as a result of this study? ◆ What might you recommend to others?
◆ Reporting results	◆ How should I make public the results of my inquiry?	◆ How will you write about what you have learned so that the findings will be useful to you and to others?

Glanz (2003, 2005) and Sullivan and Glanz (2005) explain the cyclical nature of action research and underscore that action research is an ongoing process of reflection that involves four basic and cyclical steps as illustrated in Figure 12.4 (page 253).

Figure 12.4. Action Research Steps

Action Research Steps	Processes Involved in the Steps
Step 1: Selecting a focus	a. Know what you want to investigate b. Develop some initial questions c. Establish a plan to answer or better understand these questions

Step 2: Collecting data	a. Primary
	  i. Questionnaires
	  ii. Observations
	  iii. Interviews
	  iv. Tests
	  v. Focus groups
	b. Secondary
	  i. School profile sheets
	  ii. Multimedia
	  iii. Portfolios
	  iv. Records
	  v. Other

Step 3: Analyzing and interpreting data	a. examining data b. reflecting with colleagues about the data and the meanings of the data
Step 4: Taking action	a. making decisions and taking action (changes and/ or modifications in practice) based on the results of data and the meanings of the data

Source: Adapted from Glanz (2003) and Sullivan and Glanz (2005).

In the 2003 edition of his text, *Action Research: An Educational Leader's Guide to School Improvement*, Glanz proposed a fifth step in the action research model—reflection—and this step would permeate across all steps in the action research model.

The Action of Action Research

Figure 12.5 illustrates what the steps of action research could look like in practice for a teacher, Tiffany, who is interested in how she uses manipulatives related to the sequences of her lectures, the use of guided and independent practice and the impact of manipulatives related to increased student learning and engagement. You will see that Tiffany is engaged in data collection; she is also observing other teachers and asking that others come to her classroom to observe her teach with manipulatives.

Figure 12.5. **Action Research in a Context**

Focus	Examine sequence of lecture, guided practice, and independent practice	Time frame of 3 months	Process
Data collection	1. Examine lesson plans.	Ongoing	Once every other week—both formal and informal observations.
	2. John observes Tiffany as she teaches lessons that include guided practice and independent practice.	2 months	Postobservation conferences. John tracks instructional activities and the uses of manipulatives.
	3. Teacher-generated worksheets and guides.	3 months	Match skills with activities—levels of application in both guided and independent practices.
Analyzing and interpreting data	Observation notes, worksheets, student work, postobservation notes, lesson plans, student scores on quizzes, performance-based assessments, etc.	Ongoing	Comparison of patterns over time. Tiffany examines and reexamines the intents of her lessons against the data from classroom observations.
Taking action	Tiffany discovers that she uses manipulatives in most of her instruction but that during guided and independent practice, students are required to give concrete answers.	Ongoing	Modify activities so that application of knowledge matches instruction. Revisit the problem of practice and the focus—refocusing.

Getting Started with Action Research as a Form of Professional Development

Sometimes getting started with action research can be complicated. Teachers might not have familiarity with the processes, steps, and models of action research. With professional development dollars dwindling in schools, leaders will need to provide the resources for teachers to become familiar with action research. In addition, more resources such as release time will be needed. A first step is to work with a group of teachers who want to explore some aspect of the curriculum and the instructional practices that help deliver that curriculum. There is safety in numbers, and teachers might feel more at ease working with a group that they have familiarity and an issue of practice related to student achievement.

Action research is a powerful form of professional development, and the design of action research has several benefits according to Watson and Stevenson (1989), who indicate that as a model, action research supports

♦ the opportunity to collaborate with one another;

♦ the development of a forum where interested members of the community can learn together;

♦ learning opportunities that do not attempt to influence teachers toward a predetermined point of view;

♦ the opportunity to give emotional support to one another;

♦ data-driven decision making; and

♦ more readily accepted change. (pp. 121–122)

With these potential benefits, it is common sense that action research should be championed as a form of professional development. The Madison Metropolitan School District (2004) has developed a protocol entitled *Starting Points*. This protocol (Figure 12.6) is built on the foundations that support action research.

Figure 12.6. Starting Points

1. Ask individuals to complete the "Starting Points" questions (see below, number 5). Tell them to think broadly about many areas for possible questions.

2. Go around the group one at a time and list on a flipchart all of the different areas that surface from this handout.

3. Ask each person to take one of the areas from the flipchart (could be an idea of theirs or someone else's) and practice writing a question in that area.

4. Go around the group, and one at a time, ask each person to read his or her question very slowly twice. The group should listen to the questions. Absolutely no comments are made after each question is read.

5. Ask the group to generate characteristics, qualities, and guidelines for what makes a good action research question.

   1. I would like to improve...

   2. I am perplexed by...

   3. Some people are unhappy about...

   4. I'm really curious about...

   5. I want to learn more about...

   6. An idea I would like to try out in my class is...

   7. Something I think would really make a difference is...

   8. Some I would like to do to change is...

   9. Right now, some areas I'm particularly interested in are...

   Source: Madison Metropolitan School District, 2004.

A lockstep approach to action research discourages the spontaneity to experiment with data as they emerge. Throughout the dialogue with peer or supervisor, the analysis of data, and the modification or creation of strategies, the teacher as action researcher needs the latitude to recast practices in light of new discoveries.

Data

In most of its forms, action research involves participation by others such as peer coaches and mentors; however, action research may be a solo venture. Action research can explore both qualitative and quantitative data. Data from multiple sources enrich the opportunities for interpretation and analysis. Figure 12.7 provides sample sources of data to examine. The only criterion for a useful data source should be whether it makes sense to include the information.

Figure 12.7. Possible Data Sources for Action Research

Possible data sources to consult include but are not limited to

♦ classroom observation notes (peer coach, supervisor);

♦ test results from both standardized and nonstandardized instruments;

♦ student-generated artifacts such as a final essay, project, and aggregated responses to a particular test question or a subset of questions;

♦ lesson plans, including objectives;

♦ portfolios (student, teacher) and artifacts within the portfolios;

♦ videotape and/or audiotape of teaching and/or student performance;

- journal entries;

- grade distributions on a test or quiz;

- patterns in types of questions asked during a lecture or on a test or quiz; and.

- interviews with students, team members, parents, others.

Source: Zepeda (1999, 2007b)

Action research without followup is counterproductive. Followup provides opportunities for teachers to reflect on their observations, analyze multiple sources of data, revisit practices, and plan changes based on their discoveries. Perhaps the quintessential strategy of action research is reflection—examining practices that are real.

The Importance of Reflection in the Action Research Process

Throughout the processes of action research, teachers flex their intellectual muscles. Fairbanks and LaGrone (2006) describe a "reflective spiral" that occurs throughout the action research process (p. 8). Reflection is one of the key skills of action research. Reflection encourages teachers to

- *return to experience*—by recalling or detailing salient events.

- *attend to or connect with feelings*—this has two aspects: using helpful feelings and removing or containing obstructive ones.

- *evaluate experience*—this involves reexamining experiences in the light of new knowledge. It also consists of integrating new knowledge into practice. (Jeffs & Smith, 1999)

Reflection can be private or public, or a combination of the two. Stevenson (1995) asserts that reflection occurs "*privately* as an individual action or internal dialogue with oneself or *publicly* in dialogue and reflection with others" (p. 201, emphasis in the original). When teachers write and read their own narrative about an experience in the practice of teaching, the level of understanding and comprehension about what took place increases (Fairbanks & LaGrone, 2006; Freese, 2006). McNiff and Whitehead (2005) describe reflection as "both thinking about what you are doing and also becoming critical of what you are doing" (p. 70). This implies self-evaluation through reflection and a monitoring of practice. Teachers who reflect effectively gain new perspectives on the dilemmas and contradictions inherent in classroom practices, improve judgment, and increase their capacity to take purposeful action based on the knowledge they discover.

Connecting Action Research to Teaching: The Job-Embedded Nature of Action Research

As job-embedded learning, action research allows teachers to

- examine real-life practices and experiences in the very place in which these practices and experiences occur—the classroom;

- use a systematic approach (which may become a cyclical and continuous vehicle for ongoing action research);

- develop deeper meanings about their practices with the assistance of a colleague;

- experiment with their practices based upon extended reflection and analysis of data; and,

- implement change. (Zepeda, 1999)

Action research is an approach to professional development in which teachers systematically study and reflect on their work and then make informed changes in their practices.

Leadership Needed to Support Action Research

Supervisors can help teachers become action researchers by helping develop different stages of implementation. Glanz (2005) offers the following approach:

- Identify the importance of the research and suggest ways the project will enhance student achievement.

- Identify the specific materials (primary and secondary sources) the teacher will research.

- Develop a schedule.

- Limit the project's scope. Such delimitation will promote thorough, rather than superficial, research.

- Study and analyze all materials for the project.

- Develop and implement a unit or program based on the project. (p. 25)

Supervisors can be effective in their supporting of successful action research by collaborating with teachers on the various steps of this approach. Many teachers may be timid or lack confidence in initially conducting their own action research. As this is often the case, it should be remembered by all involved that action research is a tool for professional development, not a measuring tool for teacher evaluation. It would be helpful to teachers for supervisors to assist them in clarifying the purpose of their action research by posing four sets of questions:

1. What is the purpose of the study or action research project?

2. What do I want to accomplish, or what are my objectives?

3. Why is such a study important? Why do I want to spend my time doing this?

4. How will information gleaned from my study help to improve the overall instructional program? (Glanz, 2003, p. 54)

These questions can help in guiding an initial reflection on one's teaching before a decision is made as to what the action research project will actually be. This type of reflection will provide the focus necessary to engage in action research. The role of the leader in this case would be to facilitate the reflection and to help guide the teacher to an adequate determination of a manageable action research project.

Conclusion

Action research is a valuable form of professional development for several reasons. It engages teachers in the improvement of their own practice, it is contextualized so as to suit the needs of individuals, it necessitates reflection about how and why decisions are made, and it promotes the development of collegial relationships. Additionally, because action research is job-embedded, it provides enough flexibility for teachers to investigate and analyze issues as they relate to the specific needs of unique student populations.

Principals can aid teachers in a variety of ways as they begin to improve practice through action research. A key component of effective implementation of this professional development model is the establishment of strong collegial relationships. Principals can aid in the development of such relationships by creating opportunities for discussion, data collection, and reflection. Principals can also ensure that teachers have the resources they **need** to appropriately engage in each stage of the action research process. By allotting adequate time and money to promote the professional development of their staff, principals create an optimal opportunity for improving teacher practice.

Suggested Readings

Calhoun, E. F. (1994). *How to use action research in the self-renewing school.* Alexandria, VA: Association for Supervision and Curriculum Development.

Glanz, J. (2003). *Action research: An educational leader's guide to school improvement* (2nd ed.). Norwood, MA: Christopher-Gordon Publishers.

Glanz, J. (2005). Action research as instructional supervision: Suggestions for principals. *NASSP Bulletin, 89*(643), 17–27. doi: 10.1177/019263650508964303

McNiff, J., & Whitehead, J. (2005). *Action research for teachers: A practical guide*. London: David Fulton Publishers.

Sagor, R. (2005). *The action research guidebook: A four-step process for educators and school teams*. Thousand Oaks, CA: Corwin Press.

Sullivan, S., & Glanz, J. (2005). *Supervision that improves teaching: Strategies and techniques* (2nd ed.). Thousand Oaks, CA: Corwin Press.

Portfolios

In education, the portfolio as a form of student assessment has had a rich history; the use of the portfolio for and by adults has emerged as a viable way for adults to chronicle more holistically their growth and development (St. Maurice & Shaw, 2004; Tucker, Stronge, & Gareis, 2002). Hartnell-Young and Morriss (1999) pointed to the value and benefit of the portfolio as a form of enhancing professional development:

> Many people discover that one of the most important and long-lasting outcomes of producing a portfolio is the self-esteem that comes from recording and reflecting on achievements and career success. Experienced teachers and administrators are finding that the benefits of developing a portfolio include the opportunity for professional renewal through mapping new goals and planning for future growth. (pp. 9–10)

In an era of high-stakes accountability, teacher performance is based almost exclusively on student performance on such formalized and quantifiable measures as standardized test results. The accountability era moves forward, and school systems may run the risk of falling into the trap of losing sight of what teachers do on a daily basis related to the gains in learning for both students and teachers. It is the daily work of teachers that cannot always be measured through formal assessments. Perhaps, the portfolio is a way to examine the elusive—what teachers learn from their work. Shulman (1988) believes that portfolios

[a]re messy to construct, cumbersome to store, difficult to score, and vulnerable to misinterpretation. But in ways that no other assessment method can, portfolios prove a connection to the contexts and personal histories that characterize real teaching and make it possible to document the unfolding of both teaching and learning over time. (p. 36)

Historical Context of Portfolios

Portfolios have been used in preservice education programs to chronicle growth through coursework and clinical experiences before entering teaching. The portfolio has been used as a means to evaluate teacher performance (summative evaluation) and as part of the application process for National Board certification (Tucker et al., 2002). Moreover, the portfolio is being used in some districts as part of the job application process. Many universities and colleges, accredited by the National Council for Accreditation of Teacher Education (NCATE), require students seeking both initial and ongoing certification to develop a professional portfolio. The portfolio as a tool to chronicle teacher growth and development across the career span has emerged as a practice at a much slower rate (St. Maurice & Shaw, 2004).

The Intents of the Portfolio

The intents of the portfolio are to chronicle growth and development, regardless of its use (e.g., preservice, part of an evaluation system, extension of professional development), and to capture learning through artifacts that are representative of practice. The intents of using the portfolio to extend classroom supervision, peer coaching, lesson study, and action research, for example, are grounded in the belief that people engage in more meaningful learning when they learn in the company of others and when they can concretely see the results of modifying practice. The portfolio supports the ongoing study of the teaching process by the individual teacher, alone or with collegial or supervisory support and assistance.

The Processes of Portfolio Development

There are numerous processes involved in developing a portfolio, and each process requires the application of skills. Portfolio development includes data collection (artifacts to include), analysis (the meaning of the artifacts), and then reflection on the meanings in practice that the artifacts symbolize. Danielson and Abrutyn (1997) offer a five-stage portfolio development process:

- ◆ *Collection*—save artifacts that represent the day-to-day results of teaching and learning.

- *Selection*—review and evaluate the artifacts saved, and identify those that demonstrate achievement of specific standards or goals.

- *Reflection*—reflect on the significance of the artifacts chosen for the portfolio in relationship to specific learning goals.

- *Projection (or Direction)*—compare the reflections to the standards/goals and performance indicators, and set learning goals for the future.

- *Presentation*—share the portfolio with peers and receive feedback.

The processes of portfolio development can be linked to supervision, professional development, and evaluation. All of these processes embrace as best practice—reflection, feedback, and goal setting.

Linkages of the Portfolio to Professional Development

The portfolio as a tool to chronicle professional growth is gaining a foothold as a more authentic way for teachers to construct and to reflect about their impact on student learning while simultaneously assessing their own performance. Constructing a portfolio is an interactive process, and under the best of circumstances, either a peer (coach, mentor) or a supervisor provides feedback, encouragement, and data. Feedback is needed to help the teacher extend his thinking about not only the artifacts, but also, the meaning attached in the process of including artifacts in the portfolio.

What Is a Portfolio?

Campbell, Cignetti, Melenyzer, Nettles, and Wyman (1997) assert:

A portfolio is not merely a file of course projects and assignments, nor is it a scrapbook of teaching memorabilia. A portfolio is an organized, goal-driven documentation of your professional growth and achieved competence in the complex act called teaching. (p. 3)

Regardless of whether a teacher is first-year or veteran, a portfolio is a work in progress that allows teachers to chronicle (a) teaching practices, including changes made over time; (b) attaining of long- and short-term goals; and (c) the building of knowledge through constructing artifacts.

Portfolio Construction Is an Ongoing Process

Doolittle (1994) believes that "a teacher portfolio is a document created by the teacher that reveals, relates, and describes the teacher's duties, expertise, and growth in teaching" (p. 1). The portfolio provides the opportunity for teachers to collect artifacts over an extended time period—an entire school year, even from year-to-year—and this is the strength of the portfolio.

The ongoing nature of the process of developing a portfolio makes it a natural way to extend peer coaching and the work of lesson study groups, critical friends groups, action research teams, and mentoring activities.

Portfolio Development Is Dynamic

Wolf (1991) indicates that a portfolio "represents an attitude that assessment is dynamic, and that the richest portrayals of teacher…performances are based upon multiple sources of evidence collected over time in authentic settings" (p. 129). The assessment of teaching is an ongoing process, and this assessment will only hold meaning for teachers if they are active in the processes of

- developing goals;
- selecting artifacts that offer rich portrayals of teaching;
- receiving feedback on the artifacts as they relate to "live" teaching;
- reflecting on the impact of the artifacts through data collected in classroom observations; and,
- chronicling changes in practice based on accumulating artifacts over time. (Zepeda, 2000, 2002, 2007a, 2007b)

Meanings are derived from the processes of collecting, examining, and reflecting on the contents included in the portfolio. To this end, portfolio development is a process and a product. The product is the content of the portfolio. The process is the way in which artifacts are selected, what is done with the artifacts after they are included in the portfolio, *and* what changes in practice occur as a result of these efforts.

The Contents of a Portfolio

Although there are many opinions regarding what to include in a portfolio, only one rule should dictate the contents of the portfolio: the purposes or goals targeted by the teacher (Sanborn & Sanborn, 1994). Items to be included in a portfolio might consist of written documentation (e.g., targeted student work, lesson plans, test results, curricular outlines, formal evaluations, and letters from parents) and other items such as photographs, diagrams, and audio- and videotapes. A caution on including videotape footage of classroom events in the portfolio is warranted. Many school systems have policies that prohibit videotaping without prior consent from authorities and a signed release from the parent or guardian of any child who will be in the video clip. Before beginning a formal professional growth opportunity that requires either videotape or audiotape, the supervisor should consult policy and district-level personnel. Union agreements should also be considered.

Although Wolf (1990) initially had strong reservations about the use of videotaped evidence (e.g., classroom intrusion, time-consuming evaluation, access to equipment), he reported, "A review of the portfolios suggested that the videotape, along with the teachers' descriptions of the events on the tape, was one of the most important pieces of evidence" (p. 132). This finding makes sense as videotape analysis of classroom events has been established as a means for teachers to examine their teaching practices (Amodeo & Taylor, 2004b; Ponticell, 1995; Storygard & Fox, 1995, Zepeda, 2007b). In a case study, Storygard and Fox (1995) reported, "teachers can reflect on their practice through analysis of their videotapes. Reflecting with other teachers enriches this process" (p. 25). Just like any effective practice, "teachers developed a common language for analyzing videotapes...participants were encouraged to base their comments on what they saw on the tapes, and [to look] for evidence to support their observations" (p. 26).

In the realm of supervision and peer coaching, videotape analysis of classroom events is one way to promote autosupervision, a self-directed and self-guided way for teachers to examine their own instructional practices (Zepeda, Wood, & O'Hair, 1996). Videotape analysis does not have to occur in isolation because a peer or a supervisor can readily view a teaching episode and then guide the teacher in his analysis of the teaching segment (Amodeo & Taylor, 2004b; Richardson, 2007; Zepeda & Recesso, 2007). The use of video to promote self-analysis of teaching is elaborated on by Amodeo and Taylor (2004b) who explain

> the teacher can view the archived observation alone prior to a postobservation conference or during a postobservation conference. The ability to zoom in on a particular teaching episode will enrich the conversation about best instructional practice as it relates to improved student performance. (p. 5)

Richardson (2007) confirms, "For videos to be effective professional development tools, however, requires that educators look at and discuss the videos with colleagues" (p. 2).

Zepeda and Mayers (2000) indicate that the professional teaching portfolio might include a range of topical areas in which artifacts are selected:

1. *Personal* (e.g., statement of beliefs concerning teaching);

2. *Curricular* (e.g., sample lesson plans and tests);

3. *Classroom* (e.g., samples of student work);

4. *School as a learning community* (e.g., committee work, interdisciplinary lesson artifacts); and,

5. *Professional growth* (e.g., career goals, journals, videotapes). (p. 168)

Once parameters regarding the contents of the portfolio are agreed on, an organized approach needs to be developed for selecting the contents of the portfolio. Essentially, teachers need time to work on their portfolios, and a primary responsibility of the supervisor is to find time for teachers to work on their portfolios, consult with others, and reflect on the meaning of the portfolio related to its artifacts.

Parameters for Selecting the Contents of the Portfolio

The "so what" question needs to be asked and answered while selecting artifacts for the portfolio (Van Wagenen & Hibbard, 1998). Bird (1990) suggests that grouping portfolio artifacts should center on broadly defined clusters of teaching tasks (e.g., planning, preparation; teaching the class; student evaluation; and professional exchanges). To get at the "so what" question, Van Wagenen and Hibbard (1998) propose an interrelated and circular process situated in three questions, as illustrated in Figure 13.1.

Figure 13.1. **What, So What, and Now What?**

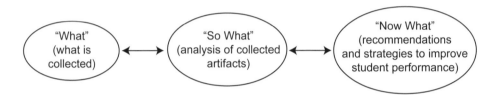

Krause (1996) suggests three processes: collection, selection, and reflection. Krause further suggests that if the process stopped with collection, the model would stagnate, but that if the portfolio contained "reflections exploring the meaning of evidence," the portfolio process could be "transformed into a powerful document representing a [more] self-aware learner" (p. 132).

Digital Portfolios

All one has to do is surf the web to see the number of digital (electronic) portfolios. The advent of technology available to most teachers includes IP-based conferencing equipment in addition to systemwide storage (web space) and storage devices such as CD-ROM. School sites can create protected spaces for teachers and staff to store electronic portfolios, create blogs, and use existing resources to create listservs.

If you have an interest in using technology to support the use of technology for teacher portfolios, consult with the system technology coordinator to ensure that the server has the space to store portfolios for the number of teachers in the building. A site visit by the technology coordinator will help that person see the big picture related to the needs of the building.

Basing their work on Lankes (1995), Weidmer (1998), and Zubizarreta (1994), Tucker et al. (2002) present in Figure 13.2 the advantages and disadvantages of digital portfolios.

Figure 13.2. Advantages and Disadvantages of Digital Portfolios

Advantages	Disadvantages
◆ Easy transfer of information among portfolio creators, colleagues, and reviewers	◆ Requires specific hardware (e.g., personal workstations, multimedia workstation, etc.)
◆ Storage and display of multiple data formats, including text, graphics, sound, pictures, and video	◆ Requires specific software (e.g., word processing, multimedia, etc.)
◆ Reduced paper and space needs	◆ Startup costs may be prohibitive
◆ Universal template can be created to provide structure and consistency among portfolios	◆ Requires technological training for portfolio creator and reviewers

Source: Tucker, P. D., Stronge, J. H., & Gareis, C. R. (2002). *Handbook on Teacher Portfolios for Evaluation and Professional Development* (p. 23). Larchmont, NY: Eye On Education. Used with permission.

Extending Peer Coaching and Instructional Supervision Through the Portfolio

Each cycle of the clinical supervision model and the peer coaching model has as its base line, the preobservation conference, the extended classroom observation, and the postobservation conference. It was the intent of the original clinical model for more than one complete cycle of supervision to occur throughout the year. By including portfolio development as part of the clinical model of supervision and peer coaching, learning can be extended.

Through overall goal setting, the teacher chooses an area to explore for the year, and under optimal conditions, all classroom observations are focused toward assisting the teacher to meet established goals. Artifact collection can become part of the data collection process used in the classroom observation. The analysis of artifacts can become part of the postobservation conference. The next section presents a model of portfolio supervision that also can be applied to peer coaching (Zepeda, 2002).

Portfolio development is both developmental and differentiated in nature. From a developmental approach, teachers begin at their current developmental level in the selection and reflective analysis of artifacts with the supervisor, peer coach, or mentor assuming either a direct or an indirect approach to working with teachers. This means that portfolio supervision can be either structured (direct) or more collaborative (indirect) between the teacher and supervisor (or colleague), or the process can be self-directed with the supervisor serving mainly as a facilitator. Career stages and principles of adult learning are addressed in Chapter 3, and the reader is encouraged to consult Chapter 3 before examining the model presented in the next section.

A Model of Portfolio Supervision—and by Extension, Peer Coaching

Based on the research of Zepeda (2002) in an extended two-year case study, a model of portfolio supervision evolved based on the practices of teachers in an elementary school. Again, this model can also be extended to peer coaching. Figure 13.3 illustrates the model and shows how portfolio development can become part of the clinical supervisory or peer-coaching process.

Figure 13.3. **Portfolio Supervision**

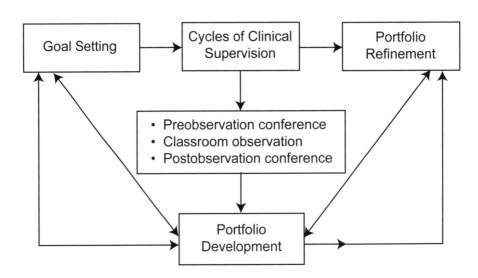

In this model, all activities—goal setting, the focus of the observation, data collection, and artifact collection, selection, and analysis—are embedded in the preobservation conference, the extended classroom observation, and the postobservation conference. This model assumes that teachers and supervisors and coaches are familiar with certain skills—the skills in guiding a teacher through portfolio development are parallel (perhaps even identical) to those skills needed to conduct meaningful classroom observations and pre- and postobservation conferences.

Essential Skills: Reflection, Goal Setting, and Decision Making

For portfolio development to be a complementary practice in the process of clinical supervision and/or peer coaching, several skills must be built into the process and include:

♦ *Reflection* about portfolio development and design;

♦ *Goal setting*; and,

♦ *Decision making* (the process of making decisions about what to include in the portfolio).

Figure 13.4 portrays the reciprocal nature of skill application when the portfolio is used as a complement to clinical supervision and peer coaching. Each of these skills works in tandem as teachers explore their practices while constructing knowledge from examining and reexamining the artifacts included in the portfolio.

Figure 13.4. Skills Inherent in Portfolio Supervision

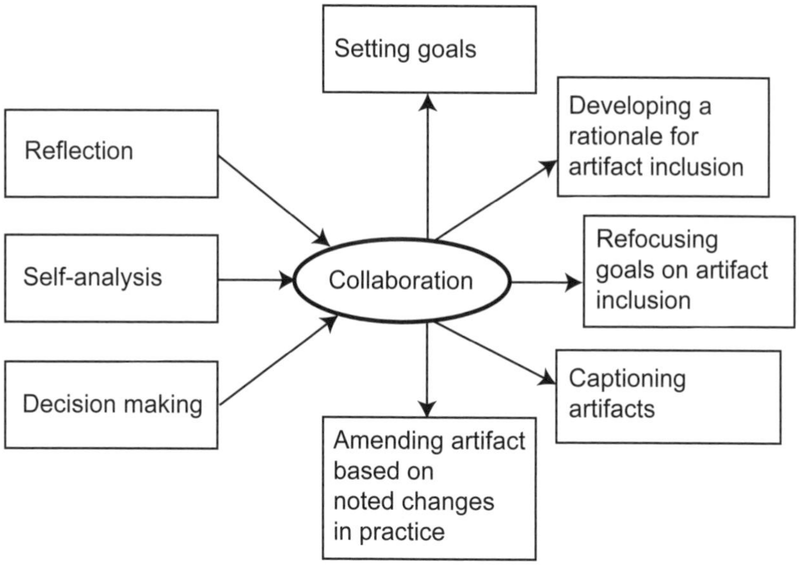

Reflection

Reflection is the primary skill involved in all of the portfolio models that have been reported in the literature, and the "power of a portfolio is found in its ability to become a tool for an individual to reflect on the real tasks" involved in teaching and learning (Murray, 1994, p. 14). Given the importance of reflection in the portfolio process, the Reflection Cycle in Figure 13.5 (page 270) illustrates the iterative and recursive nature in which people reflect following the processes inherent in the portfolio development process.

Figure 13.5. The Reflection Cycle

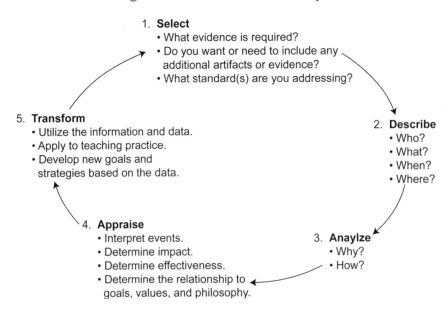

1. **Select**
   - What evidence is required?
   - Do you want or need to include any additional artifacts or evidence?
   - What standard(s) are you addressing?

2. **Describe**
   - Who?
   - What?
   - When?
   - Where?

3. **Anaylze**
   - Why?
   - How?

4. **Appraise**
   - Interpret events.
   - Determine impact.
   - Determine effectiveness.
   - Determine the relationship to goals, values, and philosophy.

5. **Transform**
   - Utilize the information and data.
   - Apply to teaching practice.
   - Develop new goals and strategies based on the data.

Source: Used with permission from the Public Schools of North Carolina, October 2, 2007. North Carolina Department of Public Instruction. Division of Communications & Information, NC Department of Public Instruction, 301 N. Wilmington St., Raleigh, NC 27601.

In their work with preservice teachers, Ward and McCotter (2004) identified four types of reflection: routine reflection, technical reflection, dialogic reflection, and critical reflection. Figure 13.6 shows the levels of reflection and what they might look like.

Figure 13.6. Levels of Reflection

Level of Reflection	Characterized By
Routine reflections	Contains very definitive statements that revealed either a lack of curiosity or a lack of attention to complexity.
Technical reflection	Can best be thought of as instrumental, in that the reflection is used as a means to solve specific problems, but does not question the nature of the problem itself. Most typically, these reflections focus on teaching tasks.
Dialogic reflection	Is best thought of as a process. The term itself connotes discussion or a consideration of the views of others. The theme of process at this level can also be seen in a focus on the process of learning and often on the process on inquiry (i.e., a sustained process of asking questions, trying new approaches, and asking new questions).

Level of Reflection	Characterized By
Critical reflection	Questions fundamental assumptions and purpose more deeply. It is rare for preservice teachers to reach this level in situated reflection. The primary focus of teachers at this level on teaching tasks and self-concerns tends to crowd out deeper questioning.

Whether through viewing videotapes, captioning artifacts, or keeping reflective logs or journals, the processes of reflection makes the difference in whether or not the portfolio becomes "simply a receptacle for disposable paper" or not (Murray, 1994, p. 9). Figure 13.7 offers a reflective log to keep alongside the portfolio. The reader is encouraged to keep this log making notations throughout the whole process of building the portfolio, but perhaps committing reflections while in the decision process of which artifacts to include and why. The reader can return to these reflections later for further reflection and even share the reflections with a peer who might be invited to view the portfolio—collaboration strengthens all professional learning.

Figure 13.7. Reflective Practice: Examining Artifacts

♦ What is the artifact and why is the artifact important?

♦ Describe how this artifact shows an instructional practice or the results from instructional efforts.

♦ How will the information contained within the artifact affect your instructional or assessment practices in the future?

♦ What changes does this artifact suggest in future practices? In other words, what (if anything) would you now do differently, if you were faced with a similar situation?

♦ Describe what you learned from studying this artifact and from discussing this artifact with a colleague or team member.

Goal Setting

Goals serve to focus the efforts of the teacher, supervisor, or coach in the process of portfolio development. The reader is directed to Chapter 9 to examine the attributes of goals. In short, goals are S.M.A.R.T. if they are

Specific in that they answer

♦ Who: Who is involved?

♦ What: What do I want to accomplish?

♦ Where: Identify a location.

♦ When: Establish a time frame.

♦ Which: Identify requirements and constraints.

- Why: Specific reasons, purpose, or benefits of accomplishing the goal.

*M*easurable in that they allow you to answer

- How much?
- How many?
- How will I know when it is accomplished?

*A*ttainable in that they allow you to answer

- Are the goals within my capabilities to attain?

*R*ealistic in that they allow you to answer

- Am I able and willing to attain the goals?

*T*imely in that they allow you to answer

- Will the goals be important in the long-run?

Decision Making

Decision making is central to portfolio development. The teacher, as an empowered professional, is constantly tinkering with artifacts, making decisions as far as what artifacts to include, what artifacts to remove, and identifying what practices have changed or will change the next time a lesson is taught. Decision making under these conditions signals thinking, and thinking signals growth and development.

Extending Action Research Through the Portfolio

Action research and the portfolio are natural complements to the work of professional development. Like action research, the portfolio "is designed to promote professional growth and accountability, both through the portfolio development process itself and through the review of the by another professional" (Tucker et al., 2002, p. 23). As a framework for growth and development, action research (see Chapter 12), peer coaching (see Chapter 7), and the portfolio complement each other by

- establishing instructional and other closely related goals (e.g., classroom management, student assessment procedures);
- encouraging ongoing self-assessment and evaluation of goals;
- refining goals and targeted activities needed to accomplish goals;
- fostering collaboration between professionals, albeit peers serving as mentors, or administrators leading teachers through more formalized supervision and evaluation processes;

- creating the conditions to examine practice through other complementary processes such as action research (e.g., tracking student achievement on standardized tests based on frequency of instructional strategies and multitiered student assessments designed by the teacher);

- pinpointing more accurately needed ongoing professional development that is situated within the learning context of the classroom, relevant to short- and long-term goals; and

- assessing the impact of professional development activities (e.g., application of staff development initiatives, professional readings, and lessons learned in graduate courses). (Zepeda, 2007a)

Conclusion

The portfolio as a means to extend supervision, peer coaching, action research and other professional development opportunities will only endure if teachers are encouraged to think out of the box as they develop and design portfolios that reflect the knowledge they are creating because of "tinkering with their practices." With the advent of sophisticated technology, teacher portfolios can be stored on school homepages available for teachers—and even parents—to view. Discussions among teachers can be posted using electronic mail.

Teacher choice plays an important part in the portfolio process. Supervisory involvement can range from directive to more collaborative approaches that place teachers in a center-stage position to regulate their own professional learning. Few forms of professional development allow for such concentrated study over extended periods with such an accurate and immediate portrayal of the contextual makeup of the teaching and learning situation—the classroom. This is the power of the portfolio.

Suggested Readings

St. Maurice, H., & Shaw, P. (2004). Teacher portfolios come of age: A preliminary study. *NASSP Bulletin, 88*(639), 15–24. doi: 10.1177/0192636506288864

Tucker, P. D., Stronge, J. H., & Gareis, C. R. (2002). *Handbook on teacher portfolios for evaluation and professional development.* Larchmont, NY: Eye On Education.

Are We There Yet?

In This Chapter...

- ◆ Looking Back Through Our Journey of Professional Development
- ◆ Learning Is at the Core of Professional Development
- ◆ Examining Standards as a Source to Frame Professional Development
- ◆ Federal Legislation—No Child Left Behind Act of 2001—and Professional Development
- ◆ Professional Development Is School Improvement
- ◆ The Cases and Notes from the Field
- ◆ So What?
- ◆ The Never-Ending Journey

Looking Back Through Our Journey of Professional Development

Our journey began with seat belts on and a full tank of gas. Our travels have taken us through the fundamentals of professional development. We made many stops along the way to refuel with knowledge. These stops were necessary to be able to reflect about the how and what of professional development.

The contents of the first half of the book focused our attention on the most foundational aspects of professional development—understanding the overall context for professional development, evaluating professional development, framing professional development, embracing a culture that supports the emergence of learning communities, exploring the very unique nature of adult learning and the need to differentiate professional development, and embracing professional development that is embedded in the primary work of educating students.

We visited many chapters that focused our attention on examining highly collaborative forms of professional development such as coaching, study groups, critical friends, lesson study, learning circles, action research, and portfolios. The journey is not over because *professional development is learning* and learning from one's practices, from colleagues, and from students is at the center of professional learning.

We are now resting at an oasis to refuel for the next leg of the journey. Befittingly, this chapter title asks the rhetorical question, "Are we there yet?" Although rhetorical questions defy absolute answers, liberty here is being exercised to answer that question with a resounding, NO—the real journey awaits us. This is exciting because we get the opportunity to check our compass, pull out the road map, and check-in with colleagues who can serve as tour guides to ensure our path is cleared for the real work of professional development.

Learning Is at the Core of Professional Development

Learning is at the core of professional development, and we must continue to focus our efforts to support and nurture teachers and other school personnel such as counselors, social workers, psychologists, nurses, paraprofessionals and support staff and personnel including secretaries, bus drivers, the maintenance crew, and any and all other personnel who impact learning. In Chapter 1, the larger landscape of schools and their contexts were examined. Learning has to be the center of professional development because teachers are in a constant state of learning. As educators, we have been firsthand witnesses to statewide reforms such as standards-based curricula, statewide academic testing systems, and, for some, value-added assessments, for example. At the federal level, the *No Child Left Behind Act of 2001* (NCLB) has elevated the notion of highly qualified teachers who can lead learning opportunities for students. With the focus on standards-based curricula, ensuring student learning, and schools making adequate yearly progress (AYP), teachers are faced with challenges and opportunities for educating a student body that continues to be more diverse.

The diversity of the teaching force also continues to change. The perennial issue of teacher shortages escalates and more alternatively certified teachers are in classrooms. As leaders, "we must do more" to support the alternatively certified teachers whose background, skills, and developmental levels are much different from their traditionally prepared teaching counterparts (Zepeda, 2006). Moreover, as the profession grays, we must continually find ways to engage our veteran teachers in professional development that honors the voices of teachers whose experience and wisdom can inform practice and support newer teachers. Veteran teachers can become a resource tapped by newer teachers. There is compelling research that points to the power dynamic of reciprocal learning that occurs when veteran teachers work with newer teachers.

Examining Standards as a Source to Frame Professional Development

Within the framework for examining the research on professional development, it is essential to examine curriculum and standards. Effective professional development is grounded in standards and the curriculum. For example, standards such as the *National Science Education Standards* not only provide the standards for the teaching of science, but also outline how professional development for science teachers must align to the standards and how this alignment points to gains in student learning. The professional development standards for science hold four major premises:

- Professional development for a teacher of science is a continuous, lifelong process.

- The traditional distinctions between "targets," "sources," and "supporters" of teacher development activities are artificial.

- The conventional view of professional development for teachers needs to shift from technical training for specific skills to opportunities for intellectual professional growth.

- The process of transforming schools requires that professional development opportunities be clearly and appropriately connected to teachers' work in the context of the school.

(Available at www.nap.edu/readingroom/books/nses/4.html)

The national organizations that set content standards should be consulted as these organizations often include professional development standards that support not only the content but also the instructional strategies and approaches to support the curriculum. One of the current trends in accountability is the call for the Common Core State Standards. These standards are rigorous and relevant to preparing young people with the knowledge and skills that will ready them for the real world.

Federal Legislation—No Child Left Behind Act of 2001—and Professional Development

Described as "the most comprehensive federal education law ever written and one that imposed serious sanctions for states and schools that failed to abide by its provisions" (Kimmelman, 2006, p. 22), the NCLB established provisions for federal funding for professional development. The mandates related to professional development include:

- All professional development must relate to the school improvement plan.

- The professional development activities must be research-based practices.

- Professional development must be tied back to student achievement.

- Professional development must also include activities related to the subject area of the individual teachers.

- Ongoing, long-term professional development activities that enhance classroom instruction must be provided.

- Evaluation of the professional development activities must be conducted.

Following the lead of the NCLB legislation, state departments of education have framed professional development standards that align with the federal guidelines for highly qualified teaching and learning. For example, the Commonwealth of Virginia, Department of Education (2004) introduces its standards with the following statements:

> High-quality professional development is defined by several interacting factors. It implies rich content that is specifically chosen to deepen and broaden the knowledge and skills of teachers, principals, administrators, paraprofessionals, and other key education staff. High-quality professional development should be based on substantive, well-defined objectives. High-quality professional development requires structure, reflecting well-thought out delivery; efficient use of time; varied and effective styles of pedagogy; discourse and application; and the use of formative and summative assessment to promote understanding. High-quality professional development demands the guidance of experienced educators and other professionals who have a thorough and up-to-date understanding of the content themselves and who can fully engage the participants in the desired learning. (p. 2)

Overall, the NCLB has been viewed as a movement toward increased educational standards for students, teachers, and administrators.

Professional Development Is School Improvement

Professional development can be targeted to support school improvement efforts. Universal rules and formulas that encompass school improvement do not exist because a plan developed for one school may not work for another school. This lack of applicability across school systems occurs, in part, because school improvement addresses gaps—needs—that are as individualistic as the schools for which the plans are developed. Development is the key word in school improvement, and Tobergate and Curtis (2002) assert, "School improvement begins with development—development of people and the school culture to keep the organization vibrant and prepared to meet new needs and challenges" (p. 771). Professional development can become the glue to support individual and collective learning; both support school improvement.

Change

School improvement is a type of purposeful change, and Harris (2002a) believes "successful school improvement is dependent upon the school's ability to manage change and development" (p. 2). The purposeful nature of change and school improvement is critical to distinguish because change as envisioned by Harris is related directly to building capacity by "…enhancing student achievement and strengthening the school's capacity for change" (p. 50). School improvement not rooted in changes in classroom practices will more than not likely endure. There are two types of school improvement—in the classroom and schoolwide—and both types of improvement need to be melded (McTighe & Thomas, 2003).

Leadership That Supports Change

Baker (1997) asserts that school leaders can increase the likelihood of long-term success through

1. Shared decision making;

2. Coordinated staff development;

3. Strategic plans and small-win tactics; and,

4. Persistence for the long-term. (p. 1)

The school improvement process provides an opportunity for the principal to share power through openness, dialogue, and a sincere desire to build trust.

Leaders build authentic relationships with teachers, students, staff, and other stakeholders, and effective leaders work to promote an environment that supports:

1. *Interaction and participation*. People have many opportunities and reasons to come together in deliberation, association, and action.

2. *Interdependence*. These associations and actions both promote and depend on mutual needs and commitments.

3. *Shared interests and beliefs*. People share perspectives, values, understandings, and commitment to common purposes.

4. *Concern for individual and minority views*. Individual differences are embraced through critical reflection and mechanisms for dissent and lead to growth through the new perspectives they foster.

5. *Meaningful relationships*. Interactions reflect a commitment to caring, sustaining relationships. (Westheimer, 1998, p. 17, emphasis in the original)

Fullan (2002) believes that building relationships is a prerequisite to efforts to improve schools:

> The single factor common to successful change is that relationships improve. If relationships improve, schools get better. If relationships remain the same or get worse, ground is lost. Thus, leaders build relationships with diverse people and groups—especially with people who think differently. (p. 18)

Given the complexities with bringing about school improvement, cohesion is needed, and cohesion is built on more than linking the work of instructional leadership and the management of school improvement tasks. A more powerful force, relationships with others, builds cohesion and this "connective leadership" is what will help to bind people and their values to the work they do in the process of working with one another.

Leaders Value Professional Development and Learning

Professional development is the primary vehicle for supporting school improvement efforts, and Joyce and Showers (2002) believe:

> Selecting the content of staff development is one of the most critical decisions in the school improvement process. If you are to attain your student achievement goals, the content of staff development needs to be aligned with those goals. And the content needs to be robust enough to effect the type of change envisioned. (p. 59)

Teachers need the opportunity and time to work with one another; they will learn more from sustained discussion on classroom practices, coaching opportunities, and the formal and informal mentoring they can provide to one another. Thompson (1992) believes "School improvement demands recognition of the link between schooling and resource effects, and the result should be a model for school improvement which places staff development at the apex of priorities" (p. 174).

Related to school improvement, Section 9101(34) of the NCLB provides guidelines for professional development (Figure 14.1).

Figure 14.1. **Professional Development Related to NCLB**

PROFESSIONAL DEVELOPMENT: *[Section 9101(34)]*

The term "professional development:"

    I. Includes activities that:

1. Improve and increase teachers' knowledge of the academic subjects the teachers teach, and enable teachers to become highly qualified;

2. Are an integral part of broad schoolwide and districtwide educational improvement plans;

3. Give teachers, principals, and administrators the knowledge and skills to provide students with the opportunity to meet challenging State academic content standards and student academic achievement standards;

4. Improve classroom management skills;

5. Are high quality, sustained, intensive, and classroom-focused in order to have a positive and lasting impact on classroom instruction and the teacher's performance in the classroom and are not one-day or short-term workshops or conferences;

6. Support the recruiting, hiring, and training of highly qualified teachers, including teachers who became highly qualified through state and local alternative routes to certification;

7. Advance teacher understanding of effective instructional strategies that are:

   a. Based on scientifically based research (except that this subclause shall not apply to activities carried out under Part D of Title II); and

   b. Strategies for improving student academic achievement or substantially increasing the knowledge and teaching skills of teachers; and

8. Are aligned with and directly related to:

   a. State academic content standards, student academic achievement standards, and assessments; and

   b. The curricula and programs tied to the standards described in subclause (a) [except that this subclause shall not apply to activities described in clauses (ii) and (iii) of Section 2123(3)(B)];

9. Are developed with extensive participation of teachers, principals, parents, and administrators of schools to be served under this Act;

10. Are designed to give teachers of limited English proficient children, and other teachers and instructional staff, the knowledge and skills to provide instruction and appropriate language and academic support services to those children, including the appropriate use of curricula and assessments;

11. To the extent appropriate, provide training for teachers and principals in the use of technology so that technology and technology applications are effectively used in the classroom to improve teaching and learning in the curricula and core academic subjects in which the teachers teach;

12. As a whole, are regularly evaluated for their impact on increased teacher effectiveness and improved student academic achievement, with the findings of the evaluations used to improve the quality of professional development;

13. Provide instruction in methods of teaching children with special needs;

14. Include instruction in the use of data and assessments to inform and instruct classroom practice; and

15. Include instruction in ways that teachers, principals, pupil services personnel, and school administrators may work more effectively with parents; and

16. May include activities that:

   a. Involve the forming of partnerships with institutions of higher education to establish school-based teacher training programs that provide prospective teachers and beginning teachers with an opportunity to work under the guidance of experienced teachers and college faculty;

   b. Create programs to enable paraprofessionals (assisting teachers employed by a local educational agency receiving assistance under Part A of Title I) to obtain the education necessary for those paraprofessionals to become certified and licensed teachers; and

   c. Provide followup training to teachers who have participated in activities described in subparagraph (A) or another clause of this subparagraph that is designed to ensure that the knowledge and skills learned by the teachers are implemented in the classroom *[Title IX, Part A, Section 9101(34)]*.

Source: *No Child Left Behind* (2002). Improving Teacher Quality State Grants. Title II, Part A Non-Regulatory Guidance. Retrieved from www2. ed.gov/programs/teacherqual/guidance.pdf

Professional Development That Supports School Improvement

Implementing school improvement requires a commitment to professional development. What should professional development that supports school improvement look like? In the report by the National Partnership for Excellence and Accountability in Teaching (1999), *What Learner-Centered Professional Development Looks Like: Revisioning Professional Development*, the authors make several suggestions (Figure 14.2).

Figure 14.2. **Professional Development,**
Research-Based Principles

♦ The content of professional development focuses on what students are to learn and how to address the different problems students may have in learning the material.

♦ Professional development should be based on analyses of the differences between (a) actual student performance and (b) goals and standards for student learning.

♦ Professional development should involve teachers in identifying what they need to learn and in developing the learning experiences in which they will be involved.

♦ Professional development should be primarily school-based and built into the day-to-day work of teaching.

♦ Most professional development should be organized around collaborative problem solving.

♦ Professional development should be continuous and ongoing, involving follow-up and support for further learning—including support from sources external to the school that can provide necessary resources and new perspectives.

♦ Professional development should incorporate evaluation of multiple sources of information on (a) outcomes for students and (b) the instruction and other processes involved in implementing lessons learned through professional development.

♦ Professional development should provide opportunities to understand the theory underlying the knowledge and skills being learned.

♦ Professional development should be connected to a comprehensive change process focused on improving student learning.

Source: *Revisioning Professional Development: What Learner-Centered Professional Development Looks Like.* National Partnership for Excellence and Accountability in Teaching (1999, p. 3). Available at www.nsdc.org/members/jsd/npeat213.pdf

School improvement signals change and one of the most important roles of the principal is to support teachers' efforts to change. A comprehensive professional development program that prepares teachers for change and supports their learning needs during change must employ a variety of learning opportunities for teachers. Professional development is essential because *"[s]tudents learn only from teachers who are themselves in the process of learning"* (McCall, 1997, p. 23, emphasis in the original). According to Abdal-Haqq (1996), effective professional development that ensures learning:

♦ is ongoing;

- includes training, practice, and feedback; opportunities for individual reflection and group inquiry into practice; and coaching or other followup procedures;

- is school-based and embedded in teacher work;

- is collaborative, providing opportunities for teachers to interact with peers;

- focuses on student learning, which should, in part, guide assessment of its effectiveness;

- encourages and supports school-based and teacher initiatives;

- is rooted in the knowledge base for teaching;

- incorporates constructivist approaches to teaching and learning;

- recognizes teachers as professionals and adult learners;

- provides adequate time and followup support; and,

- is accessible and inclusive.

Professional development should promote discussion and needs to be job-embedded and supported through peer coaching, study groups, action research, and other forms of learning from the work of teaching.

The Cases and Notes from the Field[1]

Throughout the chapters are Cases from the Field and Notes from the Field. The men and women who have shared part of their craft knowledge with us in this book have provided us with many lessons. These practices are more than just cases from beacon schools. The cases and notes from the field represent what works and why these practices work. The cases have several commonalities. The cases and notes illustrate that the long, winding journey is worth the effort and the journeys have resulted in communities of learning (for adults and students). The cases also illustrate that communities can support student success and simultaneously support organizational effectiveness because these schools are engaging adults in learning not as an add-on program but as part of the work of teaching.

The work of Kelly Nagle Causey and her teachers at Sonny Carter Elementary School to use data to frame instruction and interventions is a powerful example of job-embedded learning. The success of this program is due, in part, to the leadership that Nagle Causey provided—she knew that her teachers needed to be data savvy, and she provided professional development on two levels. First, she used time in the day to work with small groups of teachers working with them to understand data and to use data to inform

---

1 Although some educators mentioned here are no longer serving in these leadership positions, for the purposes of this book, we are keeping their names and titles to reflect the context from which these case studies were conducted.

instructional and assessment practices. Second, she and her teachers used the data and their interpretation of the data to frame professional development so that instruction would support state curricular standards. Instead of supporting teaching to the tests, teachers were led through the content of the tests, the instructional strategies used to forward the content knowledge, and the results of efforts based on data.

Dr. Scott McLeod shares numerous examples of how student work can be used as professional development. He provides a framework for how student work can be analyzed and used as a unifying effort to focus teachers on content standards, instructional strategies, and professional development. In fact, the learning that is embedded in these practices is the professional development in that teachers are learning from their work, breaking barriers of isolation through collaboration, and moving forward with modifications based on the insights they gain from the work and from the open exchanges about student work.

The work of Dr. Bill Kruskamp at Creekland Middle School illustrates how professional development was tied to the changes in demographics and the desire of the teachers to be more culturally responsive in terms of instruction, progressive discipline strategies, and the ways that teachers respond to student learning needs. Dr. Kruskamp has unified the book study program at Creekland Middle School to complement other structures, including their peer-coaching program, and by linking the books to align with the Gwinnett County Public Schools Quality-Plus Teaching Strategies.

Superintendent Judith Harvey and the director of Curriculum Services of the Maine School Administrative District No. 50 shared how this school system uses the book study as a form of professional development by connecting this learning to the districtwide improvement plan goals. Harvey and Guyer promote book studies as a means to foster data analysis and assessment to improve instruction, to improve mathematics and science instruction, and to improve literacy instruction, particularly in reference to student writing.

The work of Dr. Dana Bickmore and Kathy Ridd from the Jordan School District shows the planning efforts needed to develop a systemwide coaching program to support literacy. The systems thinking—from planning, implementing, and evaluating this program—is a stellar example of how professional development can be tied to statewide standards, how data can be used to frame the refinement of the program, and how other system-wide processes (e.g., informal classroom observations, formal classroom observations) can be used as parallel supports for this coaching program.

The work of Dr. Thomas Van Soelen with Critical Friends as an induction support program shows how professional development is tied to the context of the school in which he supported beginning teachers' thinking about student issues and the myriad issues that beginning teachers experience. Reflection, dialogue, and open exchanges are the hallmark of this case from the field. Moreover, Dr. Van Soelen describes how the superintendent of the City Schools of Decatur incorporates the use of Critical Friends strategies to guide the work of the central office administrative staff and their work within schools.

So What?

In Chapter 1 and throughout this book, the key research about professional development has been offered. Practical applications have been added to give cues on how professional development at the site can be adapted to reflect the research base. The reader is encouraged to refer to Chapter 1 and review Figure 1.1, *Lessons Learned from Key Research on Professional Development* (page 9). There are a few other lessons that can support professional development.

These lessons are especially important to ponder because of the layout of this book. This book is designed as a resource book. The chapters can be read very much like you would read an encyclopedia—by topic (e.g., peer coaching, book study) or an area of interest (e.g., learning circles, examining student work, evaluating professional development). Two important items must be kept at the forefront.

First, professional development must be viewed as more than a "pull-out" program. To be effective, professional development must be systemic and embedded in the work that teachers and other personnel conduct on a daily basis. Professional development is planned, purposeful, and comprehensive in its scope, and in its totality, professional development aims to support "productive change" (Bellanca, 1995). Systemic thinking moves beyond individual thinking and focuses on the development of the organization and all of its subsystems. Professional development that is systemic looks to improve not only individual practice but also to improve collective practices of teachers and others in the school.

Second, professional development must be coherent. Effective professional development is more than the "flavor of the month." School personnel must begin thinking about how and why professional development is important, focusing on the work adults do to enhance student learning. Professional development should be the core work that teachers do, working in tandem with teaching. However, coherence is needed to help align professional development needs with the system. Coherence is needed to build purposeful relationships among and across activities, offerings, and initiatives. Alignment is needed to ensure coherence. Professional development might very well be a way to achieve coherence with tackling local, state, and national expectations for student achievement.

Third, professional development must be ongoing. Jurasaite-Harbison and Rex (2010) analyzed a form of career long professional development—informal teacher learning as expressed by teachers in the United States and Lithuania. The authors emphasized the impact of school culture framed by school mission, traditions, architectural features, organizational arrangement, and professional relationships on teacher learning. Jurasaite-Harbison and Rex (2010) summarized that "sociocultural infrastructures and cultures are needed for continual and consistent implementation of educational reforms and to better respond to the needs of ever-changing societies" (p. 277).

The Never-Ending Journey

Professional development is not easy work. Getting to the destination is a never-ending journey because the work associated with professional development that makes a difference emphasizes continuous learning. As architects of change, leaders need to be warriors of professional development, championing programs, processes, and opportunities for teachers to grow and to develop. The more teachers grow, the more students grow.

It is the hope that this book is your boarding pass and that the information presented in this text can serve to stoke and fan the imaginations of teachers, leaders, and others who care about professional development.

References

Abdal-haqq, I. (1996). *Making time for teacher professional development*. Washington, DC: ERIC Clearinghouse on Teaching and Teacher Education. (Document Reproduction Service No. ED400259). Retrieved from http://sdiplus.tie2.wikispaces.net/file/view/MakingTimeforTPD.pdf

Adelman, N. E. (1997). Framing the cases: Time for change. In N. E. Adelman, K. P. Walking Eagle, & A. Hargreaves (Eds.), *Racing with the clock: Making time for teaching and learning in school reform* (pp. 1–7). New York, NY: Teachers College Press.

Alterio, M. (2004). Collaborative journaling as a professional development tool. *Journal of Further and Higher Education, 28*(3), 321–332. doi:10.1080/0309877042000241788

American Educational Research Association. (2005). Teaching teachers: Professional development to improve student achievement. *Research Points: Essential Information for Educational Policy, 3*(1), 1–4. Retrieved from www.aera.net/

Amodeo, A. J., & Taylor, A. (2004a). Virtual supervision model tips the scales in favor of instructional leadership. *T.H.E. Journal*. Retrieved from http://web.ebscohost.com/

Amodeo, A. J., & Taylor, A. (2004b). A virtual supervision model. Retrieved from www.techlearning.com/article/1804

Ancess, J. (2000). The reciprocal influence of teacher learning, teaching practice, school restructuring and student learning outcomes. *Teachers College Record, 102*(3), 590–619. Retrieved from www.tcrecord.org/

Annenberg Institute for School Reform (n.d.). *Professional learning communities: Strategies that improve instruction*. Providence, RI: Annenberg Institute for School Reform at Brown University.

Ashur, N., Babayco, M., Fullerton, J., Jackson, T., & Smith, K. (1991). Staff development program evaluation. (ERIC Document Reproduction Service No. ED 345771).

ATLAS Learning Communities. (2007a). *Learning from student work*. Cambridge, MA: Author.

ATLAS Learning Communities. (2007b). *Thinking, listening and reflecting with colleagues about student work*. Cambridge, MA: Author.

Atonek, J., McCormick, D. E., & Donato, R. (1997). The student teacher portfolio as autobiography: Developing a professional identity. *The Modern Language Journal, 81*(1), 15–27. Retrieved from http://web.ebscohost.com/

Aubel, J. (1999). *Evaluation manual: Involving program stakeholders in the evaluation process*. (2nd ed). Calverton, MD: Child Survival Technical Support Project/Catholic Relief Services.

Avery, C. S. (1990). Learning to research/researching to learn. In M. W. Olson (Ed.), *Opening the door to classroom research* (pp. 32–44). Newark, NJ: International Reading Association.

Baker, P. J. (1997). Building better schools: How to initiate, sustain and celebrate school improvement. *Planning & Changing: A Journal for School Administrators, 28*(3), 130–138.

Bambino, D. (2002). Critical friends. *Educational Leadership, 59*(6), 25–27. Retrieved from http://web.ebscohost.com/

Bandura, A. (1982). Self-efficacy mechanism in human agency. *American Psychologist*, *37*(2), 122–147. doi:10.1037/0003–066X.37.2.122

Bandura, A. (1986). *The social foundations of thought and action*. Englewood Cliffs, NJ: Prentice-Hall.

Bandura, A. (1995). *Self-efficacy in changing societies*. New York, NY: Cambridge University Press.

Baron, D. (n.d.). *Success analysis protocol*. Bloomington, IN: National School Reform Faculty. Retrieved from www.nsrfharmony.org/protocol/doc/success_ana_individuals.pdf

Barott, J., & Raybould, R. (1998). Changing schools into collaborative organizations. In D. G. Pounder (Ed.), *Restructuring schools for collaboration: Promises and pitfalls* (pp. 27–42). Albany, NY: State University of New York Press.

Basom, R., & Crandall, D. (1991). Implementing a redesign strategy: Lessons from educational change. *Educational Horizons, 69*(2), 73–77.

Baumgartner, L. M. (2001). An update on transformational learning. In S. B. Merriam (Ed.), *The new update on adult learning theory. New Directions for Adult and Continuing Education, No. 89* (pp. 15–24). San Francisco, CA: Jossey-Bass.

Beck, L. G. (1992). Meeting the challenge of the future: The place of a caring ethic in educational administration. *American Journal of Education, 100*(4), 454–496. Retrieved from www.jstor.org/

Bellanca, J. (1995). *Designing professional development for change. A systemic approach*. Palatine, IL: IRI/Skylight Publishing.

Birchak, B., Connor, C., Crawford, K. M., Kahn, L., Kaser, S., Turner, S., & Short, K. G. (1998). *Teacher study groups: Building community through dialogue and reflection*. Urbana, IL: National Council of Teachers of English.

Bird, T. (1990). The schoolteacher's portfolio: An essay on possibilities. In J. Millman, & L. Darling-Hammond (Eds.), *The new handbook of teacher evaluation: Assessing elementary and secondary school teachers* (2nd ed.) (pp. 241–256). Newbury Park, CA: Sage.

Birman, B., Desimone, L., Porter, A. C., & Garet, M. (2000). Designing professional development that works. *Educational Leadership, 57*(8), 28–33. Retrieved from http://web.ebscohost.com/

Bjerkaker, S. (2003). *The study circle: A method for learning, a tool for democracy*. Paper presented at the FACE Annual Conference, Stirling, UK. Retrieved from www.face.stir.ac.uk/documents/Paper109Bjerkader.pdf

Blachowicz, C. L. Z., Obrochta, C., & Fogelberg, E. (2005). Literacy coaching for change. *Educational Leadership, 62*(6), 55–58. Retrieved from http://web.ebscohost.com/

Blase, J., & Blase J. (2000). *Empowering teachers: What successful principals do* (2nd ed.). Thousand Oaks, CA: Corwin.

Boggs, H. (1996, October). *Launching school change through teacher study groups: An action research project*. Paper presented at the annual meeting of the Mid-Western Educational Research Association Conference, Chicago, IL.

Bogler, R., & Somech, A. (2004). Influence of teacher empowerment on teachers' organizational commitment, professional commitment, and organization citizenship behavior in schools. *Teaching and Teacher Education, 20*(3), 277–289. doi:10.1016/j.tate.2004.02.003

Bolam, R., McMahon, A., Stoll, L., Thomas, S., Wallace, M, Greenwood, A., Hawkey, K., Ingram, M., Atkinson, A., & Smith, M. (2005). *Creating and sustaining effective professional learning communities*. Research Report RR637. University of Bristol,

UK. Retrieved from www.mpn.gov.rs/resursi/dokumenti/dok267-eng-DfES_professional_learning_communities.pdf

Boreen, J., Johnson, M. K., Niday, D., & Potts, J. (2000). *Mentoring beginning teachers: Guiding, reflecting, coaching.* York, ME: Stenhouse.

Borko, H. (2004). Professional development and teacher learning: Mapping the terrain. *Educational Researcher, 33*(8), 3–15. Retrieved from www.jstor.org/

Boud, D. (2001). Using journal writing to enhance reflective practice. *New Directions for Adult and Continuing Education, 2001*(90), 9–17. Retrieved from http://web.ebscohost.com/

Bransford, J. D., Brown, A. L., & Cocking, R. (1999). *How people learn: Brain, mind, experience, and school.* Washington, DC: National Academies Press. Retrieved from http://books.nap.edu/openbook/0309065577/html/index.html

Brinkerhoff, R. O., Brethower, D. M., Hluchyj, T., & Nowakowski, J. R. (1983). *Program evaluation: A practitioner's guide for trainers and educators.* Boston, MA: Kluwer-Nijhoff.

Brookfield, S. D. (1986). *Understanding and facilitating adult learning.* San Francisco, CA: Jossey-Bass.

Brookfield, S. D. (1995). *Becoming a critically reflective teacher.* San Francisco, CA: Jossey- Bass.

Bryk, A. S., & Schneider, B. (2002). *Trust in schools: A core resource for improvement.* Thousand Oaks, CA: Sage.

Bucher, R., & Strauss, A. (1961). Professions in process. *American Journal of Sociology, 66*(4), 325–334. Retrieved from www.jstor.org/

Burden, P. (1982a, February). *Developmental supervision: Reducing teacher stress at different career stages.* Paper presented at the Association of Teacher Educators National Conference, Phoenix, AZ. Retrieved from http://www.eric.ed.gov:80/PDFS/ED218267.pdf

Burden, P. (1982b). Implications of teacher career development: New roles for teachers, administrators and professors. *Action in Teacher Education, 4*(4), 21–25. Retrieved from http://eric.ed.gov/

Burke, P. J., Christensen, J. C., & Fessler, R. (1984). *Teacher career stages: Implications for staff development* (No. 214). Bloomington, IN: Phi Delta Kappa Educational Foundation.

Calderon, M. (2007). *Teaching reading to English language learners, grades 6–12: A framework for improving achievement in the content areas.* Thousand Oaks, CA: Corwin.

Campbell, D. M., Cignetti, P. B., Melenyzer, B. J., Nettles, D. H., & Wyman, R. M. (1997). *How to develop a professional portfolio: A manual for teachers.* Needham Heights, MA: Allyn & Bacon.

Casey, K. (2006). *Literacy coaching: The essentials.* Portsmouth, NH: Heinemann.

Cayuso, E., Fegan, C., & McAlister, D. (2004). *Designing teacher study groups: A guide for success.* Gainesville, FL: Maupin.

Cervero, R. M. (1988). *Effective continuing education for professionals.* San Francisco, CA: Jossey-Bass.

Chance, P. L., & Chance, E. W. (2002). *Introduction to educational leadership and organizational behavior: Theory into practice.* Larchmont, NY: Eye On Education.

Chase, B., Germundsen, R. Brownstein, J. C., & Distad, L. S. (2001). Making the connection between increased student learning and reflective practice. *Educational Horizons, 79*(3), 143–147. Retrieved from www.pilambda.org/styles/pilambda/defiles/chase.pdf

Chokshi, S., & Fernandez, C. (2004). Challenges to importing lesson study: Concerns, misconceptions, and nuances. *Phi Delta Kappan, 85*(7), 520–525. Retrieved from http://web.ebscohost.com/

Christensen, J., Burke, P., Fessler, R., & Hagstrom, D. (1983). *Stages of teachers' careers: Implications for professional development.* Washington, DC: National Institute of Education (ERIC Document Reproduction Services No. ED 227 054).

Clark, C. (Ed.). (2001). *Talking shop: Authentic conversation and teacher learning.* New York, NY: Teachers College Press.

Clarke, J. C. (2006). The nexus of learning: The intersection of formal and informal education. *Chief Learning Officer, 5*(2), 22–25. Retrieved from http://web.ebsco-host.com/

Clarke, M., & Otaky, D. (2005). Reflection "on" and "in" teacher education in the United Arab Emirates. *International Journal of Educational Development, 26*(1), 111–122. doi:10.1016/j.ijedudev.2005.07.018

Clarke, M., Shore, A., Rhoades, K., Abrams, L., Miao, J., & Li, J. (2003). *Perceived effects of state-mandated testing programs on teaching and learning: Findings from interviews with educators in low-, medium-, and high-stakes states.* Retrieved from http://eric.ed.gov/

Clutterbuck, D. (2005). *Creating a Coaching Climate.* Retrieved from http://pc4p.com.au/j15/images/stories/Clutterbuck3.pdf

Coalition of Essential Schools Northwest. (n.d.). *Critical friends groups.* Retrieved from www.smallschoolsproject.org/PDFS/Planning_Resources/summer2003/summer2003-adapting.pdf

Cochran-Smith, M., & Fries, M. (2001). Sticks, stones, and ideology: The discourse of reform in teacher education. *Educational Researcher, 30*(8), 3–15. Retrieved from www.jstor.org/

Collay, M., Dunlap, D., Enloe, W., & Gagnon, G. W. (1998). *Learning circles: Creating conditions for professional development.* Thousand Oaks, CA: Corwin.

Committee on Institutional Cooperation. (2005). *Critical friends: A process built on reflection.* Retrieved from https://www.ohrd.wisc.edu/

Commonwealth of Virginia, Department of Education. (2004). *High quality professional development criteria.* Retrieved from www.doe.virginia.gov/teaching/regulations/high_quality_prof_dev_criteria.pdf

Conlan, J., Grabowski, S., & Smith, K. (2003). Adult Learning. In M. Orey (Ed.), *Emerging perspectives on learning, teaching, and technology.* Retrieved from http://projects.coe.uga.edu/epltt/

Corcoran, T. B. (1995). *Helping teachers teach well: Transforming professional development.* Philadelphia, PA: Consortium for Policy Research in Education Publications. Retrieved from www.ed.gov/pubs/CPRE/t61/index.html

Costa, A. L., & Garmston, R. J. (1987). Student teaching: Developing images of a profession. *Action in Teacher Education, 9(3),* 5–11.

Costa, A. L., & Garmston, R. J. (1994). *Cognitive coaching: A foundation for Renaissance Schools.* Norwood, MA: Christopher-Gordon.

Costa, A. L., & Garmston, R. J. (2002). *Cognitive coaching: A foundation for Renaissance Schools.* (2nd ed). Norwood, MA: Christopher-Gordon.

Costa, A. L., & Kallick, B. (1993). Through the lens of a critical friend. *Educational Leadership, 51*(2), 49–51. Retrieved from http://web.ebscohost.com/

Covey, S. R. (1989). *Seven habits of highly successful people.* New York, NY: Simon & Schuster.

Covey, S. R. (1992). *Principle-centered leadership.* New York, NY: Simon & Schuster.

Cowley, K. S., & Meehan, M. L. (2001, July). *Assessing teacher efficacy and professional learning community in 19 elementary and high schools.* Paper presented at the Tenth Annual Meeting of the CREATE National Evaluation Institute, Wilmington, NC.

Cross, K. P. (1992). *Adults as learners: Increasing participation and facilitating learning.* San Francisco, CA: Jossey-Bass.

Crowther, F., Kaagan, S. S., Ferguson, M., & Hann, L. (2002). *Developing teacher leaders.* Thousand Oaks, CA: Corwin.

Curry, M. W. (2008). Critical friends groups: The possibilities and limitations embedded in teacher professional communities aimed at instructional improvement and school reform. *Teachers College Record, 110*(4), 733–774. Retrieved from www.tcrecord.org/

Cushman, K. (1998). How friends can be critical as schools make essential changes. *Coalition of Essential Schools.* Retrieved from www.essentialschools.org/resources/45

Dalellew, T., & Martinez, Y. (1988). Andragogy and development: A search for the meaning of staff development. *Journal of Staff Development, 9*(3), 28–31.

Danielson, C. (1996). *Enhancing professional practice: A framework for teaching.* Alexandria, VA: Association for Supervision and Curriculum Development.

Danielson, C., & Abrutyn. L. (1997). *An introduction to using portfolios in the classroom.* Alexandria, VA: Association for Supervision and Curriculum Development.

Dantonio, M. (2001). *Collegial coaching: Inquiry into the teaching self* (2nd ed). Bloomington, IN: Phi Delta Kappa.

Darling-Hammond, L. (1989). Accountability for professional practice. *Teachers College Record, 91*(1), 59–80.

Darling-Hammond, L. (1997a). School reform at the crossroads: Confronting the central issues of teaching. *Educational Policy, 11*(2), 51–66.

Darling-Hammond, L. (1997b). *Doing what matters most: Investing in quality teaching.* Kutztown, PA: National Commission on Teaching and America's Future.

Darling-Hammond, L. (1999). Target time toward teachers. *Journal of Staff Development, 20*(2), 31–36.

Darling-Hammond, L. (2003). Keeping good teachers: Why it matters, what leaders can do. *Educational Leadership, 60(8),* 6–13.

Darling-Hammond, L. (2004). Standards, accountability, and school reform. *Teachers College Record, 106*(6), 1047–1085. Retrieved from www.tcrecord.org/

Darling-Hammond, L., & Goodwin, A. L. (1993). Progress toward professionalism in teaching. In G. G. Cawelti (Ed.), *Challenges and achievements of American education: 1993 Yearbook of the Association for Supervision and Curriculum Development* (pp. 19–52). Alexandria, VA: Association for Supervision and Curriculum Development.

Davies, M. A., & Willis, E. (2001). Through the looking glass…Preservice professional portfolios. *The Teacher Educator, 37*(1), 27–36. doi:10.1080/08878730109555278

Dawes, L. (1999). Enhancing reflection with audiovisual playback and trained inquirer. *Studies in Continuing Education, 21*(2), 197–215. Retrieved from http://web.ebscohost.com/

Dede, C., Breit, L., Ketelhut, D. J., McCloskey, E., & Whitehouse, P. (2006). An overview of current findings from empirical research on online teacher professional development. In C. Dede (Ed.), *Online professional development for teachers: Emerging models and methods* (pp. 13–29). Cambridge, MA: Harvard Education Press.

Deno, S., & Mirkin, P. (1977). *Data-based program modification.* Minneapolis, MN: Leadership Training Institute for Special Education.

References ◆ 291

Dewey, J. (1929). *Sources of science education*. New York, NY: Liverisht.

Dewey, J. (1933). *How we think*. Boston, MA: D. C. Heath.

Dewey, J. (1938). *Experience and education*. New York, NY: Macmillan.

Dick, B. (1999). *What is action research?* Santa Clara, CA: Santa Clara University. Retrieved from www.scu.edu.au/schools/gcm/ar/whatisar.html

Doolittle, P. (1994). *Teacher portfolio assessment*. Washington, DC: Clearinghouse on Assessment and Evaluation. (ERIC Document Reproduction Services No. ED385608).

Doyle, L. H. (2004). Leadership for community building: Changing how we think and act. *The Clearing House, 77*(5), 196–199. Retrieved from http://web.ebscohost.com/

Dozier, C. (2006). *Responsive literary coaching: Tools for creating and sustaining purposeful change*. Portland, ME: Stenhouse.

DuFour, R. (2004a). Leading edge: The best staff development is in the workplace not in a workshop. *Journal of Staff Development, 25*(2). Retrieved from www.learningforward.org/news/jsd/dufour252.cfm

DuFour, R. (2004b). What is a "professional learning community?" *Educational Leadership, 61*(8), 6–11. Retrieved from http://web.ebscohost.com/

DuFour, R., & Eaker, R. (1998). *Professional learning communities at work: Best practices for enhancing student achievement*. Bloomington, IN: Solution Tree.

DuFour, R., DuFour, R., Eaker, R., & Karhanek, G. (2004). *Whatever it takes: How professional learning communities respond when kids don't learn*. Bloomington, IN: Solution Tree.

DuFour, R., DuFour, R., Eaker, R., & Many, T. (2006). *Learning by doing: Handbook for professional learning communities at work*. Bloomington, IN: Solution Tree.

Duke, D., & Corno, L. (1981). Evaluating staff development. In B. Dillion-Peterson (Ed.), *Staff development/organization development* (pp. 93–112). Alexandria, VA: Association for Supervision and Curriculum Development.

Dunne, F., & Honts, F. (1998, April). *"That group really makes me think!" Critical friends groups and the development of reflective practitioners*. Paper presented at the annual meeting of the American Educational Research Association.

Dunne, F., Nave, B., & Lewis, A. (2000). Critical friends groups: Teachers helping teachers improve student learning. *Research Bulletin, 28*. Retrieved from www2. spokaneschools.org/ProfessionalLearning/Initiatives/Book_Study-04–2006/ ProLibwebpage/Articles/Collaboration/CF_Teachers_Helping_Teachers_to_ Improve_Student_Learning.pdf

Dyer, W.G. (1995). *Team building: Current issues and new alternatives* (3rd ed.). Reading, MA: Addison-Wesley.

Easton, L.B. (1999). Tuning protocols. *Journal of Staff Development, 20*(3). Retrieved from www.pds-hrd.wikispaces.net/file/view/Tuning+Protocols.pdf

Fairbanks, C. M., & LaGrone, D. (2006). Learning together: Constructing knowledge in a teacher research group. *Teacher Education Quarterly, 33*(3), 7–25. Retrieved from http://web.ebscohost.com/

Fairfax County Public Schools. (2007). *Professional learning and training*. Retrieved from www.fcps.edu/plt/tresearch.htm

Feiman, S., & Floden, R. (1980). *What's all this talk about teacher development?* East Lansing, MI: The Institute for Research on Teaching. (ERIC Document Reproduction Service No. ED189088).

Fenstermacher, G. D. (1990). Some moral considerations on teaching as a profession. In J. I. Goodlad, R. Soder, & K. A. Sirotnik, (Eds.), *The moral dimensions of teaching* (pp. 130–151). San Francisco, CA: Jossey-Bass.

Fenwick, T. J. (2004). Teacher learning and professional growth plans: Implementation of a provincial policy. *Journal of Curriculum and Supervision, 19*(3), 259–282. Retrieved from http://web.ebscohost.com/

Ferguson, R. F. (2006). Five challenges to effective teacher professional development. *Journal of Staff Development, 27*(4), 48–52.

Fernandez, C., Cannon, J., & Chokshi, S. (2003). A US–Japan lesson study collaboration reveals critical lenses for examining practice. *Teaching and Teacher Education, 19*(2), 171–185. doi:10.1016/S0742–051X(02)00102–6

Fernandez, C., & Chokshi, S. (2002). A practical guide to translating lesson study for a U.S. setting. *Phi Delta Kappan, 84*(2), 128–135.

Fisher, D., & Frey, N. (2010). *Enhancing RTI: How to ensure success with effective classroom instruction & intervention.* Alexandria, VA: Association for Supervision and Curriculum Development.

Flexner, A. (1915, May). *Is social work a profession?* Paper presented at the annual meeting of the National Conference of Charities and Corrections, Baltimore, MD. Retrieved from www.hhs.csus.edu/homepages/

Franzak, J. K. (2002). Developing a teacher identity: The impact of critical friends practice on the student teacher. *English Education, 34*(4), 258–280. Retrieved from www.jstor.org/

Frazier, A. (1997). *A roadmap for quality transformation in education.* Boca Raton, FL: St. Lucie Press.

Frechtling, J. (2002). *The 2002 user-friendly handbook for project evaluation.* Arlington, VA: The National Science Foundation. Division of Research, Evaluation, and Communication. Retrieved from www.nsf.gov/pubs/2002/nsf02057/nsf02057.pdf

Freese, A. R. (2006). Reframing one's teaching: Discovering our teacher selves through reflection and inquiry. *Teaching and Teacher Education, 22*(1), 100–119. doi:10.1016/j.tate.2005.07.003

Freiberg, J. (1998). Measuring school climate. *Educational Leadership, 56*(1), 22–26. Retrieved from http://web.ebscohost.com/

Frome, P., Lasater, B., & Cooney, S. (2005). *Well-qualified teachers and high quality teaching: Are they the same?* Southern Regional Education Board. Retrieved from http://publications.sreb.org/2005/05V06_Research_Brief_high-quality_teaching.pdf

Fullan, M. (1982). *The meaning of educational change.* New York, NY: Teachers College Press.

Fullan, M. (2001). *Leading in a culture of change.* San Francisco, CA: Jossey Bass.

Fullan, M. (2002). The change leader. *Educational Leadership, 59*(8), 16–20. Retrieved from http://web.ebscohost.com/

Fullan, M. (2007). *The new meaning of educational change* (4th ed.). New York, NY: Teachers College Press.

Funk, C. (2002). *Creating learning communities through circles of learning.* Unpublished opinion paper. Huntsville, TX: Sam Houston State University. (ERIC Document Reproduction Service No. ED481623).

Gage, N. L., & Berliner, D. (1998). *Educational psychology* (6th ed.). Boston, MA: Houghton-Mifflin.

Garet, M. S., Porter, A. C., Desimone, L., Birman, B. F., & Yoon, K. S. (2001, Winter). What makes professional development effective? Results from a national sample of teachers. *American Educational Research Journal, 38*(4), 915–945. Retrieved from www.jstor.org/

Garmston, R. J. (1987). How administrators support peer coaching. *Educational Leadership, 44(5),* 18–26. Retrieved from http://web.ebscohost.com/

Garmston, R. J., & Wellman, B. M. (1999). *The adaptive school: A sourcebook for developing collaborative groups.* Norwood, MA: Christopher-Gordon.

Garmston, R., Linder, C., & Whitaker, J. (1993). Reflections of cognitive coaching. *Educational Leadership, 51*(2), 57–60. Retrieved from http://web.ebscohost.com/

Garrison, D. R. (1997). Self-directed learning: Toward a comprehensive model. *Adult Education Quarterly, 48*(1), 18–34. doi:10.1177/074171369704800103

Gephart, M. A., Marsick, V. J., Van Buren, M.E., & Spiro, M.S. (1996). Learning organizations come alive. *Training & Development, 50*(12), 35–45. Retrieved from http://web.ebscohost.com/

Gingiss, P. L. (1993). Peer coaching: Building collegial support for using innovative health programs. *Journal of School Health, 63(2),* 79–85. Retrieved from http://proquest.umi.com/

Glanz, J. (1999). Action research. *Journal of Staff Development, 20*(3), 22–25.

Glanz, J. (2003). *Action research: An educational leader's guide to school improvement* (2nd ed.). Norwood, MA: Christopher-Gordon.

Glanz, J. (2005). Action research as instructional supervision: Suggestions for principals. *NASSP Bulletin, 89*(643), 17–27. doi:10.1177/019263650508964303

Glickman, C. D., Gordon, S. P., & Ross-Gordon, J. M. (2009). *Supervision of instruction: A developmental approach* (7th ed.). Boston, MA: Allyn and Bacon.

Goldsmith, M., Lyons, L., & Freas, A. (2000). *Coaching for leadership: How the world's greatest coaches help leaders learn.* San Francisco, CA: Jossey-Bass.

Golja, T., & Schaverien, L. (2007). *Theorising professional development in the academy: A conversational approach.* Sydney, AU: Institute of Interactive Media and Learning and Faculty of Education and University of Technology. doi:10.1.1.114.5339

Good, J. M. (2002). Encouraging reflection in preservice teachers through response journals. *The Teacher Educator, 37*(4), 254–267. doi:10.1080/08878730209555299

Gordon, S. P. (2004). *Professional development for school improvement: Empowering learning communities.* Boston, MA: Allyn & Bacon.

Gottesman, B. L., & Jennings, J. O. (1994). *Peer coaching for educators.* Lancaster, PA: Technomic.

Gredler, M. (1996). *Program evaluation.* Englewood Cliffs, NJ: Prentice-Hall.

Guba, E. G., & Lincoln, Y. S. (1981). *Effective evaluation.* San Francisco, CA: Jossey-Bass.

Guskey, T. R. (1999). Moving from means to ends. *Journal of Staff Development, 20*(1), 48.

Guskey, T. R. (2003). Analyzing lists of the characteristics of effective professional development to promote visionary leaders. *NASSP Bulletin, 87*(637), 4–20. doi:10.1177/019263650308763702

Guskey, T. R. (2000). *Evaluating professional development.* Thousand Oaks, CA: Corwin.

Guskey, T. R. (2005/2006). A conversation with Thomas R. Guskey. *The Evaluation Exchange, 11*(4). Retrieved from www.gse.harvard.edu/hfrp/eval/issue32/qa-nda.html

Hargreaves, A. (1994). *Changing teachers, changing times: Teachers' work and culture in the postmodern age.* London, UK: Cassell.

Hargreaves, A. (1997). Cultures of teaching and educational change. In M. Fullan (Ed.), *The challenge of school change* (pp. 57–84). Arlington Heights, IL: Skylight Training and Publishing.

Harris, A. (2002a). *School improvement: What's in it for schools?* London, UK: Routledge/Falmer.

Harris, A. (2002b). Effective leadership in schools facing challenging contexts. *School Leadership and Management, 22*(1), 15–26. doi:org/10.1080/13632430220143024a

Harris, A. (2003). Teacher leadership as distributed leadership: Heresy, fantasy, or possibility? *School Leadership and Management, 23*(3), 313–325. doi:10.1080/1363243032000112801

Hartnell-Young, E., & Morriss, M. (1999). *Digital professional portfolios for change.* Arlington Heights, IL: Skylight Professional Development.

Haycock, K. (1998). Good teaching matters…a lot. *Thinking K-16, 3*(2), 3–14. Retrieved from www.edtrust.org/

Heflich, D. A. (1997, March). *Online interviews: Research as a reflective dialogue.* Paper presented at the Annual Meeting of the American Educational Research Association. Chicago, IL.

Heller, J. I., Daehler, K. R., & Shinohara, M. (2003). Mosaic approach to evaluation makes a complete picture: Connecting all the pieces. *Journal of Staff Development, 24*(4), 36–41.

Herzberg, F. (1968). One more time: How do you motivate employees? *Harvard Business Review, 46*(4), 53–62. Retrieved from http://gaounion.net/

Heydenrych, J. (2001). Improving educational practice: Action research as an appropriate methodology. *Progressio, 23*(2). Retrieved from www.unisa.ac.za/

Hill, D. (2003). E-folio and teacher candidate development. *The Teacher Educator, 38*(4), 256–266. doi:10.1080/08878730309555322

Hipp, K. A. (1996, April). *Teacher efficacy: Influence of principal leadership behavior.* Paper presented at the Annual Meeting of the American Educational Research Association, New York.

Hirsh, S., & Ponder, G. (1991). New plots, new heroes in staff development. *Educational Leadership, 49*(3), 43–48. Retrieved from http://web.ebscohost.com/

Hlavaty, K. (2001). *Differentiated supervision for veteran teachers.* Unpublished comprehensive exam. Athens, GA: University of Georgia.

Hodges, N. J., & Franks, I. M. (2002). Learning as a function of coordination bias: Building upon pre-practice behaviours. *Human Movement Science, 21*(2), 231–258. doi:10.1016/S0167–9457(02)00101-X

Holloway, K., & Long, R. (1998). Teacher development and school improvement: The use of "shared practice groups" to improve teaching in primary schools. *Journal of Inservice Education, 24*(3), 535–545. doi:10.1080/13674589800200056

Hord, S. M., Rutherford, W. L., Huling-Austin, L., & Hall, G. E. (1987). *Taking charge of change.* Alexandria, VA: Association for Supervision and Curriculum Development.

Hord, S. M., Rutherford, W. L., Huling-Austin, L., & Hall, G. E. (2005). *Taking charge of change.* Austin, TX: Southwest Educational Development Laboratory.

Howden, B. J. (1998). Using action research to enhance the teaching of writing. *Queensland Journal of Educational Research, 14*(1), 45–58. Retrieved from http://iier.org.au/

Hu, C., Sharpe, L., Crawford, L., Gopinathan, S., Khine, M. S., Moo, S. N., & Wong, A. (2000). Using lesson video clips via multipoint desktop video conferencing to facilitate reflective practice. *Journal of Information on Technology for Teacher Education, 9*(3), 377–388. doi:10.1080/14759390000200093

Hudson, R. (1999). Subject-verb agreement in English. *English Language and Linguistics, 3*(2), 173–207.

Hudson, J., & Gray, J. (2006). Renewal through collaborative inquiry: The critical friends group process. *New Horizons for Learning Online Journal, 12*(2). Retrieved from www.newhorizons.org/spneeds/inclusion/staff/gray_hudson.htm

Huffman, D., & Kalnin, J. (2003). Collaborative inquiry to make data-based decisions in schools. *Teaching and Teacher Education, 19*(6), 569–580. doi:10.1016/S0742-051X(03)00054-4

Huntress, J., & Jones, L. (2000, April). *Reflective process tools.* A presentation made at the annual meeting of the Association for Supervision and Curriculum Development for the Instructional Supervision Network, New Orleans, LA.

IBM Learning Solutions. (2006, January). *Learning infrastructure: Architecting a formal and informal learning environment* (executive brief). Somer, NY: IBM.

International Reading Association. (2006). *Standards for middle and high school literacy coaches.* Newark, DE: Author.

Iowa Department of Education. *Iowa professional development model training manual, part 2-model components.* (n.d.). Des Moines, IA: Author. Retrieved from www.iowa.gov/educate/pdmtm/pdfs/part_2-i.pdf

Israel, S. E., Block, C. C., Bauserman, K. L., & Kinnucan-Welsch, K. (2005). *Metacognition in literacy learning: Theory, assessment, instruction, and professional development.* Mahwah, NJ: Lawrence Erlbaum.

Jacobson, D. (2010). Coherent instructional improvement and PLCs: Is it possible to do both? *Phi Delta Kappan, 91*(6), 38–45. Retrieved from http://web.ebscohost.com/

Jay, J. K. (1999, February). *Untying the knots: Examining the complexities of reflective practice.* Paper presented at the annual meeting of the American Association of Colleges for Teacher Education, Washington, DC.

Jeffs, T., & Smith, M. K. (1999). *Informal education: Conversation, democracy and learning.* Nottingham, UK: Educational Heretics Press.

Joint Committee on Standards for Educational Evaluation (1994). *Program evaluation standards: How to assess evaluations of educational programs* (2nd ed.). Thousand Oaks, CA: Sage.

Jolly, A., & Evans, S. (2005). Teacher assistants move to the front of the class. *Journal of Staff Development, 26*(3), 8–13.

Joyce, B. (2004). How are professional learning communities created? History has a few messages. *Phi Delta Kappan, 86*(1), 76–83.

Joyce, B., & Showers, B. (1981). Transfer of training: The contribution of "coaching". *Journal of Education, 163*(2), 163–172. Retrieved from http://web.ebscohost.com/

Joyce, B., & Showers, B. (1982). The coaching of teaching. *Educational Leadership, 40*(1), 4–10. Retrieved from http://web.ebscohost.com/

Joyce, B., & Showers, B. (1995). *Student achievement through staff development: Fundamentals of school renewal* (2nd ed.). White Plains, NY: Longman.

Joyce, B., & Showers, B. (2002). *Student achievement through staff development: Fundamentals of school renewal* (3rd ed.). Alexandria, VA: Association for Supervision and Curriculum Development.

Jurasaite-Harbison, E., & Rex, L. A. (2010). School cultures as contexts for informal teacher learning. *Teaching and Teacher Education, 26*(2), 267–277. doi:10.1016/j.tate.20099.03.012

Katzenmeyer, M., & Moller, G. (2001). *Awakening the sleeping giant: Helping teachers develop as leaders.* Thousand Oaks, CA: Corwin.

Kazemi, E., & Franke, M. (2003). *Using student work to support professional development in elementary mathematics* (Document No. W-03–1). Seattle, WA: University of Washington, Center for the Study of Teaching and Policy.

Keefe, J., & Jenkins, J. (1997). *Instruction and the learning environment.* Larchmont, NY: Eye On Education.

Kelly, K. (2002). Lesson study: Can Japanese methods translate to U.S. schools? *Harvard Education Letter, 18*(3), 4–7.

Kemmis, S., & McTaggart, R. (Eds.). (1988). *The action research planner.* Victoria, AU: Deakin University Press.

Kent, A. M. (2004). Improving teacher quality through professional development. *Education, 124*(3), 427–435. Retrieved from http://findarticles.com/

Killion, J. (2002a). *Assessing impact: Evaluating staff development.* Oxford, OH: National Staff Development Council.

Killion, J. (2002b). *What works in the high school results-based staff development.* Oxford, OH: National Staff Development Council.

Killion, J. (2003). Solid footwork makes evaluation of staff development programs a song. *Journal of Staff Development, 24*(4), 15–21.

Kimmelman, P. L. (2006). *Implementing NCLB: Creating knowledge framework to support school improvement.* Thousand Oaks, CA: Corwin.

Kirkpatrick, D. L., & Kirkpatrick, J. D. (1994). *Evaluating training programs: The four levels* (3rd ed). San Francisco, CA: Berrett-Koehler.

Kise, J. (2006). *Differentiated coaching: A framework for helping teachers change.* Thousand Oaks, CA: Corwin.

Knight, J. (2007). *Instructional coaching: A partnership approach to improving instruction.* Thousand Oaks, CA: Corwin.

Knowles, M. S. (1977). *The modern practice of adult education: Andragogy versus pedagogy.* New York, NY: Association Press.

Knowles, M. S. (1990). *The adult learner: A neglected species* (4th ed.). Houston, TX: Gulf Publishing.

Knowles, M. S., Holton, E. F., & Swanson, R. (2005). *The adult learner: The definitive classic in adult education and human resource development* (6th ed.). New York, NY: Elsevier.

Koshy, V. (2005). *Action research for improving practice: A practical guide.* Thousand Oaks, CA: Sage.

Krause, S. (1996). Portfolios in teacher education: Effects of instruction on preservice teachers' early comprehension of the portfolio process. *Journal of Teacher Education, 47*(2), 130–138. doi:10.1177/0022487196047002006

Kruse, S. D., & Louis, K. S. (2007). Professional communities and learning communities: What school leaders need to know. *Orbit Magazine, 30*(1).

Lambert, L. (1995). Toward a theory of constructivist leadership. In L. Lambert, D. Walker, D. Zimmerman, J. Cooper, M. Lambert, M. Gardner, & P. J. Ford-Slack (Eds.), *The constructivist leader* (pp. 28–51). New York, NY: Teachers College Press.

Lambert, L. (2005). *Leadership capacity for lasting school improvement.* Alexandria, VA: Association for Supervision and Curriculum Development.

Langer, J. A., & Applebee, A. (1986). Reading and writing instruction: Toward a theory of teaching and learning. *Review of Research in Education, 13,* 171–194.

Lankau, M. J., & Scandura, T. A. (2002). An investigation of personal learning in mentoring relationships: Content, antecedents, and consequences. *Academy of Management Journal, 45*(4), 1–18. Retrieved from http://web.ebscohost.com/

Larson, M. S. (1977). *The rise of professionalism.* Berkeley, CA: University of California Press.

Laursen, P. F. (1996). Professionalism and the reflective approach to teaching. In M. Kompf, R. Bond, D. Dworet, & R. T. Boak (Eds.), *Changing research and practice: Teachers' professionalism, identities and knowledge* (pp. 48–55). Bristol, PA: Falmer Press.

Learning Forward. (2011). *Standards for staff development.* Retrieved from www.nsdc. org/standards/index.cfm

Learning Forward. (2011). *Standards for professional learning.* Oxford, OH: Author.

Lefever-Davis, S., Wilson, C., Moore, E., Kent, A., & Hopkins, S. (2003). Teacher study groups: A strategic approach to promoting students' literacy development. *The Reading Teacher, 56*(8), 782–784. Retrieved from http://web.ebscohost.com/

Leitch, R., & Day, C. (2000). Action research and reflective practice: Towards a holistic view. *Educational Action Research, 8*(1), 179–193. doi:10.1080/09650790000200108

Lesson Study Research Group. *What is lesson study?* New York, NY: Teachers College, Columbia University. Retrieved from www.tc.edu/lessonstudy/whatislesson-study.html

Levin, B. B. (2003). *Case studies of teacher development: An in-depth look at how thinking about pedagogy develops over time.* Mahwah, NJ: Lawrence Erlbaum.

Levine, T. H. (2010). Tools for the study and design of collaborative teacher learning: The affordances of different conceptions of teacher community and activity theory. *Teacher Education Quarterly, 37*(1), 109–130. Retrieved from http://web.ebscohost.com/

Levine, T. H., & Marcus, A. S. (2010). How the structure and focus of teachers' collaborative activities facilitate and constrain teacher learning. *Teacher and Teacher Education, 26*(3), 389–398. doi:10.1016/j.tate.2009.03.001

Lewis, C. (2002). What are the essential elements of lesson study? *CSP Connection, 2*(6), 1–4. Retrieved from www.lessonresearch.net/newsletter11_2002.pdf

Lewis, C., Perry, R., & Hurd, J. (2004). A deeper look at lesson study. *Educational Leadership, 61*(5), 18–22. Retrieved from http://web.ebscohost.com/

Lewis, C., Perry, R., & Murata, A. (2006). How should research contribute to instructional improvement? The case of lesson study. *Educational Researcher, 35*(3), 3–14. Retrieved from www.jstor.org/

Lewis, C., Perry, R., Hurd, J., & O'Connell, M. P. (2006). Lesson study comes of age in North America. *Phi Delta Kappan, 88*(4), 273–281.

Lick, D. W. (2001). The principal as study group leader. *Journal of Staff Development, 22*(1), 37–38.

Lick, D. W., & Murphy, C. U. (Eds.). (2007). *The whole-faculty study groups fieldbook: Lessons learned and best practices from classrooms, districts, and schools.* Thousand Oaks, CA: Corwin.

Lindeman, E. C. (1926). *The meaning of adult education.* New York, NY: New Republic.

Lindsey, D. B., Martinez, R. S., & Lindsey, R. B. (2007). *Culturally proficient coaching: Supporting educators to create equitable schools.* Thousand Oaks, CA: Corwin.

Lipka, J., & McCarty, T. (1994). Changing the culture of schooling: Navajo and Yup'ik cases. *Anthropology & Education Quarterly, 25*(3), 266–284. Retrieved from www.jstor.org/

Liptak, L. (2002, November). *It's about time: A principal's perspective on lesson study.* Paper presented at the annual meeting of the Research for Better Schools, Lesson Study Conference. Stamford, CT. Retrieved from www.rbs.org/Special-Topics/Lesson-Study/Lesson-Study-Conference-2002/204/

Little, J. W. (1994). Teacher's professional development in a climate of educational reform. Systemic reform: Perspectives on personalizing education. Retrieved from www2.ed.gov/pubs/EdReformStudies/SysReforms/little1.html

Lortie, D. C. (1975). *Schoolteacher: A sociological study.* Chicago, IL: University of Chicago Press.

Loucks-Horsley, S., Hewson, P. W., Love, N., & Stiles, K. E. (1998). *Designing professional development for teachers of science and mathematics.* Thousand Oaks, CA: Corwin.

Lovett, S., & Gilmore, A. (2003). Teachers' learning journeys: The quality learning circle as a model of professional development. *School Effectiveness and School Improvement,14*(2), 189–211. doi:0924-3453/03/1402-189

Lunenburg, F.C. (1995). *The principalship: Concepts and applications.* Englewood Cliffs, NJ: Merrill.

Macintyre, C. (2000). *The art of action research in the classroom.* London, UK: Fulton.

Madison Metropolitan School District. (2004). *Classroom action research: What is action research?* Retrieved from http://staffdevweb.madison.k12.wi.us/node/233

Mahon, J. P. (2007). Enhancing the principal's instructional leadership role. In D. W. Lick, & C. U. Murphy (Eds.), *The whole-faculty study groups fieldbook: Lessons learned and best practices from classrooms, districts, and schools* (pp. 27–33). Thousand Oaks, CA: Corwin.

Makibbin, S., & Sprague, M. (1991). *Study groups: Conduit for reform.* St. Louis, MO: National Staff Development Council. (ERIC Document Reproduction Service No. ED 370 893).

Marks, H. M., & Printy, S. M. (2003). Principal leadership and school performance: An integration of transformational and instructional leadership. *Educational Administration Quarterly, 39*(3), 370–397. doi:10.1177/0013161X03253412

Marshak, D. (1996). The emotional experience of school change: Resistance, loss, and grief. *NASSP Bulletin, 80*(577), 72–77. doi:10.1177/019263659608057713

Marzano, R. (2003). *What works in schools: Translating research into action.* Alexandria, VA: Association for Supervision and Curriculum Development.

Maslow, A. H. (1954). *Motivation and personality.* New York, NY: Harper & Row.

Maslow, A. H. (1968). *Toward a psychology of being.* New York, NY: D. Van Nostrand.

McBride, R., Reed, J., & Dollar, J. (1994). Teacher attitudes toward staff development: A symbolic relationship at best. *Journal of Staff Development, 15*(2), 36–41.

McCall, J. (1997). *The principal as steward.* Larchmont, NY: Eye On Education.

McDonald, J. (2001). Students' work and teachers' learning. In A. Lieberman, & L. Miller (Eds.), *Teachers caught in the action: Professional development that matters* (pp. 209–235). New York, NY: Teachers College Press.

McEntee, G., Appleby, J., Dowd, J., Grant, J., Hole, S., & Silva, P. (2003). *At the heart of teaching: A guide to reflective practice.* New York, NY: Teachers College Press.

McGreal, T. (1983). *Effective teacher evaluation.* Alexandria, VA: Association for Supervision and Curriculum.

McIntyre, D. J., & Byrd M. (Ed.). (1996). *Teacher Education Yearbook IV*. Thousand Oaks, CA: Corwin.

McLaughlin, M. & Oberman, I. (Eds.). (1996). *Teacher learning: New policies, new practices*. New York, NY: Teachers College Press.

McLeod, S. (2005). *Data-driven teachers*. Minneapolis, MN: Center for the Advanced Study of Technology Leadership in Education.

McLeod, S. (2006). *Pyramid of interventions packet* (Draft; updated June 14, 2006).

McNamara, C. (2007). *Basic guide to program evaluation*. Minneapolis, MN: Authenticity Consulting. Retrieved from www.managementhelp.org/evaluatn/fnl_eval.htm

McNiff, J., & Whitehead, J. (2005). *Action research for teachers: A practical guide*. London, UK: David Fulton.

McTighe, J., & Thomas, R. S. (2003). Backward design for forward action. *Educational Leadership, 60*(5), 52–55. Retrieved from http://web.ebscohost.com/

Merriam, S. (2001). Andragology and self-directed learning: Pillars of adult learning theory. In S. Merriam (Ed.), *The new update on adult learning theory: New directions for adult and continuing education* (No. 89). San Francisco, CA: Jossey-Bass.

Merriam, S. B., Caffarella, R. S., & Baumgartner, L.M. (2007). *Learning in adulthood: A comprehensive guide* (3rd ed.). San Francisco, CA: John Wiley.

Mezirow, J. (1991). *Transformative dimensions of adult learning*. San Francisco, CA: Jossey Bass.

Midcontinent Research for Education and Learning. (2002). Sustaining school improvement. Professional learning community. Retrieved from http//www.mcrel.org/pdf/leadershiporganizationdevelopment/5031TG_proflrncommfolio.pdf

Middleton, J. A. (1999). Curricular influences on the motivational beliefs and practices of two middle school mathematics teachers: A followup study. *Journal for Research in Mathematics Education, 30*(3), 349–358. Retrieved from www.jstor.org/

Miles, K. H., Odden, A., Fermanich, M., & Archibald, S. (2004). Inside the black box of school district spending on professional development: Lessons from five urban districts. *Journal of Education Finance, 30*(1), 1–26. Retrieved from www.tqsource.org/issueforums/plantoAction/resources/7_PlenarySessions/PDSpending/BlackBoxofPDSpending.pdf

Milstein, M. M. (1993). *Restructuring schools: Doing it right*. Thousand Oaks, CA: Corwin.

Mizell, H. (2003). Facilitator: 10, Refreshments: 8, Evaluation 10. *Journal of Staff Development, 24*(4), 10–13.

Moller, G., & Pankake, A. (2006). *Lead with me: A principal's guide to teacher leadership*. Larchmont, NY: Eye On Education.

Moon, J. A. (1999). *Reflection in learning and professional development*. Sterling, VA: Stylus Publishing.

Moore, R. (1999). *Preservice teachers engaged in reflective classroom research*. The Teacher Educator, 34(4) 259–275.

Morey, M. K., Satchwell, L. E., & Loepp, F. L. (2006). Unlocking the National Science Education Standards with IMaST. In R. E. Yager (Ed.), *Exemplary science in grades 5–8: Standards-based success stories*. Arlington, VA: NSTA.

Moxley, D. E., & Taylor, R.T. (2006). *Literacy coaching: A handbook for school leaders*. Thousand Oaks, CA: Corwin.

Murphy, C. U., & Lick, D. W. (1998). *Whole-faculty study groups: Creating professional learning communities that target student learning*. Thousand Oaks, CA: Corwin.

Murphy, C. U., & Lick, D. W. (2005). *Whole-faculty study groups: Creating professional learning communities that target student learning* (3rd ed.). Thousand Oaks, CA: Corwin.

Murphy, J., Murphy, C., Joyce, B., & Showers, B. (1988). The Richmond County school improvement program: Preparation and initial Phase. *Journal of Staff Development, 9*(2), 36–41.

Murray, J. P. (1994, February). *The teaching portfolio: The department chairperson's role in creating a climate of teaching excellence.* A paper presented at the annual International Conference for Community College Chairs, Deans, and Other Instructional Leaders. Phoenix, AZ.

Musanti, S. I., & Pence, L. P. (2010). Collaboration and teacher development: Unpacking resistance, constructing knowledge, and navigating identities. *Teacher Education Quarterly, 37*(1), 73–89. Retrieved from http://web.ebscohost.com/

Nan, S. A. (2003). Formative evaluation. Beyond Intractability. In G. Burgess, & H. Burgess (Eds.), *Conflict Research Consortium.* Boulder, CO: University of Colorado. Retrieved from www.beyondintractability.org/essay/formative_evaluation/

National Association of Elementary School Principals. (2001). *Leading learning communities: Standards for what principals should know and be able to do.* Alexandria, VA: Author.

National Board for Professional Teaching Standards (NBPTS). (n.d.). *What teachers should know and be able to do: The 5 core propositions of the National Board.* Retrieved from www.nbpts.org/about/coreprops.cfm#policy

National Commission on Excellence in Education. (1983). *A nation at risk: The imperative for educational reform.* Washington, DC: U.S. Department of Education.

National Commission on Teaching and America's Future. (1996). *What matters most: Teaching for America's future.* New York, NY: Author.

National Education Association Foundation for the Improvement of Education. (2003). *Using data about classroom practice and student work to improve professional development for educators.* Washington, DC: Author.

National Partnership for Excellence and Accountability in Teaching. (1999). *Revisioning professional development: What learner-centered professional development looks like.* Oxford, OH: National Staff Development Council.

National School Reform Faculty at the Harmony Education Center. (n.d.). *Critical friends groups: Purpose and work.* Retrieved from www.nsrfharmony.org/articles.html

National School Reform Faculty. (2006). *Critical friends groups: Frequently asked questions.* Retrieved from www.nsrfharmony.org/faq.html

Newman, K., Burden, P., & Applegate, J. (1980). *Helping teachers examine their long-range development.* Washington, DC: Association of Teacher Educators. (ERIC Document Reproduction Service No. ED204321).

Newman, K., Dornburg, B., Dubois, D., & Kranz, E. (1980). *Stress to teachers' midcareer transitions: A role for teacher education.* (ERIC Document Reproduction Service No. ED196868).

Nieto, S. (2000). Placing equity front and center: Some thoughts on transforming teacher education for a new century. *Journal of Teacher Education, 51*(3), 180–187. doi:10.1177/0022487100051003004

No Child Left Behind Act of 2001, Pub. L. No. 107-110, 115 Stat. 1425 (2002).

Nolan, M. (2007). *Mentor coaching and leadership in early care and education.* New York, NY: Thomson Delmar Learning.

References

North Central Regional Educational Laboratory. (n.d.). *Action research*. Retrieved from www.ncrel.org/sdrs/areas/issues/envrnmnt/drugfree/sa3act.htm

Northeastern Nevada Regional Professional Development Program. (2009). Effective models of professional development. *Northeastern Nevada Regional Professional Development Program Chronicle, 3*(3). Retrieved from www.nnrpdp.org/newsletters/march_09.pdf

Northwest Regional Educational Laboratory. (2005). Having another set of eyeballs: Critical friends groups. *Northwest Education, 11*(1). Retrieved from www.nwrel.org/nwedu/11–01/cfg/

Noyce, P. (2006). Professional development: How do we know if it works? [commentary] *Education Week, 26*(3), 36–37. Retrieved from www.educationresourcestrategies.org/documents/EdweekPD13Sept06.pdf

O'Neil, J. (1998). Constructivism—wanted: Deep understanding. In J. O'Neil, & S. Willis (Eds.), *Transforming classroom practice* (pp. 49–70). Alexandria, VA: Association for Supervision and Curriculum Development.

Oliver, B. (2007). Send me in a coach! *Just for the ASKing!* Retrieved from www.ask-education.com/newsletter.htm

Olivero, G., Bane, K. D., & Kopelman, R. E. (1997). Executive coaching as a transfer of training tool: Effects on productivity in a public agency. *Public Personnel Management, 26*(4), 461–469. http://proquest.umi.com/

Olson, M. R. (2000). Linking personal and professional knowledge of teaching practice through narrative inquiry. *The Teacher Educator, 35*(4), 109–127. doi:10.1080/08878730009555241

Orland-Barak, L. (2005). Portfolios as evidence of reflective practice: What remains "untold." *Educational Research, 47*(1), 25–44. doi:10.1080/0013188042000337541

Palmer, P. J. (1998). *The courage to teach: Exploring the inner landscape of a teacher's life*. San Francisco, CA: Jossey-Bass.

Pankake, A., & Moller, G. (2007). What the teacher leader needs from the principal. *Journal of Staff Development, 28*(1), 32–36.

Pascarelli, J. T., & Ponticell, J. A. (1994). *Trust-blocking responses*. Training Materials Developed for Co-Teaching. Chicago, IL.

Patterson, J., & Patterson, J. (2004). Sharing the lead. *Educational Leadership, 61*(7), 74–78.

Patton, M. Q. (1996). *Utilization-focused evaluation: The new century text* (3rd ed.). Thousand Oaks, CA: Sage.

Peterson, K. D. (1999). Time use flows from school culture. *Journal of Staff Development, 20*(2), 16–19.

Peterson, K. D. (2002). Positive or negative? *Journal of Staff Development, 23*(3), 10–15.

Phi Delta Kappa Educational Foundation. (2005). *How to conduct a book study group*. Retrieved from www.pdkintl.org/index.htm

Poe, A.C. (2000, September). *Launching a mentor program: SHRM white paper*. Retrieved from www.shrm.org/

Polly, D., & Hannafin, M. (2010). Reexamining technology's role in learner-centered professional development. *Educational Technology Research & Development, 58*(5), 557–571. doi:10.1007/s11423–009–9146–5

Ponticell, J. A. (1995). Promoting teaching professionalism through collegiality. *Journal of Staff Development, 16(3),* 13–18.

Ponticell, J. A., & Zepeda, S. J. (1996). Making sense of teaching and learning: A case study of mentor and beginning teacher problem solving. In D. J. McIntyre, & D.

M. Byrd (Eds.), *Preparing tomorrow's teachers: The field experience* (pp. 115–129). Thousand Oaks, CA: Corwin.

Ponticell, J. A., & Olivarez, A. (2000). Evaluating the block schedule. In S. Zepeda, & R. S. Mayers (Eds.), *Supervision and staff development in the block* (pp. 197–225). Larchmont, NY: Eye On Education.

Porter, A. C., Garet, M. S., Desimone, L. M., & Birman, B. F. (2003). Providing effective professional development: Lessons from the Eisenhower Program. *Science Educator, 12*(1), 23–40.

Porter, A. C., Garet, M. S., Desimone, L. M., Yoon, K. S., & Birman, B. F. (2000). *Does professional development change teaching practice? Results from a three-year study. Executive Summary*. Washington, DC: American Institutes for Research in the Behavioral Sciences. Retrieved from www2.ed.gov/rschstat/eval/teaching/epdp/report.pdf

Portner, H. (1998). *Mentoring new teachers*. Thousand Oaks, CA: Corwin.

Prawat, R. S. (1992). From individual differences to learning communities—Our changing focus. *Educational Leadership, 49*(7), 9–13.

Printy, S. M., & Marks, H. M. (2004). Communities of practice and teacher quality. In W. K. Hoy, & C. G. Miskel (Eds.), *Educational administration, policy, and reform: Research and measurement* (pp. 91–122). Greenwich, CT: Information Age.

Puchner, L. L., & Taylor, A. R. (2006). Lesson study, collaboration and teacher efficacy: Stories from two school-based math lesson study groups. *Teaching and Teacher Education, 22*(7), 922–934. doi:10.1016/j.tate.2006.04.011

Rae, S., & O'Driscoll, T. (2004). Contextualized learning: Empowering education. *Chief Learning Officer Magazine*. Retrieved from http://clomedia.com/articles/view/contextualized_learning_empowering_education

Randi, J., & Zeichner, K. M. (2004). New visions of teacher professional development. In M. A. Smylie, & D. Miretzky (Eds.), *Developing the Teacher Workforce* (pp. 180–227). Chicago, IL: University of Chicago Press.

Razik, T. A., & Swanson, A. D. (2001). *Fundamental concepts of educational leadership* (2nd ed.). Upper Saddle River, NJ: Prentice Hall.

Reiman, A. J., & Peace, S. D. (2002). Promoting teachers' moral reasoning and collaborative inquiry performance: A developmental role-taking and guided inquiry study. *Journal of Moral Education, 31*(1), 51–66. doi:10.1080/03057240120111436

Richardson, J. (2001). *Student work at the core of teacher learning: Results*. Alexandria, VA: National Staff Development Council. Retrieved from www.nsdc.org/library/publications/

Richardson, J. (2007). Learning through a lens: Classroom videos of teachers and students prove to be a powerful professional learning tool. *Tools for Schools for a Dynamic Community of Learners and Leaders, 10*(4), 1–2. Retrieved from www.learningforward.org/news/

Riel, M. (1997). *Learning circle teachers' guide*. Retrieved from www.iearn.org/circles/lcguide/

Riel, M., Cheng, B., Polin, L., Wiske, S., Koch, M., Harasim, L., Hsi, S., Haavind, S., & Bonk, C. (2002). Research learning circle: Online learning and teaching. *InterLearn*. Retrieved from http://members.cox.net/mriel/circle.html

Robbins, P. (1991). *How to plan and implement a peer coaching program*. Alexandria, VA: Association for Supervision and Curriculum Development.

Roberts, S. M., & Pruitt, E. Z. (2003). *Schools as professional learning communities: Collaborative activities and strategies for professional development*. Thousand Oaks, CA: Corwin.

Rosemary, C. A., Roskos, K. A., & Landreth, L. K. (2007). *Designing professional development in literacy: A framework for effective instruction.* New York, NY: Guilford.

Rourke, J. (2007). *From my classroom to yours: reflection on teaching.* Lanham, MD: Rowman & Littlefield Education.

Royse, D., Thyer, B. A., & Padgett, D. K. (2010). *Program evaluation: An introduction* (5th ed.). Belmont, CA: Wadsworth.

Rutherford, W. (1989) *NASSP TIPS for Principals.* Reston, VA: National Association of Secondary Principals.

Saavedra, E. (1996). Teachers study groups: Contexts for transformative learning and action. *Theory into Practice, 35*(4), 271–276. Retrieved from http://web.ebscohost.com/

Sagor, R. (2000). *Guiding school improvement with action research.* Alexandria, VA: Association for Supervision and Curriculum Development.

Sanborn, J., & Sanborn, E. (1994). A conversation on portfolios. *Middle School Journal, 26*(10), 26–29.

Sanders, J. R., & Sullins, C. D. (2005). *Evaluating school programs: An educator's guide* (3rd ed.). Thousand Oaks, CA: Corwin.

Saphier, J., & King, M. (1985). Good seeds grow in strong cultures. *Educational Leadership, 42*(6), 67–74.

Schlechty, P. (1997). *Inventing better schools.* San Francisco, CA: Jossey-Bass.

Schmuck, R. A. (2006). *Practical action research for change* (2nd ed.). Thousand Oaks, CA: Corwin.

Schön, D. (1983). *The reflective practitioner.* New York, NY: Basic Books.

Schön, D. (1987). *Educating the reflective practitioner.* San Francisco, CA: Jossey-Bass.

Schulz, B. C. (2008). Teacher perspectives of how high-stakes testing influences instructional decisions and professionalism. In S. J. Zepeda (Ed.), *Real world supervision: Adapting theory to practice* (pp. 145–166). Norwood, MA: Christopher-Gordon.

Scriven, M. (1967). The methodology of evaluation. In R. E. Stake (Ed.), *Curriculum evaluation. American Educational Research Association Monograph Series on Evaluation, No. 1* (pp. 39–83). Chicago, IL: Rand McNally.

Seng, S., & Seng, T. (1996, November). *Reflective teaching and the portfolio approach in early childhood staff development.* Paper presented at the Joint Conference of the Australian Association of Singapore and the Australian Association for Research in Education. Singapore.

Senge, P. M. (1990). *The fifth discipline: The art and practice of the learning organization.* New York, NY: Currency Doubleday.

Senge, P. M. (1996). Leading learning organizations. In F. Hesselbein, M. Goldsmith, & R. Beckhard (Eds.), *The leader of the future: New visions, strategies, and practices for the next era* (pp. 41–58). San Francisco, CA: Jossey-Bass.

Senge, P. M., Kleiner, A., Roberts, C., Ross, R. B., & Smith, B. J. (1994). *The fifth discipline fieldbook: Strategies and tools for building a learning organization.* New York, NY: Doubleday.

Sergiovanni, T. J. (1994). *Building community in schools.* San Francisco, CA: Jossey-Bass.

Sergiovanni, T. J. (1996). *Leadership for the schoolhouse.* San Francisco, CA: Jossey-Bass.

Shiffman, B. (1991, March). The best education in the biggest cities. *Forbes Magazine.* The article is found online at: http://www.forbes.com/2004/02/13/cx_bs_0213home.html

Shulman, L. S. (1988). A union of insufficiencies: Strategies for teacher assessment in a period of educational reform. *Educational Leadership, 46*(4), 36–41.

Siegel, W., Kappaz, C., & Dowell, P. (2006). *Learning circles: An effective model for professional development and organizational capacity building.* Chicago, IL: Millennia Consulting.

Skerrett, A. (2010). "There's going to be community. There's going to be knowledge": Designs for learning in a standardised age. *Teacher and Teacher Education, 26*(3), 648–655. doi:10.1016/j.tate.2009.09.017

Smith, C., & Beno, B. (1993). *Guide to staff development evaluation.* Sacramento, CA: Community College League of California. (ERIC Document Reproduction Service No. ED363381)

Smith, T. M., Desimone, L. M., & Ueno, K. (2005). Highly qualified to do what? The relationship between NCLB teacher quality mandates and the use of reform-oriented instruction in middle school mathematics. *Educational Evaluation and Policy Analysis, 27*(1), 75–109. Retrieved from www.jstor.org/

Spalding, E., & Wilson, A. (2002). Demystifying reflection: A study of pedagogical strategies. *Teachers College Record, 104*(7), 1393–1421. Retrieved from www.tcrecord.org/

Sparks, D. (1995). Focusing staff development on improving student learning. In G. Cawelti (Ed.), *Handbook of research on improving student achievement* (pp. 163–169). Arlington, VA: Educational Research Service.

Sparks, D. (2005). *Leading for results: Transforming teaching, learning, and relationships in schools.* Thousand Oaks, CA: Corwin.

Sparks, D., & Hirsh, S. (1997). *A new vision for staff development.* Oxford, OH: National Staff Development Council.

Speck, M. (1996). Best practice in professional development for sustained educational change. *ERS Spectrum, 14*(2), 33–41.

Speck, M. (2002). Balanced and year-round professional development: Time and learning. *Catalyst for Change, 32,* 17–19.

Spillane, J. (2006). *Distributed leadership.* San Francisco, CA: Jossey-Bass.

Spillane, J. P., Halverson, R., & Diamond, J. B. (2001). Investigating school leadership practice: A distributed perspective. *Educational Researcher, 30*(3), 23–28.

Spillane, J., Halverson, R., & Diamond, J. (2004). Towards a theory of leadership practice: A distributed perspective. *Journal of Curriculum Studies, 36*(1), 3–34. doi:10.1080/0022027032000106726

St. Maurice, H., & Shaw, P. (2004). Teacher portfolios come of age: A preliminary study. *NASSP Bulletin, 88*(639), 15–24.

Stepanek, J., Appel, G., Leong, M., Mangan, M. T., & Mitchell, M. (2007). *Leading lesson study: A practical guide for teachers and facilitators.* Thousand Oaks, CA: Corwin.

Stevenson, R. B. (1995). Action research and supportive school contexts: Exploring the possibilities for transformation. In S. E. Noffke, & R. B. Stevenson (Eds.), *Educational action research: Becoming practically critical* (pp. 197–209). New York, NY: Teachers College Press.

Stewart, R., & Brendefur, J. (2005). Fusing lesson study and authentic achievement. *Phi Delta Kappan, 86*(9), 681–687.

Stone, S. J. (1995). Teaching strategies: Empowering teachers, empowering children. *Childhood Education, 71*(5), 294–295. Retrieved from http://findarticles.com/

Storygard, J., & Fox, B. (1995). Reflection on video: One teacher's story. *Journal of Staff Development, 16*(3), 25–29.

References

Strahan, D. (2003). General patterns and particular pictures: Lessons learned from reports from beating the odds schools. *Journal of Curriculum and Supervision, 18*(4), 296–305. Retrieved from http://web.ebscohost.com/

Sullivan, S., & Glanz, J. (2005). *Supervision that improves teaching: Strategies and techniques* (2nd ed.). Thousand Oaks, CA: Corwin.

Sullivan, W. (1995). *Work and integrity: The crisis and promise of professionalism in North America.* New York, NY: Harper Collins.

Symonds, K. W. (2003). *Literacy coaching: How school districts can support a long-term strategy in a short-term world.* San Francisco, CA: Bay Area School Reform Collaborative. (ERIC Document Reproduction Service No. ED477297)

The Teal Trust. (2002). *Team process.* Retrieved from www.teal.org.uk/et/teampro.htm

Thompson, D. C. (1992). School improvement and student outcomes: A resource perspective. *Planning & Changing: A Journal for School Administrators, 23*(3), 174–188.

Thompson, D. P. (1996). *Motivating others: Creating the conditions.* Larchmont, NY: Eye On Education.

Thompson, S. C., Gregg, L., & Niska, J. M. (2004). Professional learning communities, leadership, and student learning. *Research in Middle Level Education Online, 28*(1). Retrieved from www.nmsa.org/Publications/RMLEOnline/tabid/426/Default.aspx

Thompson-Grove, G. (2005, January). *A call to action.* Speech presented at the 9th annual Winter meeting of the National School Reform Faculty. Cambridge, MA.

Thompson-Grove, G. (2005). *Connections tuning protocol.* Bloomington, IN: National School Reform Faculty. Retrieved from www.nsrfharmony.org/protocol/doc/connections.pdf www.nsrfharmony.org/connections_auth_arch.html

Thompson-Grove, G. (n.d.). The Consultancy Protocol. Bloomington, IN: National School Reform Faculty. Retrieved from www.nsrfharmony.org/protocol/doc/consultancy.pdf

Tienken, C. H., & Stonaker, L. (2007). When every day is professional development day. *Journal of Staff Development, 24*(2), 24–29.

Tillema, H. H. (2001). Portfolios as developmental assessment tools. *International Journal of Training and Development, 5*(2), 126–135. Retrieved from http://web.ebscohost.com/

Tobergate, D. R., & Curtis, S. (2002). There is a crisis! And failure is not an option. *Education, 122*(4), 770–776.

Tucker, P. D., Stronge, J. H., & Gareis, C. R. (2002). *Handbook on teacher portfolios for evaluation and professional development.* Larchmont, NY: Eye On Education.

Tuckman, B. W. (1965). Developmental sequence in small groups. *Psychological Bulletin, 63*(6), 384–399.

U. S. Department of Education. *No child left behind.* (2002). Improving Teacher Quality State Grants. Title II, Part A Non-Regulatory Guidance. Washington, DC: Author. Retrieved from www.ed.gov/offices/OESE/SIP/TitleIIguidance2002.doc

U. S. Department of Education. (1995). *Building bridges: The mission and principles of professional development.* Washington, DC: Author. Retrieved from www.ed.gov/G2K/bridge.html

Valli, L. (1997). Listening to other voices: A description of teacher reflection in the United States. *Peabody Journal of Education, 72*(1), 67–88. Retrieved from http://web.ebscohost.com/

Van Wagenen, L. V., & Hibbard, K. M. (1998). Building teacher portfolios. *Educational Leadership, 55*(5), 26–29.

Vella, J. K. (2001). *Taking learning to task: Creative strategies for teaching adults.* San Francisco, CA: Jossey-Bass.

Vinson, J. B. (2006). *The perspectives of central office personnel examining professional development for veteran teachers as specified in the highly-qualified guidelines of the No Child Left Behind Act of 2001.* Published doctoral dissertation, University of Georgia, Athens, GA. Retrieved from http://dbs.galib.uga.edu/

Walpole, S., & McKenna., M. C. (2004). *The literacy coach's handbook: A guide to research-based practice.* New York, NY: Guilford.

Ward, J. R., & McCotter, S. S. (2004). Reflection as a visible outcome for preservice teachers. *Teaching and Teacher Education, 20*(3), 243–257. doi:10.1016/j.tate.2004.02.004

Watson, D., & Stevenson, M. (1989). Teacher support groups: Why and how. In G. S. Pianet, & M. L., Matlin (Eds.), *Teachers and researchers: language learning in the classroom* (pp. 118–129). New York, NY: International Reading Association.

Westheimer, J. (1998). *Among school teachers: Community, autonomy and ideology in teacher's work.* New York, NY: Teacher's College Press.

Wheelan, S. A., Tilin, F., & Sanford, J. (1996). School group effectiveness and productivity. *Research/Practice Newsletter, 4*(1). Retrieved from www.cehd.umn.edu/carei/reports/rpractice/Spring96/group.html

Whiteworth, L., Kimsey-House, H., & Sandahl, P. (1998). *Co-active coaching: New skills for coaching people toward success in work and life.* Palo Alto, CA: Davies-Black.

Wiburg, K. M., & Brown, S. (2006). *Lesson study communities: Increasing achievement with diverse students.* Thousand Oaks, CA: Corwin.

Wiggins, G., & McTighe, J. (2006). Examining the teaching life. *Educational Leadership, 63*(6), 26–29. Retrieved from http://web.ebscohost.com/

Wolf, K. (1991). The schoolteacher's portfolio: Issues in design, implementation, and evaluation. *Phi Delta Kappan, 73* (2), 129–136.

Wolf, R. (1990). *Evaluation in education: foundations of competency assessment and program review* (3rd ed.). New York, NY: Praeger.

Wood, F. H., & Killian, J. E. (1998). Job-embedded learning makes the difference in school improvement. *Journal of Staff Development, 19*(1), 52–54.

Wood, F. H., & McQuarrie, F. (1999). On-the-job learning. *Journal of Staff Development, 20*(3), 10–13.

Worthen, B. R., & Sanders, J. R. (1987). *Educational evaluation: Alternative approaches and practical guidelines.* New York, NY: Longman.

Worthen, B. R., Sanders, J. R., & Fitzpatrick, J. L. (1997). *Program evaluation: Alternative approaches and practical guidelines.* New York, NY: Longman.

Youngs, P. (2001). District and state policy influences on professional development and school capacity. *Educational Policy, 15*(2), 278–301. doi:10.1177/0895904801015002003

Youngs, P., & King, M. B. (2002). Principal leadership for professional development to build school capacity. *Educational Administration Quarterly, 38*(5), 643–670. doi:10.1177/0013161X02239642

Zepeda, S. J. (1999). *Staff development: Practices that promote leadership in learning communities.* Larchmont, NY: Eye On Education.

Zepeda, S. J. (2000, October). *Portfolio development as supervision.* Paper presented the annual meeting of the League of Professional Schools, Athens, GA.

Zepeda, S. J. (2002). Linking portfolio development to clinical supervision: A case study. *The Journal of Curriculum and Supervision, 18*(1), 83–102.

References ◆ 307

Zepeda, S. J. (2004a). *Annotated bibliography on performance coaching for Georgia's Leadership Institute for School Improvement*. Atlanta, GA: Georgia's Leadership Institute for School Improvement.

Zepeda, S. J. (2004b). *Instructional leadership for school improvement*. Larchmont, NY: Eye On Education.

Zepeda, S. J. (2006). High stakes supervision: We must do more. *The International Journal of Leadership in Education, 9*(1), 61–73. doi:10.1080/13603120500448154

Zepeda, S. J. (2007a). *Instructional supervision: Applying tools and concepts* (2nd ed.). Larchmont, NY: Eye On Education.

Zepeda. S. J. (2007b). *The principal as instructional leader: A handbook for supervisors* (2nd ed.). Larchmont, NY: Eye On Education.

Zepeda, S. J., & Mayers, R. S. (2000). *Supervision and staff development in the block*. Larchmont, NY: Eye On Education.

Zepeda. S. J., Mayers, R. S., & Benson, B. N. (2003). *The call to teacher leadership*. Larchmont, NY: Eye On Education.

Zepeda, S. J., & Recesso, A. (2007, June). *Video-tape analysis at Creekland Middle School*. A workshop presented to the faculty. Snellville, GA.

Zepeda, S. J., Wood, F., & O'Hair, M. J. (1996). A vision of supervision for 21st century schooling: Trends to promote change, inquiry, and reflection. *Wingspan, 11*(2), 26–30.

Zeus, P., & Skiffington, S. (2001). *The complete guide to coaching at work*. New York, NY: McGraw-Hill.

National School Reform Faculty. (n.d.). *Zones of comfort, risk and danger: Constructing your zone map*. Bloomington, IN: Retrieved from www.nsrfharmony.org/protocol/doc/zones_of_comfort.pdf

Zweibel, B. (2005). *GottaGettaCoach! Incorporated*. Retrieved from www.ggci.com

Index

Index

Index

Marsick, V. J. 87
Martinez, Y. 145
Martinez, R. S. 47, 48, 52
Marzano, R. 6
Maslow, A. H. 58, 59, 95
Mayers, R. S. 40, 113
McAlister, D. 180, 203
McBride, R. 73
McCall, J. 62, 282
McCarty, T. 186
McCloskey, E. M. 242, 245
McCormick, D. E. 116
McCotter, S. S. 270
McDonald, J. 235
McEntee, D. 116, 121, 122
McGreal, T. 169
McKenna, M. C. 151, 152
McLaughlin, M. 126
McLeod, S. 97, 98, 103, 104, 105, 107,
     108, 109, 110, 111, 112, 284
McMahon, A. 114
McNamara, C. 21, 34, 39
McNiff, J. 246, 247, 251, 257, 260
McTaggart, R. 249
McTighe, J. 66, 67, 278
McQuarrie, F. 9, 75, 128, 129, 141
Meehan, M. L. 231
Melenyzer, B. J. 263
Mentor Coaching 165
Merriam, S. B. 47, 63
Mezirow, J. 61
Miao, J. 14
Middleton, J. A. 130, 131
Miles, K. H. 17
Milstein, M. M. 26
Mirkin, P. 106
Mitchell, M. 230
Mizell, H. 22
Moller, G. 5, 105, 115, 174
Moo, S. N. 120
Moon, J. A. 119, 121
Moore, E. 121
Moore, R. 180

Morey, M, K. 65
Morriss, M. 261
Murata, A. 226
Murphy, C. U. 54, 180, 186, 187
Murphy, J. 180
Murray, J. P. 269, 271
Musanti, S.I. 178

N

Nan, S. A. 30
National Association of Elementary
     School Principals 65
National Board for Professional
     Teaching Standards (NBPTS) 11
National Commission on Excellence
     in Education 11
Education Standards and Assess-
     ment 11, 14, 15, 42, 64, 66, 68, 92,
     136, 212, 263
National Commission on Teaching
     and America's Future 4, 49
National Education Association
     Foundation for the Improvement
     of Education 96, 225
National Partnership for Excellence
     and Accountability in Teaching
     281
National Science Education Stan-
     dards 276
National School Reform Faculty 205
National School Reform Faculty at
     the Harmony Education Center
     207
Nave, B. 204
Nettles, D. H. 263
Newman, K. 56, 57
Niday, D. 165
Nieto, S. 206
Niska, J. M. 82, 96
No Child Left Behind Act of 2001 11,
     14, 18, 52, 276
Nolan, M. 145, 165

Rex, L. A. 285
Rhoades, K. 14
Richardson, J. 204, 212, 265
Ridd, K. 152, 284
Riel, M. 242, 243
Risk-Taking 113
Roberts, C. 47, 48, 63
Roberts, S. M. 88
Ross, R. B. 53
Ross-Gordon, J. M. 53
Royse, D. 19, 20, 45
Rutherford, W. 25, 31, 155

S

Saavedra, E. 184
Sagor, R. 250, 251, 260
Sanborn, E. 264
Sanborn, J. 264
Sanders, J. R. 10, 20, 29, 35, 36, 37, 41, 44, 45
Sanford, J. 209
Saphier, J. 90
Scandura, T. A. 131
Schaverien, L. 4
Schlechty, P. 26
Schmuck, R. A. 247
Schneider, B. 91
Schön, D. 89
School Improvement and Professional Development 192, 277
Schulz, B. C. 11, 14
Scriven, M. 19
Seng, S. 87, 116
Seng, T. 87, 116
Senge, P. M. 83, 85, 87, 88, 93
Sergiovanni, T. J. 83, 85, 86, 87
Sharpe, L. 120
Shaw, P. 261, 262
Shiffman, B. 153
Shinohara, M. 25
Shore, A. 14
Showers, B. 9, 158, 166, 168, 180, 279

Shulman, L. S. 261
Siegel, W. 240
Silva, P. 116, 121, 122, 224
Skiffington, S. 169
Smith, B. J. 88
Smith, C. 40
Smith, K. 35, 47
Smith, M. K. 257
Smith, R. 197
Smith, T. M. 53
Somech, A. 89
Sonny Carter Elementary School 131
Sparks, D. 141, 142
Speck, M. 49, 76, 125, 142
Spillane, J. P. 86
Spiro, M. S. 87
Sprague, M. 192
St. Maurice, H. 261, 262, 273
Standards 11, 14, 15, 42, 64, 66, 68, 92, 136, 212, 263
    Curricular 384
    Joint Committee on Standards for Educational Evaluation 42
    Learning Forward Standards 15, 66–69
    No Child Left Behind Act of 2001 14, 18, 52, 276
    Professional Development 276
Stepanek, J. 230, 231, 238
Stevenson, M. 255
Stevenson, R. B. 257
Stewart, R. 233
Stiles, K. E. 9
Stoll, L. 114
Stone, S. J. 114
Stonaker, L. 2
Storygard, J. 265
Strahan, D. 52
Strauss, A. 12, 13
Stronge, J. H. 261, 267, 273

Index

X, Y, Z

Notes

Notes

Notes

Notes

Notes

Notes

Notes